(continued from front flap)

- Build alliances with suppliers and customers
- Use new policy deployment techniques to align all work activity to your business strategy
- Create a "learning organization" through benchmarking and creative-thinking techniques
- Acquire the essential leadership skills to manage organizational change
- Leverage the full potential of information technologies
- And much more

The challenges of today's marketplace are daunting, but as William Band makes abundantly clear, the patterns for success have begun to emerge. Now, *Touchstones* arms you with the cutting-edge strategies and techniques for reproducing those patterns in *your* organization.

About the author

WILLIAM A. BAND is a Vice President of Rath & Strong, Inc., the management consulting firm based in Lexington, Massachusetts. Formerly a partner with The Coopers & Lybrand Consulting Group where he led the firm's Center for Excellence in Customer Satisfaction, Mr. Band specializes in helping organizations facing complex change achieve success through developing customer value-creating strategies. He is also the author of the bestselling Wiley business book, *Creating Value for Customers: Designing and Implementing a Total Corporate Strategy*.

Touchstones

NEW DIRECTIONS IN BUSINESS

New Directions in Business books provide managers and business profession-als with authoritative sources of ideas and information. They're designed to be a convenient and effective way to upgrade your skills in today's fast-changing world of business.

New Directions in Business books cover current topics that leaders in every business need to know about. They focus on applied techniques that can be used today and they are written by leading-edge authors with academic and professional experience.

OTHER TITLES IN NEW DIRECTIONS IN BUSINESS

Touchstones: Ten New Ideas Revolutionizing Business by William A. Band

The Smarter Organization: How to Build a Business That Learns and Adapts to Marketplace Needs by Michael E. McGill and John W. Slocum

Hands-On Strategy: The Guide to Crafting Your Company's Future by William C. Finnie

New Product Success Stories: Lessons from the Leading Innovators by Robert J. Thomas

The New Competitor Intelligence: The Complete Resource for Finding, Analyzing, and Using Information about Your Competitors by Leonard M. Fuld

Touchstones

Ten New Ideas Revolutionizing Business

William A. Band

John Wiley & Sons, Inc.
New York • Chichester • Brisbane • Toronto • Singapore

This text is printed on acid-free paper.

Copyright © 1994 by William A. Band
Published by John Wiley & Sons, Inc.

Library of Congress Cataloging-in-Publication Data:

Band, William A.
    Touchstones : ten new ideas revolutionizing business / William
Band.
        p.   cm.
    Includes index.
    ISBN 0-471-31096-4
    1. Management—United States.   2. Quality of products—United
States—Management.   3. Customer service—United States—Management.
I. Title.
HD70.U5B34   1994
658.4—dc20   94-12182

Printed in the United States of America

10 9 8 7 6 5 4 3 2 1

This book is dedicated to Charlene Band.

Acknowledgments

Writing a book requires having the support of numerous individuals who are willing to help toward the achievement of difficult goals. I am indebted to my friends and business acquaintances for their unselfish support of my efforts.

Julia Woods, vice president of John Wiley & Sons Canada Limited, was an enthusiastic sponsor of this book and provided important advice on how to organize my ideas for publication. John Mahaney, senior editor at John Wiley & Sons in New York, professionally guided me through the manuscript development process, giving appropriate criticism and encouragement to keep the writing process on track. I am thankful to both of these individuals for supporting me in my writing projects during the past five years.

This book builds on the ideas of many other business writers, consultants, and practitioners. I have tried to acknowledge my sources throughout the text and in the endnotes. Credit is due to these many leaders in their respective disciplines. Errors and omissions are my own.

I am also grateful to my clients, who have helped me shape and refine my ideas about the critical abilities that organizations must develop in order to achieve success. The commitments to confidentiality that govern a consulting relationship prevent me from identifying many of the most important contributors. In no case does this book contain data that have not been obtained from public sources or that have not been modified to prevent the identification of my clients.

I was fortunate to have the help of two hard-working and cheerful editorial assistants. Mark Hacking synthesized my research material and helped me locate important sources. Sara Rosenthal worked very hard to give my prose a more engaging style. I could not have finished this project without their professional advice and support.

Finally, I would like to thank my wife, Charlene, who critiqued early drafts of the book and cheered me along through every step of the publishing process.

WILLIAM A. BAND

Lexington, Massachusetts
August 1994

Contents

Touchstones

INTRODUCTION

Ten New Ideas
Revolutionizing Business

It is very easy to manage our neighbor's business, but our own sometimes bothers us.

Josh Billings

Imagine having at your fingertips the very best ideas for elevating you, and your organization, to previously unheard-of levels of performance. Think what it would be like to sweep aside the clutter of the current "new age" management jargon and penetrate to the heart of the success secrets of today's most successful enterprises. Imagine yourself knowing how to apply these prescriptions quickly, effectively, and with confidence. I have written *Touchstones* for action-oriented executives who know they need the best, most up-to-date, and proven strategies for winning in today's competitive and chaotic marketplace.

In this book, you will find a potent distillation of ten new ideas that are revolutionizing business. These ten capabilities are fast becoming recognized as "critical competencies"—the prerequisites for success. Understanding these concepts will change the way you think, act, and do business. Make these ideas your enduring touchstones for achievement.

THE SHIFTING BALANCE OF POWER

The business press is currently full of accounts of firings and "early retirements" of CEOs in some of North America's largest and best known business

1

organizations. These departures are merely the more visible indications of the fact that the very nature of business competition has changed. Foremost among these changes is the shifting balance of power between producers and buyers. Most industries today are no longer constrained by supply. There is, in fact, an overabundance of suppliers crowding into every part of the market. This gives customers, who, every day, are becoming more astute in their buying practices, tremendous choice in deciding whom to do business with.

The 1990s have become the "value decade"; buyers carefully examine a producer's total offering to determine whether it represents the best overall value compared to alternatives. Today's business challenge is to give customers all of what they want and none of what they do not; the best quality *and* the best prices; make it quick *and* serve it with a smile! Provide superior value or be driven from the marketplace. Find new and better ways to compete, or become another victim of the business version of natural selection.

During the past ten years, the search for a better way of leading and managing has produced a torrent of new ideas. The traditional thinking about what makes for a high-performing enterprise is no longer legitimate. New "logic" is emerging piecemeal in its place, and some early implementers of the new logic are already gaining a competitive advantage. Which elements of this unconventional thinking have enduring merit? What will the successful organization of the future look like?

THE HIGH-PERFORMING ENTERPRISE

There is little argument, among the executives I work with, that their organizations must change. Indeed, they can readily define the necessary capabilities for high performance. In my consulting work, I have seen how some organizations have successfully transformed and others, which took different paths, ended in failure. I believe powerful new principles and practices have emerged that businesses can seize and capitalize on. This "new wisdom" comprises ideas that will become the dominant pattern of success in the decades ahead.

Today's high-performing enterprises are filled with people who are:

- Relentless in their focus on creating superior value for the customer;
- Obsessed with quality and service;
- Cost-effective in the ways they serve targeted market segments;
- Effective in working in cross-functional teams across organizational "silos";

- Driven to do essential tasks faster and more flexibly in response to changing competitive conditions;
- Insistent on continuous learning and improvement.

If you're concerned with improving the competitive position of your organization, or if you fear that your enterprise cannot transform itself successfully, the strategies in *Touchstones* will help you.

PARADIGM PRISON

Evidence of the need for new approaches is everywhere. Why, then, is it so difficult to put better methods in place? Because existing patterns of success can prevent businesses from conceiving the solutions to new challenges. A sort of "paradigm paralysis" blocks many executives from making the changes necessary to move their organizations closer to the high-performing model.

If you want to escape your paradigm prison, you need a clear view of what the future will look like:

- The average company will become smaller, employing fewer people;
- The traditional hierarchical organization will give way to a variety of organizational forms, and chief among them will be networks of specialists;
- Technicians will replace manufacturing operatives as the worker elite;
- The vertical division of labor will be replaced by a horizontal view of enterprise management;
- The paradigm of doing business will shift from making a product to providing a service;
- Work itself will be redefined to mean constant learning, more high-order thinking, and less "nine-to-five" behavior.

To come out on top in the value decade, an organization must have a new set of proficiencies and the personal skills to match. It is not enough to know what and why change is necessary; you need to know *how*.

THE TEN CRITICAL COMPETENCIES

I have been unraveling the success secrets of high-performing enterprises for nearly 20 years. Most of what I will share with you is a result of practical experience gained by working with my clients to improve their competitive position. I specialize in helping organizations that face complex change create success through customer value-driven solutions. I have been fortunate to have been asked to assist clients in the United States, Canada, Mexico, and Europe.

As a result of my experience, I have concluded that the ten critical competencies listed below are the foundation capabilities necessary for any business that seeks to become a high value-delivering organization. In this book, I will define these ten touchstones and show you how to apply them in your business through real-world examples and specific prescriptions.

Touchstone 1: The Four Keys to Creating Extraordinary Value

I'll identify the four criteria that today's sophisticated customer uses when deciding to do business with an organization: (1) quality, (2) service, (3) cost, and (4) time. You'll learn how all four of these factors must be delivered *simultaneously* in the marketplace, to beat the competition. You'll discover how to detect the specific requirements that define value in the mind of the customer.

Touchstone 2: Redesigning Business Processes

I'll explain the importance of core business processes—flows of cross-functional activity that differentiate the performance of your enterprise from the competition and create value for customers. You'll learn how to define previously unidentified business processes: how to map them, how to measure their performance, how to redesign them to improve quality and customer service, and how to eliminate the waste that adds to cost and contributes to slow response. The advantages and pitfalls of attempting radical performance improvement through business process "reengineering" are also discussed.

Touchstone 3: The New Enterprise Architecture

What are the most effective organizational frameworks that support competitive success in the value decade? I'll describe some new enterprise designs that are beginning to replace today's conventional organizational hierarchies. You'll see new possibilities for your own business. You'll also discover how to upgrade your own workplace to include emerging patterns.

Touchstone 4: The High-Involvement Workplace

Leading companies are developing new methods for promoting employee participation. By doing this, they find and harness the best ideas from employees in all parts of the enterprise. I'll describe the right team structures for promoting collaboration, effective staff recruiting, reward and recognition programs, and the types of employee communications programs that empower employees. You'll also learn about the benefits and drawbacks of high-involvement management practices.

Touchstone 5: Partnerships for Prosperity

How can you build partnership relationships with customers, suppliers, and, perhaps, competitors? I'll explain the benefits of leveraging the resources of other organizations. Topics discussed will include joint ventures, alliances, comarketing arrangements, co-op R&D, employee exchange programs, technology agreements, and other forms of cooperation among enterprises that are mutually advantageous.

Touchstone 6: Transforming through Technology

Often, as enterprises struggle to make the transition to the high-performing enterprise model, they find their computing systems are holding them back. I'll show you how new information technologies are creating open-network enterprises. I'll discuss work-group computing; enterprise computing and the integrated organization; and interenterprise computing, which extends the reach of companies to their customers, suppliers, and other business partners.

Touchstone 7: Strategy Alignment

"Hoshin planning," a Japanese method of strategy deployment, is a system that helps an enterprise achieve strategic breakthroughs in the marketplace. The techniques explained here will enable an organization to involve all employees in achieving a few critical business objectives that promote long-term competitive advantage. You'll also learn how to apply the seven steps of strategy deployment and the specific tools and techniques used at each stage in the process.

Touchstone 8: Fostering the Learning Organization

What is a learning organization? How can it be fostered? The learning organization is one that *continually enhances its capability to create its future*. I'll explain how enterprises are finding ways to meet rapidly shifting market conditions. I'll discuss the use of benchmarking as a systematic way to learn more quickly from other organizations. Finally, I'll describe "creativity" techniques that accelerate the pace of learning for people in the enterprise and simultaneously resolve critical business problems.

Touchstone 9: Mastering Change Management

A mere desire for organizational transformation is not sufficient for success. You must know how to influence the change process that will bring your organization from its current state to your future vision of a high-performing enterprise. What strategy for change fits the history, corporate culture, and unique competitive challenges of your business? I'll explain how to "diagnose" your enterprises's readiness for change, the roles of the various participants in the change process, and how to overcome "change rejection"—the natural resistance to change.

Touchstone 10: The New Spirit of Leadership

I'll identify the key leadership skills necessary for a high-performing enterprise. You'll be shown the most effective ways of promoting a new vision and value system, and you'll learn how to communicate the need for change. The role of the "change agent" is discussed and you'll understand how to lead the "revolution from within" even when you're not in a formal position of authority.

The need to create "extraordinary value" is not new. Years ago, Peter Drucker, the dean of management consultants and a critic of outdated practices reminded us:

> Quality and service is not what the supplier puts in. It is what the customer gets out and is willing to pay for. A product is not quality because it is hard to make or costs a lot of money. Customers pay for what is of use to them and gives them value. Nothing else constitutes quality.

Although the need for value is not new, the pressure to deliver it has never been more urgent. You can do it if you master the ten critical capabilities presented here as touchstones.

TOUCHSTONE
1

The Four Keys to Creating Extraordinary Value

He profits most who serves best.

Anonymous

To survive into the next century and not be driven from the marketplace, your enterprise must provide superior value to its customers. Value is giving customers all of what they want and none of what they do not; the best quality *and* the best prices; make it quick *and* serve it with a smile! Today's sophisticated and wary customers make four judgments when deciding to do business with an organization: (1) quality, (2) service, (3) cost, and (4) time. It is no longer sufficient to achieve distinction through high performance in one area alone. To deliver superior value and beat the competition, your enterprise must learn how to execute all four of these benefits *simultaneously* in the marketplace while also fostering an enterprise culture that supports the primacy of value creation. The ability to effectively harness these four "drivers" of value comprises the first and most fundamental competency of the high-performing enterprise.

SOLVING THE "VALUE EQUATION"

If you understand the secrets of customers' perception of superior value, your organization can translate this insight into a powerful enterprise strategy that addresses the value equation—the relationship between customer value and financial performance (Figure 1.1). Better value delivered to the

$$\frac{\textit{Value for}}{\textit{Customers}} = \frac{\text{Increase Quality} \times \text{Increase Service}}{\text{Decrease Cost} \times \text{Decrease Time}} = \frac{\textit{Value for}}{\textit{Shareholders}}$$

Figure 1.1   The value equation.

customer results in greater long-term returns to the owners of the business. Let value for the customer erode, and you will suffer the consequences of declining profits and, ultimately, the demise of the organization.

The value equation illustrates the four critical factors that create value in the eyes of customers: (1) quality, (2) service, (3) cost, and (4) time. Improve the numerators in the equation (quality and service), and the customer benefits from increased product utility and personal attention from your organization. Your enterprise benefits through improved customer loyalty, which lowers marketing costs. You also gain a larger share of the market, which contributes to better operation efficiencies.

Attacking the denominators in the equation (cost and time) will also increase the value delivered. By eliminating waste to reduce cost, your organization can offer more benefits to the customer at a lower price. Or, the cost savings can be retained to improve profit margins for those who have a financial stake in the enterprise. Reducing cycle time helps customers by getting new, improved products and services to market faster. Speeding-up business processes usually means eliminating non-value-adding activities and realizing lower cost and improved profits.

Your organization must master *all four* of the key factors in the value equation. Customers want quality and service, but at the right price and at the right time.

Edwin L. Artzt, Chairman of the Board and CEO of Procter & Gamble, once said that although consumers still want good product performance, quality now has a stronger value-for-the-money component. He believes that what consumers are looking for is *affordable* quality—better quality at a better price. In other words, to satisfy customers, businesses have to deliver value and concentrate on promoting customer loyalty:

> The demand for greater value isn't restricted only to consumer products. In fact, it goes beyond business altogether and reaches into government, education, non-profit organizations—every institution that provides a product or service to the consumer. People want to know that they're getting what they pay for, whether that payment comes in the form of taxes or tuition or a charitable donation.

Who's Winning with a Value Strategy?

Michael Treacy and Fred Wiersema studied 40 companies to discover the most important factors in a successful business strategy. Their findings, reported in the *Harvard Business Review,* indicated a number of important elements. Dell Computers, Nike, and Home Depot gained market share through three key achievements: (1) they redefined value in their respective markets; (2) they built powerful, cohesive business systems that could deliver more of that value than their competitors could, and (3) by doing so, they raised customers' expectations beyond the competition's reach. These authors concluded:

> Today's customers . . . have an expanded concept of value that includes convenience of purchase, after-sale service, dependability, and so on.

Dell Computer's Michael Dell established an objective for his company to lead the computer industry in price and convenience. By cutting dealers out of the distribution process, Dell outperformed Compaq and was able to offer better prices to customers. The company pioneered new operational approaches to offer exceptional delivery service and technical support. It's able to execute these effectively because of close contact with product users—without having to rely on an insufficiently trained or undermotivated intermediary.

Nike is an example of a company that is constantly pushing the "outside of the envelope" in product technical advances. The athletic shoe industry is intensely competitive; in order to stay at or near the top, Nike believes it must push itself to innovate *before* it feels pushed by the competition.

> Product leaders are their own fiercest competitors. They continually cross a frontier, then break more new ground. They have to be adept at rendering obsolete the products and services that they have created because they realize that if they do not develop a successor, another company will.

Personal service is Home Depot's forte. Its "business strategy is built not just around selling home-repair and improvement items inexpensively, but also around the customer's needs for information and service." In other words, by offering free advice as well as reasonably priced products, Home Depot achieves a competitive edge. In a major growth industry such as home renovation, it is imperative that customers are not treated as one-time purchasers of a bag of nails at 13 cents apiece. Treat them well and they will return, possibly to buy all the building supplies for the rest of the home additions they're planning.

Treacy and Wiersema concluded that, for companies to become industry leaders, not only must they become champions in at least one area that creates value, but they must also meet industry standards for other customer requirements. A company can't be outstanding in one area and be way below the mark on additional performance attributes that are important to customers. Superb companies will be those that become masters of several of the "value disciplines" in their industry.

"Golden Handcuffs"

In a nutshell, creating value means building trust with customers. Trust is developed by reducing perceived risks, creating a unique offering, rewarding loyalty, and shackling the customer with "golden handcuffs." Customers who trust your enterprise are more loyal. Customers who perceive greater value in an organization's offerings are, in turn, more valuable to it because:

- They are likely to use the services more often;
- They are willing to pay more for them;
- They require lower marketing and service costs;
- They provide referrals and word-of-mouth advertising;
- They are less likely to defect to competitors.

In short, make it tough for your established customers to leave. "When a company consistently delivers superior value and wins customer loyalty, market share and revenues go up, and the cost of acquiring and serving customers goes down."

A loyalty-based business strategy must target the "right" customers—those who are the most profitable in the long term. They are not necessarily the easiest customers to attract initially, nor are they the most profitable in the short term.

> For various reasons, some customers don't ever stay loyal to one company, no matter what value they receive. The challenge is to avoid as many of these people as possible in favor of customers whose loyalty can be developed.

An example of the devastating results of losing customers' trust is Word-Star Corporation. An industry leader in word processing software up to 1984, the company allowed its brand equity to deteriorate. After gaining an initial degree of customer loyalty through innovative products, WordStar created new products that were incompatible with its old ones. Furthermore, customers were not only forced to make a long-distance call for technical assistance, but were often put on hold and kept waiting.

In contrast to WordStar's indifference to its customer base, WordPerfect entered the marketplace in 1984 with toll-free customer support lines and new software that didn't force the customer to learn how to use their products all over again. All of WordPerfect's software packages were "backward compatible." The result? By 1990, WordStar was worth an estimated $10 million, while WordPerfect was worth an estimated $1 billion.

In one word, the secret to success in the 1990s is *value*. The way to provide value is to solve the value equation as it applies to your industry. Let's examine the value formula in more detail to see how the winners in today's markets are succeeding and to gain insight to how a value strategy can work for your enterprise.

VALUE FOR CUSTOMERS

Instead of going forward to predict what the next customer trend is, we need to go backward and remember the First Commandment of any company: "The customer is always right." Today, putting a new twist on that sacred truth, a successful organization understands: "The customer is never wrong." What's the difference? The First Commandment is arrogant and trite. It contains a subtext: "We won't *argue* with the customer, but we all know that the customer is really a pain in the neck." The new statement is humble and has this subtext: "Hey—maybe there really *is* a problem that we don't know about. Maybe we should listen to the customer for a change." "The customer is never wrong" is the true touchstone for an enterprise's success: a determination to truly understand what customers value.

More Demanding Shoppers

The need for a deep understanding of the customer has never been more important. Customer expectations are changing. A recent study of the auto industry, conducted by Yankelovich Clancy Shulman, probed Americans' changing needs for satisfaction. The study uncovered a major shift away from the "conspicuous consumerism" of the late 1980s:

- Consumers no longer buy products to impress others;
- People feel less need to buy more than they really need;
- Buyers are looking for "value" in all price ranges;
- Consumers are aware of sales and of deals;
- Comfort and utility are important selling points;
- Consumers are interested in technology that makes life easier;
- Service is critically important.

This trend among customers—to evaluate their suppliers more and to examine the "total value offering"—is evident among buyers of business goods and services as well. REM Associates, of Princeton, New Jersey, conducted a survey for a multinational industrial products firm. The survey concluded that the five most important factors leading to customer satisfaction are: (1) responsiveness, (2) customer service, (3) delivery, (4) product quality, and (5) price.

Responsiveness was judged on whether there was follow-up on customer inquiries, how well changing needs were met, and problem solving. Customer service was examined for ease of order placement, availability of product/order status information, and response to emergency situations. Delivery was measured according to order cycle time, dependability, and order condition. Product quality was based on consistency, how well the product conformed to specifications, and whether it performed as intended. Price was rated on competitiveness: its relationship to the value of products/services, the willingness to honor contracts (i.e., not spring price increases on the customer), and the willingness to provide a rationale for price levels and increases.

These characteristics are important because, when it comes to value, not all benefits are created equal in the minds of customers. There is a hierarchy: core elements that must be performed well to be in the business at all; expected elements any good provider should offer; and breakthrough elements that surprise and delight the customer. Focusing on breakthroughs without delivering core or expected elements is a recipe for disaster.

Xerox shows a refreshing clarity in its understanding of the hierarchy of value for its customers of after-sales service. The company's service value strategy, shown in Figure 1.2, has three levels. The top level, represented by the outer band, is made up of supplementary services, those that build-in great value to ensure ongoing satisfaction—account management and consultative support, for example. The middle level focuses on value-added services that help customers receive the maximum possible return on their investment in a Xerox product. This level includes such elements as customer education, planned maintenance, prioritized responsiveness, and so on—all part of the design to either prevent repairs or provide timely repairs. The inner or core level has just two words: FIX IT. Xerox clearly understands that fixing a machine and getting it back into service quickly is the most important priority to the customer. Only then, will customers have any interest in additional "customer delight" factors.

Earning Trust

Trend watchers at Grey Advertising have tried to determine what delights customers. Surprisingly, they report, customer delight is comprised of some pretty basic expectations. Customers want to do business with enterprises they trust. Successful companies should:

- Ensure their products and services perform as promised;
- Give more than the customer expects;
- Give guarantees;
- Avoid unrealistic pricing;

Figure 1.2 Xerox service: Value added throughout.

■ **Remedial Maintenance**
Our core business is to repair your equipment quickly and efficiently.

□ **Value Added Services**
Service today is more than just fixing equipment. It's maximizing your investment to the fullest. Xerox Service provides total value performance.

▨ **Ancillary Services**
Building on great service value are supplementary services to ensure your ongoing satisfaction.

- Give the customer the facts necessary to make informed decisions;
- Build relationships.

These suggestions boil down to offering the customer trustworthy behavior. Product performance that lives up to advertising claims builds trust and is a basic expectation of the customer. Guarantees ensure that if the company does make a mistake, it is prepared to fix it. Reality pricing reassures customers that they are really getting what they are paying for. Plain-facts advertising helps to instill confidence and allows customers to feel that they are able to make the best choice for their needs.

The bottom line for you? Trust equals relationships—just as it does in your personal life. Would you, for example, sell a used computer to your best friend without leveling to that friend about the true performance of the computer? Would you not give that friend a personal guarantee that if the computer didn't work when he or she took it home, you would take it back? Would you not offer that computer at a realistic price? You would, because you value the friendship and want the relationship to continue.

During the 1980s, much was written about the magic of "relationship marketing," a fancy way of saying that companies that truly embrace their customers will win in the long term. Philip Kotler, International Marketing Professor at the Kellogg Graduate School of Management at Northwestern University, says:

> Relationship marketing is a sometimes overused notion because it suggests you bond with the customer . . . . The truth is any business relationship will break up if value evaporates. You've got to continue to generate more value for the customer but not give away the house. It's a very delicate balance.

Building true bonds with customers means involving them in your enterprise, letting their "voice" drive your business decisions. At the Jacksonville Naval Aviation Depot, customers are involved in every step of the product development and production process. In this case, customers include the Navy, other military services, foreign governments, and civilian agencies such as NASA.

The Jacksonville depot was bidding on a large defense contract, competing against private aerospace firms. The depot knew that its productivity and cost performance had improved greatly as a result of working with the Naval Industrial Improvement Program, reducing overhead, and improving material management and management information systems.

In open competition, Jacksonville won the contract, offering the highest level of service at the lowest price. The job was to upgrade 30 antisubmarine aircraft and was worth $50 million over five years.

To make sure the Jacksonville depot could live up to its bid, a policy of on-site customer presence was put in place. Managers invited customers to spot-check quality at any time, and performance reports were discussed with customers to solicit their suggestions. Supervisors were allowed to make customer-authorized changes without having to wait for higher-level clearances. This approach saved time, money, and confusion, and had the added bonus of letting the customers feel they were playing a part in the company's continuous improvement strategy. The beauty of this policy is that there are no costly problems to deal with once the customer takes delivery of the product, because the customer is on-site to help detect problems before they become too expensive.

By the time they began work on the fifth aircraft, Jacksonville workers had trimmed 500 worker-hours off the production schedule; by the ninth, they had exceeded their best-case projection for worker-hours, with record-breaking quality-check results; by the last aircraft, the required worker-hours were 40 percent less than the original bid amount—and they continued to decrease.

WHAT'S IN IT FOR SHAREHOLDERS?

"Sure, customers are important," you agree, "but what about making money?" Ultimately, happy customers lead to improved profitability—better value for the owners or for others who have a financial stake in the enterprise. As shown in several studies, companies that focus on providing true value to the customer will deliver the most value to the shareholder—and, in the end, create the strongest competitive advantage.

Happy Customers Are Profitable

PIMS Associates conducted one of the most authoritative studies linking quality (and value) with business results. Using a database of over 3,000 businesses in Europe and North America, they were able to evaluate the effect of "relative customer perceived quality"—the perception of quality by customers relative to the offerings of competitors.

PIMS reported: "There is a clear, positive correlation between quality and profit. . . . The higher the relative quality, the higher both the average return on investment and return on sales." The businesses in the PIMS database were divided into groups according to quality and financial performance. The group with low relative quality fared poorly; only one-fifth achieved a return on investment of more than 25 percent. Of the high-quality group, over half achieved a return on investment of more than 25 percent.

The reason for this higher profitability in companies with greater quality is easy to understand. With higher quality comes a greater degree of desirability for those products or services on the part of the customer. As a result, the company can charge higher prices for its products or services; or, it can choose to offer better value without charging more, and build greater market share. The PIMS study concluded:

In the long run, the most important factor affecting a business unit's performance is the quality of its products and services, relative to those of the competitors.

The consulting firm, Bain & Company, conducted a somewhat different study and came up with a similar result: there is a direct link between customer satisfaction and profitability. Bain looked at companies' customer retention rate (defined simply as the percentage of customers at the beginning of the year who remain customers at the end of the year), inferring that customers staying with one company are, by definition, satisfied customers. Increasing the retention rate means that customers remain loyal for longer. High rates of customer retention reduce costs, add to revenue and prices, and protect market share:

- The cost of acquiring a new customer can be substantial; higher retention rates mean fewer new customers are needed; established customers place frequent, consistent orders and therefore usually cost less to serve.

- Existing customers tend to order more and will often refer new customers to the company, thereby reducing, again, the cost of attracting new customers.

- Satisfied customers are often willing to pay a premium price for products and services from a company they know and trust.

- Retaining customers makes market entry or share gain more difficult for competitors.

A good example of a company that understands the economics of customer retention is the Canadian hardware chain, Aikenhead's. Says Stephen Bebis, President, "Ultimately, we're in the service business, not the hardware or home improvement business." The store puts every executive to work on the store floor. Carpenters, plumbers, and tradespeople all participate in serving and advising customers. This is done because the real power behind most businesses today is not the CEO but the customer; employees are the obvious and important link between the organization and its customers.

Bebis believes that, over a lifetime, the average North American home owner spends at least $50,000 on house improvement. Bebis concludes:

The way I see it, every time we make a special effort to satisfy a customer, we're gaining a $50,000 order. If we disappoint that customer in his search for a ladder, or a caulking compound, or a can of paint, we've lost that $50,000 order.

Very smart!

An Interesting Study

Although somewhat limited in scope, a study published by the U.S. General Accounting Office (GAO) in May 1990 looked at the "quality management" programs in 20 companies. Each of the organizations was a high scorer in the competition for either the 1988 or 1989 Malcolm Baldrige National Quality Award. Using a detailed survey and extensive follow-up interviews, the GAO concluded that there was a positive "cause-and-effect" relationship between total quality management (TQM) practices and corporate performance, as measured by profitability, customer satisfaction, internal efficiencies, and employee satisfaction.

Spend Now or Pay Later

Investors in a business are continually faced with a trade-off: maximize profits today, or build for the future? In today's fast-changing market, this trade-off may no longer exist. Investments in value improvement must be made today or there will be no tomorrow for the enterprise. Intel CEO Andy Grove emphasizes the need for investing enormous amounts of time and money to produce long-term profitability. Grove estimates that Intel spent between $30 million and $40 million, and between 200 and 300 worker-years, on three major product development projects that didn't work out at all.

The man who fled his native Hungary in 1956 with only $20 in his pocket believes that any company doing business in a fast-changing market can't afford *not* to risk:

> [You can't] hesitate or hedge your bets. You can have the best product in the world, but if you fail to invest in enough plant and equipment to satisfy demand for it, all your efforts are wasted. All you've done is create an opportunity for someone else.

Grove doesn't see companies structured the old way thriving in the future. In these difficult economic times, the shareholder is often obsessed with budgets. Yet, to attract customers in the future, money must be spent now. It's a "got-to-spend-money-to-make money" scenario, and it's perhaps more true now than at any time in the postindustrial age. Says Grove:

> First, you have to start with a better product than the other guy's. Second, it has to be better in a way that your customers can appreciate. Third, your customers have to *know* it's a better product in a way they can appreciate. . . . We have to figure out what their [customers'] needs will be years from now . . . .

BRINGING COST INTO THE EQUATION

Companies can no longer choose between offering low prices *or* top quality. Instead, they must be able to offer both. Len Schlesinger, an associate professor at the Harvard Business School, cites the case of Intuit Software, makers of the *Quicken* software package. Intuit owns 60 percent of the market for small business and personal financial planning. The strategy to gain a competitive edge ". . . absolutely drenches the product in customer research. Instead of designing products to the taste of software engineers, the company designs products with the customer in mind." This means software designs are efficient from the customer's perspective.

Another good example is Taco Bell. The fast-food chain asked customers what they wanted, and discovered that preparing the food in front of the customer at each retail location was a "non-value-adding activity." Taco Bell removed the practice by preparing more of its food off-site, cut 15 work-hours per day per location, and was able to cut prices by 25 to 35 percent. The message is: Let the customers decide what is valuable to them, what is worth paying for.

Blinded by Outdated Financial Systems

The financial management systems of most corporations are ill-equipped to handle the demands of the much more competitive future. Outdated management accounting systems are not providing timely and detailed information on process efficiencies. Managers have become disconnected from the real value-creating operations of the organization.

In *Relevance Lost: The Rise and Fall of Management Accounting*, H. Thomas Johnson and Robert S. Kaplan observe:

> With vigorous global competition, rapid progress in product and process technology, and wide fluctuations in currency exchange rates and raw material prices, an organization's management accounting system must provide timely and accurate information to facilitate efforts to control costs, to measure and improve productivity, and to devise improved production processes.
>
> • • •
>
> For the purposes of process and cost control, allocating costs not directly affected by activity levels in the cost center has no apparent value.

What this means is: There are only two kinds of costs when you get down to it: (1) those that add value to the company's end products and services and (2) those that don't add value.

Traditional cost information systems have a number of shortcomings. They provide an "account" perspective rather than a "management" perspective;

the links between the cost incurred and the activity that required the cost are not clear. Truly understanding cost dynamics involves documenting the relationship between activities and their causes *and* the relationship between activities and their costs. This type of approach is called "total cost management" or "activity-based costing."

Innovative enterprises are revamping their cost management approaches to provide better management control and more value for the customer. Here are some examples:

- *Speeding service to the customer.* A large life insurance company employed a total cost management team to analyze the time, quality, and cost of its services. The team looked at processes such as new policy applications, loan applications, policy surrenders, premium receipts, and customer inquiries. Calculations included the activities necessary for each process and the average cost of completion. Activities that the policyholder did not value were further analyzed, and the question of why the activity was necessary at all was addressed. The team also analyzed the data to identify the greatest opportunities for improving speed of response and quality.

  The team then grouped recommendations into three implementation phases: (1) short-term "hits," (2) system changes and (3) people/organization changes. A typical suggestion on the short-term "hit" list was to change the format of premium notices so they could be processed with scanning equipment rather than manual input. Because the company had excess scanning equipment capacity it already owned, the only investment required to implement this change was a redesign of the standard form and some programming to automate the scanning.

  The system in use for processing universal life policies had been in place for only a few years, but it seemed to be the source of many problems identified by the team. Further investigation revealed that the system had been poorly implemented; many important features were not included at all. The recommended system changes were largely a reimplementation of the system already used in-house.

  People changes centered on better training and on reorganizing work spaces for improved work flow. In addition to achieving reduced cycle-time goals, the effect of all these changes was to achieve cost savings of 30 to 35 percent of the insurance company's expense base for these processes.

- *Improving quality within a planning organization.* In a high-technology services corporation, the director of a product planning division worked with an analyst to estimate the travel expenses required to support commitments within the business plan. Managers developed travel budgets based on activity, and noted the expenses that corresponded to each activity. From this analysis, they were able to identify poor-quality travel: spending money on trips that turned out to be a waste of time because of a lack of clear objectives, premature technical reviews, or key personnel missing from meetings.

- *Getting close to profitable customers.* A management team used activity-based cost analysis to gain a better understanding of which combinations of products, services, and customers represented its most profitable business. The team identified services that were both costly and ineffective, discovered ways to develop business alliances and more personalized service, and were able to effectively eliminate non-value-adding waste.

Avoiding Pricing Mistakes

Your pricing decisions are likely weakened by having both a distorted view of your costs and a poor understanding of perceptions of price by the customer. Your correct focus for pricing decisions should be: Marketplace first, cost second. In other words, you should not just ask what a product or service costs. Instead, you should be asking questions like:

- Which customers should we pursue?
- Which products and services should we include in our offering to our targeted customers?
- What is the perceived value by the customer of each element of our offering to the market?

After these questions are addressed, you can determine what the market will bear with regard to your specific products and services. Your next question to yourself should be: "Can we meet the pricing target in our selected markets at a profit margin we can live with?"

What do you do if the pricing target is too low in comparison to your costs? Determine why the cost is what it is and what can be done to bring it in line with market demands. In other words:

- Make your cost information support your strategy;
- Try to see your organization as a collection of business processes, not as a set of organizational charts or cost centers;
- Once you've made the fundamental shift to "process thinking," manage your costs by managing your activities;

- Organize your information by identifying the value of activities to your customers;
- Monitor your business by aligning process performance measures with the important factors that affect customer value perceptions.

For example, the Little Rock, Arkansas, plant of Chicopee, a Johnson & Johnson subsidiary, was dependent on internal suppliers (other companies in the Johnson & Johnson family) who had operational problems and could not be counted on for reliable delivery. Therefore, Chicopee was forced to keep inventory high to meet its own customers' demands.

In response to this problem, a project team made up of financial, engineering, manufacturing, and production planning personnel interviewed managers and gathered shop-floor reports to evaluate the company's work activities. They divided activities into value-added and non-value-added categories. Mark Rose, project manager and team leader, calls a value-added activity one that "converts resources into products or services consistent with customer requirements" and "one that the customer is willing to pay for." A non-value-added activity is "one that can be eliminated with no deterioration of product attributes, namely performance, quality or perceived value." Using this information, the team identified cost reduction opportunities to offset the inventory carrying costs.

QUALITY IN THE 1990s

Cost and quality are interdependent. Taking shortcuts on costs doesn't pay if the quality is compromised. Indeed, progressive enterprises have learned that a focus on product quality also results in lower costs—better value for the customer *and* the shareholders.

Defect Free

Motorola's obsession with quality has paid off. In 1987, Motorola set a target of "zero defects" in manufactured components by 1992. It missed the target, but still achieved an astounding performance of 3.4 defects per million, an enormous improvement over the 6,000 defects per million of five years before.

Richard Buetow, Director of Quality at Motorola, believes that quality improvement, as measured by an absence of product defects, has saved the company more than $700 million in manufacturing costs over the five-year period. Fewer defects means less rework—sometimes called "doing it right the first time." The company's next goal is to cut manufacturing defects by

90 percent every two years through the 1990s. By the year 2001, the company wants its defect rate to be one per million. Motorola has learned:

- *Quality is in the eye of the customer.* Motorola "grades" customers to determine those who are the most demanding, then questions them in detail to learn about their well-above-average needs, setting ever higher standards for itself.

- *Redundancy costs money that is well spent.* Building redundancy into products such as transistors (through spare capacity, alternative signal paths, and so on) causes an increase in costs as well as in complexity, but customers' perception of quality is boosted. Complaints and product returns are eliminated, thus reducing the heavy costs of customer dissatisfaction.

- *Responsibility can be pushed down the ranks.* Motorola spends $30 million per year training employees in order to meet stringent quality targets. Motorola also emphasizes the need for quality partnerships with suppliers. Any suppliers that don't see eye-to-eye on quality with Motorola are dropped.

TQM Going Sour?

The increasing recognition that product (and service) quality is a prerequisite in today's marketplace has fueled the rapid growth of the total quality management (TQM) movement during the past decade. TQM has many definitions. *Report on Business Magazine* says:

> Essentially, TQM boils down to a process-oriented system based on the belief that quality is conformance to the requirements of the end-user of the product or service. It is believed that these requirements can be isolated and measured. Deviations can be assigned a dollar value, and, more important, prevented through process improvement or redesign.

The promised benefits of TQM, however, are sometimes elusive. For example, Douglas Aircraft, a subsidiary of McDonnell Douglas Corporation, launched its TQM program in 1989; some 8,000 employees were sent to two-week seminars. In less than two years, the quality effort was a shambles, largely because of massive layoffs that poisoned management–labor relations. "At Douglas, TQM appeared to be just one more hothouse Japanese flower never meant to grow on rocky American ground." TQM programs have often stumbled badly because of inflated expectations. TQM has been sold as a cure-all—and an instant one to boot.

Florida Power & Light, the first American company to win Japan's Deming Prize for quality management, has slashed its TQM program because of employee complaints of excessive paperwork.

The Wallace Company, a Houston oil-supply company that won the U.S. Department of Commerce's Malcolm Baldrige National Quality Award, has since filed for Chapter 11 bankruptcy protection.

Making TQM Work

Despite these problems, thoughtful observers recognize the promise of the total quality approach. The issue is not the concept, but impatience and faulty implementation. Here are five barriers to effective TQM:

1. *Insufficient executive commitment.* Employees need constant reinforcement; executives often don't manage the TQM initiative properly.
2. *Unrealistic expectations.* Immediate and significant results are expected, when it actually takes at least two to three years.
3. *Primary focus on serving the internal customer, which neglects the external customer.* Too much initial emphasis is placed on team building and on solving internal problems; it's crucial to focus on improving first the work processes that are important to achieving sales increases and improved customer satisfaction.
4. *Lack of prioritization.* Teams are formed to "get things done" but management takes a "hands-off" stance, and projects are not prioritized according to their importance to customer satisfaction or profitability.
5. *Weak measurement methods.* Enterprises need to continuously measure performance to keep track of progress.

The Quality and Productivity Management Association (QPMA) warns against these common "quality mistakes":

- *A focus on changing culture versus changing behavior.* Some companies use all the TQM "buzz words," but never get down to the specifics of what continuous improvement, teamwork, or empowerment means to the organization.
- *Failure to fully and accurately define performance requirements.* If it is not willing to define specific, measurable areas of performance improvement, a company will not succeed with TQM.
- *Failure to perform a "gap analysis" and develop a strategic plan prior to implementing TQM.* An organization's existing quality practices should be assessed against best-in-class practices and plans tailored to close the specific short-comings which are revealed.
- *Failure to establish a functioning executive-quality management structure.* Enterprises need to establish a TQM Council that devotes 50

percent of its time to the effort, holds monthly meetings, and has the personal "hands-on" involvement of the most senior executives of the organization.

- *Failure to establish key quality measures and goals for every level of the organization and to link them to organizationwide requirements for market leadership.* A company needs to make sure that all quality improvement initiatives are linked together in a way that supports its business strategy.

- *Failure to change compensation systems so as to hold senior executives and middle managers responsible for quality leadership and for achieving quality results.* This refers, for example, to retaining compensation bonus systems that are linked to short-term results such as monthly sales instead of long-term results such as customer retention.

- *Failure to place managers, supervisors, and employees physically and emotionally close to the customers they serve.* TQM requires a "Mom and Pop store" mentality: close interaction with customers, and personalized service.

- *Too much reliance on training in quality improvement tools and techniques as THE way to implement TQM.* TQM is a holistic, management paradigm change that occurs as a result of a multiyear, coordinated, and planned effort that touches every facet of the organization; it's not just one thing, it's *everything*.

- *Failure to do just-in-time (JIT) training and to provide follow-up coaching to ensure that skills taught in the training are immediately applied on the job.* For the training to sink in, it must be taught using the JIT approach—just before it's applied.

- *Focus on short-term breakthroughs versus long-term continuous improvement.* Spectacular, immediate breakthroughs are possible but unlikely; significant long-term improvement is the goal.

New and Improved

Products and services that are reliable and defect-free are obviously of value to customers. Finding new ways to serve customers better is also important to increasing value.

ChemLawn, a $355-million-per-year company, had a virtual lock on the lawn-care market until smaller, more responsive companies began to steal customers away. In May 1991, ChemLawn asked its biggest commercial customers about their perception of the organization, and it discovered—to its surprise—that ChemLawn wasn't perceived as a "total" lawn-care provider. Instead, customers thought of ChemLawn as a company that maintained *only the grass*. Customers were looking elsewhere for their other landscape needs. Using this information, ChemLawn took a new approach: it emphasized its customers' "total grounds look" as a marketing edge. "We can improve your bottom line by making your [grounds] appearance a marketing tool," pitched ChemLawn. ChemLawn began selling this "grounds look" idea to customer marketing personnel instead of maintenance personnel. Commercial clients—banks, restaurants, and hotels—responded. Sales in the targeted segment starting growing at 20 percent per year.

In another example of seeing new opportunities to create value, Baxter International, an $8.9-billion-per-year hospital products company, observed that hospitals were spending huge amounts of money storing and distributing supplies on-site. Baxter listened. It developed ValueLink, a computerized service that helps hospitals reduce costly inventory while improving the distribution of supplies. Baxter charges the hospital a service fee of 3 to 6 percent of sales, and it gains better control over the supplies and the accounts.

For example, Saint Barnabas Hospital, which used to order from many suppliers, would order only about $500,000 worth per year from Baxter. On ValueLink, the hospital orders exclusively from Baxter, to the tune of about $5 million per year. In exchange, Saint Barnabas gets better, more personalized service, and no longer wastes valuable storage space on surplus inventory or spends administrative time juggling several suppliers.

Renewing the Faith

How your company handles the consequences of a quality lapse is also important. Take, for example, the case of Great Plains Software, a company that faced potential catastrophe because of the type of quality problem that keeps CEOs up at night.

Great Plains, a software developer, is the largest seller of high-end software for accountants. The company has built an enviable reputation for "getting close to the customer" and providing great customer support. "Great Plains has an incredible reputation for service," says *The Soft Letter,* an industry newsletter. "That's an important competitive advantage in an industry where the products are a lot alike."

Great Plains has 45,000 buyer profiles in the database it uses to keep in touch with customers. The company regularly is in contact with users to ensure that the software they purchased is working well and to ask for ideas about improvements. This close association resulted in an astounding 42 percent of the owners of Great Plains Accounting Version 6 upgrading to the new Version 7 when it was introduced in 1993.

Then disaster struck! Version 7 turned out to contain bugs. The company's carefully maintained reputation was on the line. CEO Doug Bergum launched an all-out effort to rebuild trust with his customers. He first spent $250,000 to mail out new, bug-free disks to every Version 7 buyer. He then wrote to his 2,500 dealers, admitting that the company had failed to test the Version 7 properly. He even offered to compensate any dealer who suffered a loss because of the problem.

Great Plains's response to its quality failure may have made customers more loyal! Many dealers wrote to praise the company for its actions. Very few asked for restitution. The company had to pay only $25,000 in claims, less than 0.5 percent of Version 7 revenues. *Accounting Today* magazine commended the company for being "a model of how problems should be handled."

The Great Plains story is a vivid contrast to the infamous Audi automobile incident. When a television news program reported that Audi drivers were having accidents caused by a "sudden acceleration" problem, Audi claimed it was nothing more than driver error. Its own studies concluded that there were no technical difficulties with the cars, Audi suffered through an enormous amount of bad public relations. The German carmaker's sales dropped from 74,000 in 1985 to 26,000 in 1987. Research indicated that customers felt insulted and betrayed by Audi's "We're right, you're wrong" stance. Although all indications point to the fact that Audi was correct in its findings, it underestimated the power of both the media and customer disapproval of Audi's failure to take responsibility for its products.

When Lexus first entered the American market, it turned a minor fault into a major public relations coup. About 8,000 new vehicles had to be recalled for some insignificant adjustment. What could have turned into a tidal wave of customer dissatisfaction emerged as approval. Lexus staff retrieved the cars from the owners' homes to make the adjustment, and returned them quickly, cleaned and polished. Customers were flabbergasted by Lexus' very visible attempt to take full responsibility, going the extra mile to regain customer trust.

SERVICE WITH A SMILE

Low costs (and prices) along with high-quality products certainly build value for the customer, but excellence in customer service is also a powerful competitive advantage. Service adds value through the personal relationship and support provided to the customer above and beyond the performance of the product itself. When a woman shops at Nordstrom, the much publicized retailer, she's not there just for the wide merchandise selection or good prices, but because of the exceptional—no, *extraordinary*—service that Nordstrom offers. We all remember a report that aired on "60 Minutes," showing an ordinary Nordstrom salesperson taking a cab across town—using his own money—to return a parcel to a customer who had left it behind in the store.

Another example of a company of "service heroes" is Southwest Airlines. CEO Herbert Kelleher explains why other airlines are losing money while his is posting a profit: "We dignify the customer. The bigger we get, the smaller I want my employees to think and act." Here's a list of what Southwest Airlines does to dignify its customers:

- The average cost of fares is $1/3$ of the competitions'—real value;
- The word "customer" is capitalized in all printed material;
- Frequent fliers get birthday cards;
- The 1,000 customer letters received every week get personal responses, not form letters, within four weeks;
- Frequent fliers sit in on flight attendant job interviews!

The Right Philosophy Needed

In many industries, excellent customer service is critical to survival; it is the competitive edge over competitors with similar products. To achieve service excellence, satisfying customers must be the first priority of everyone in the organization, from the CEO on down. Jeffrey E. Disend describes customer service as "an attitude, an obsession, a way of life, an ongoing process." Every aspect of the customers' experience must be managed; when these "moments of truth" are unmanaged, service deteriorates. He recites these examples of internally focused organizations—enterprises that put their own needs ahead of customers:

- Banks that are open only from 9:00 A.M. to 4:00 P.M., never late at night, forcing enormous line-ups at other times when they are open (Saturdays, Thursday nights);
- Companies that provide the closest available parking to executives, next closest to employees, and farthest spaces to customers;
- Doctors and dentists who don't keep their offices open past regular "business" hours and overbook appointment times;
- Auto service centers that aren't open past 5 P.M. on weekdays and don't offer loaner cars or shuttle services;
- Automated telephone answering services that require the caller to listen to a long list of options before arriving at the needed extension.

Poor service by public sector agencies contributes to taxpayers' frustration and their perception of poor value received for their tax dollars. In a 1986 study of customer service in the public sector, the Technical Assistance Research Programs Institute (TARP) compared 643 private businesses to state and local governments and private volunteer agencies (SLVs). TARP found that many consumers have difficulty gaining access to public sector agencies because there are no toll-free telephone lines, nor can agency staff direct people to proper extensions. Very few agencies conduct customer surveys or use other methods to gauge customer satisfaction.

The TARP study also found that SLV front-line employees receive relatively little training. Budgets for complaint handling are low in the public sector, even though the public sector handles more complaints than the private sector and uses fewer people, who are paid less money.

L.L. Bean, a noted service leader whose practices have been studied closely by many leading companies, represents an excellent example of how service can be used to enhance value for customers. Its motto is: "Sell good merchandise at a reasonable profit, treat your customers like human beings, and they will always come back for more."

L.L. Bean infuses each employee with the following company beliefs:

- Customer service is an investment, not a cost. "Every dollar we spend on customer service is a capital dollar for the future."

- Customer service is dealing effectively with one call at a time, one letter at a time, one order at a time.

- Everyone has a role to play in customer service. "Research has shown us that customers who complain tend to be your most loyal customers and have a greater propensity for ordering from you again."

This last belief—that the *people* make a difference in delivering outstanding service—is the bedrock of companies that excel in finding new ways of adding value. For example, Susan Gagnon, a service representative at Polaroid, received a request for a special instant camera on behalf of a little girl who couldn't use her right hand. Gagnon didn't ignore the request, nor did she write a return letter expressing her regret that the camera was not suited to anyone who was exclusively left-handed.

What Gagnon *did* do was to send a camera to the little girl free of charge. Then she brought together a group of technicians to create a special shutter system for Polaroid's instant camera that allowed it to be operated by the left hand. Gagnon went on to help develop a program called Special Needs Adapted Photography (SNAP). Polaroid set up a toll-free phone line and encouraged customers to make similar special requests. The result: Polaroid is now reaching a new market of 32 million disabled people because it started to think more deeply about ways to serve customers better.

Listening and Learning

Delivering good service means turning a sensitive ear to the "voice of the customer"—making it easy for customers to tell you what they want and when they are unhappy. When General Motors conducted research on its customers, the company made some startling findings:

- Of 100 customers with genuine complaints, only 40 will voice them; of the remaining 60, 54 will go to the competitor. Out of the 40 complainants, 16 will stay with you if their complaint is resolved satisfactorily, and another 16 will stay if they are listened to but not satisfied. The final 8 are lost forever.

- Satisfied customers tell 8 to 10 people about positive experiences; dissatisfied customers tell 16 to 20.

- People place twice the value on negative product or service information as on positive information.

- It costs five times as much to gain one new customer as it does to retain one customer.

- Almost 70 percent of consumers make a purchasing decision based on prior personal experience with the product, knowing someone who owns a similar product, knowing someone who is knowledgeable about the product, or reading an objective consumer-advice article.

The proof of GM's findings can be found at Amica Mutual Insurance Company, named by *TIME Magazine* as one of the top providers of service in the United States. Of its new business, 90 to 95 percent comes through referrals from satisfied customers. Amica has 5,000 policyholders who have been with the company for 50 years, and an additional 6,000 policyholders who have remained for 25 years: Amica focuses on consumer insurance needs and doesn't handle commercial business at all. The company concentrates on being the best, not the biggest, in serving a specific target market.

Excellence in customer service is not really complicated, particularly in addressing problems and complaints. Experience and empirical data reveal consumers have these very simple expectations:

- Being called back when promised;
- Receiving an explanation of how a problem happened;
- Being provided with the right phone numbers to call to get information about the company;
- Being contacted promptly when a problem is resolved;
- Being allowed to talk to someone in authority;
- Being told how long it will take to resolve a problem;

- Being given useful alternatives if a problem can't be solved;
- Being treated like people, not account numbers;
- Being told about ways to prevent future problems;
- Being given progress reports if a problem can't be solved immediately.

SPEED: VALUE IN THE FAST LANE

Companies that are successful in the value decade will attack the consumption of time throughout their organization with the same intensity that they used to focus on cost. Companies that reduce time-to-market establish market share and brand position earlier. "Fast followers" can often recoup a significant share and carve an alternate position, but slow-paced competitors are left behind "in the dust."

Ed Hay, a vice president with the Boston-based management consulting firm, Rath & Strong, Inc., believes that few executives have an appreciation for the magnitude of the opportunity to "speed up" business processes. In his experience, only 5 to 15 percent of the steps of a typical work process add value. Indeed, he says that during the elapsed time of a typical process, value is being added only 1 percent of the time!

To compress "cycle times," an enterprise must seek out the causes of lack of quickness—the factors that typically increase cost and reduce quality at the same time. Through the reduction of waste and non-value-adding activities, cost and quality will improve, increasing value for the customer. Reducing time-to-market also increases competitors' obsolescence and raises the benchmark that they must meet to compete. Kellogg's, the cereal maker, for example, can take products developed by competitors and produce the equivalent within weeks, even as it is developing entirely new products ahead of the competition.

> Markets based on style, fashion, or fads have always felt this pressure, but today producers of semiconductors, industrial vehicles and equipment, and chemicals, to name a few, feel its effects.

Authors George Stalk, Jr. and Thomas M. Hout point out, in their book, *Competing against Time: How Time-Based Competition Is Reshaping Global Markets,* that compression of time brings about:

- *Productivity increases.* Cycle time is inversely proportional to work-in-progress turns; as work-in-progress turns increase, cycle times decrease.

- *Increases in prices.* Customers are willing to pay 20 to 100 percent more for products and services delivered with increased response rates.

- *Reduced risks.* The cost of over or underforecasting demand can be high; forecasts made closer to the time of sale are more accurate.

- *Market share increases.* Traditional approaches such as price cuts to gain market share often won't differentiate to the degree that quick time-to-market can.

It's easy to observe companies that profit from "speed-to-market"—giving customers what they want *when* they want it. Wal-Mart has honed its warehousing and inventory management process and is able to replenish its stock in stores twice weekly—far above the industry average. Compared to its rivals, it also offers customers four times the choice of product range.

Competitors such as K mart, Sears, and Zayres, on other hand, only re-stock every two weeks and must carry far larger inventories. As a result of offering customers a broad selection of the very latest products, Wal-Mart is growing three times faster than the retail discount store industry average. Efficient inventory management, which boosts the "velocity" of product moving through the system, dramatically lowers costs and helps Wal-Mart achieve a return on capital that it twice the industry benchmark.

Other companies are enjoying the benefits of speed-based advantages. Thomasville Furniture ships out-of-stock items within 30 days of the order; the industry average is three months. The company is growing four times as fast as its competitors and is twice as profitable. Atlas Door fills orders for non-standard overhead doors in three to four weeks, one-third faster than the industry average; these special orders often command a 20 percent price premium. Atlas is growing three times faster than its competitors, and its profits are five times higher than the industry average.

Accelerating

A better word to explain the notion of time-to-market is "accelerator." How many "accelerators" are in place in your organization in engineering, production, sales response, or customer service? A McKinsey & Company study showed that a product that is six months late to market will miss out on one-third of its potential profit over its lifetime. The study concluded:

> Speed-to-market requires a major or total change in traditional operations. That is, after the changes are applied, the original procedures (and accompanying deficiencies) are no longer recognizable.

The changes in how you work may have to be large, but the payoff can be equally dramatic. Ballistic Systems Division of Boeing Aerospace Corporation implemented a "Developmental Operations" program to simplify its design and product development processes in order to increase speed. A multifunctional product development team was formed to utilize process simplification techniques to expedite the ways a specific new product was developed and brought to the market. The results:

- Design analysis was reduced from two weeks to 38 minutes (goal: four minutes);

- The average number of engineering changes was reduced from 15 to 20 down to 1;

- The ratio of shop floor inspection hours to direct labor was reduced from 1:15 to 1:20.

Flexibility and "S t r e t c h"

Speed-to-market is important, but time has another dimension: flexibility. Flexibility is the ability to change and to cope rapidly with fluctuations in customer demand and preferences. The Japanese are already investing heavily to improve their flexibility and competitive agility: they are "stretching" to fit the requirements of the market. As U.S. business works to narrow the "quality gap" with Japan, Japan is redefining the rules of the game through flexibility: changing fast and keeping costs low, while still responding quickly to customers.

Aleda Roth, manufacturing expert at Duke University's business school, comments that "most American companies are a generation behind [on flexibility]—as far behind as they were on quality." Flexibility is the ability not only to read the market more quickly, but also to manufacture many different products on the same production line, switching back and forth at low cost.

In a Deloitte & Touche survey of 900 U.S. and Japanese companies, the differences in approach between the two nations' companies were startling:

- Japan stresses flexibility; America emphasizes product quality (durability, conformance to specifications, on-time delivery). The Japanese take product quality as a "given" and now focus on more and better product features, expanded customer service, flexible factories, and rapid development of new products.

- Japan is committed to staying ahead in flexibility sweepstakes through advanced technology. This includes the use of computer-aided design (CAD), automated materials handling, robotics, and similar innovations.

- Compared to U.S. firms, Japanese companies are 25 percent more likely to have bigger investment plans for 33 out of 42 advanced manufacturing technologies studied.

- Japan places emphasis on "agile production": small, modular factories employ reprogrammable machinery to make an almost infinite variety of new or customized goods at low unit cost.

Using Speed to Deliver Value

Stalk and Hout nicely sum up the methods of organizations that have learned to make time a competitive weapon:

1. *They choose time consumption as the critical management and strategic parameter.* They determine how much time is needed to give their customers what they want and to perform vital internal chores.

2. *They use responsiveness to stay close to customers, increasing the customers' dependence on them.* How long must the customer wait for the product or service? The longer the wait, the higher the chance the customer will go elsewhere.

3. *They direct their value delivery system to the most attractive customers, which forces competitors toward less attractive customers.* The most attractive customers are those who cannot wait for what they want and will therefore pay a premium for not waiting.

4. *They set the pace of innovation in their industry.* Time-based companies that have extended the response advantage throughout the organization almost always lead the field in the areas of technological and product leadership.

5. *They grow faster and have higher profits than their competitors.* A response advantage three to four times faster than the average almost always results in growth three times faster than the average.

6. *They baffle competitors.* Constant quick-paced innovation keeps slow companies on the defensive.

To become an effective time-based competitor, make the value delivery systems of your company two to three times more flexible and faster than those of your competitors. Determine how your customers value variety and responsiveness, focus on customers with more sensitivity to these issues, and price accordingly. Have a strategy for surprising your competitors by using your new time-based advantage.

ARE YOU LISTENING?

High-value-producing enterprises are obsessive listeners. John Sharpe, Executive Vice President of Operations, Four Seasons Hotels, reminds us:

> Customers don't buy a product, they buy what the product does for them. Quality in product or service is not what *we* think it is. It's what our customers perceive it is—and what they need and want. If we don't give customers what they expect, they'll perceive our service as poor. If we give them what they expect, they'll perceive it as good. If we give them more than they expect, they'll perceive it as excellent.

Does your organization know what customers value? What is their preference for quality, service, cost, and speed? What are the specific attributes they use to judge your performance in each of these "four keys" to value? Figure 1.3 is a simple tool to help you define customer value requirements. Evaluate your performance against customer needs; include an assessment of competitor performance. Once you have isolated the important leverage points for value, you will know where to target your enterprise improvement efforts.

Author and consultant Jim Clemmer advises:

> Your customers' perceptions of the value they are receiving must become the common yardstick against which all activities throughout your entire organization are measured.

He suggests some excellent customer listening techniques:

- *"Close up and personal."* Meet people and ask them what they look for in your type of product and service.

- *Participate in your own market research.* Identify patterns and changes in markets on a regular basis. Keep a clipping file for insights, articles, comments/letters from customers, and competitors' materials.

- *Conduct focus groups and advisory panels.* Through these media, customers can provide feedback on product design, pricing, expectations, and so on.

- *Conduct customer surveys.* On a regular basis, contact a cross-section of buyers and prospects and ask what they expect from your type of product or service, and how well your enterprise stacks up when compared to the competition.

- *Install customer hotlines.* Toll-free 800 telephone numbers make it easy for customers to contact your company.

- *Elicit customer complaints.* Less than 5 percent of customers complain; the others say it's too much "trouble" and believe no one cares

Quality	Rating			Service	Rating		
	Your Company	*Competitor #1*	*Competitor #2*		*Your Company*	*Competitor #1*	*Competitor #2*
Value Attribute				*Value Attribute*			
1				1			
2				2			
3				3			
4				4			

Cost	Rating			Time	Rating		
	Your Company	*Competitor #1*	*Competitor #2*		*Your Company*	*Competitor #1*	*Competitor #2*
Value Attribute				*Value Attribute*			
1				1			
2				2			
3				3			
4				4			

Figure 1.3 Customer value evaluation.

anyway. The key is to provide customers with an effective complaint outlet, then win them back through quick resolution of problems.

- *Organize "team visits."* Send your own people out to watch how your products are used by customers.

- *Organize user groups and conferences.* Get customers to meet together with you to share ideas and experiences about the use of particular products or services. This is common in the computer field.

New and ever more innovative methods of customer "listening" are emerging. Did you hear the story about the architect who built a cluster of office buildings, but waited until people wore paths on the lawn to decide where to put the walkways?

Canadian Airlines pays customers to fly together with a researcher; they go through the entire travel procedure as the researcher gathers feedback. The Ritz Carlton, the first hotel operator to win the coveted Malcolm Baldrige National Quality Award, keeps repeat customers happy through use of its database system to keep track of guests' preferences: what newspapers they read, their favorite breakfasts, and so on.

In Argentina, Diner's Club, concerned about the fact that its virtual monopoly on the credit card market had eroded, responded by having its top 130 executives telephone 80 customers each to find out why. The company discovered that its customers were tired of repeatedly inaccurate billings, being kept too long on hold when calling, and the arrogant and high-handed manner in which they were treated. Diner's Club used the input to make changes in customer service, has prevailed over both American Express and Mastercard, and is now second only to Visa in the credit card wars in Argentina. The 10,000 cardholders who were personally telephoned have an attrition rate less than half that of regular customers, and their card use is 30 percent higher.

In summary, to develop an effective strategy for delivering superior value requires a sensitive ear tuned to the "voice of the customer." As you listen, keep these questions in mind:

- What attributes of the customer experience are of particular value?
- How desirable is each attribute relative to the others?
- How well does your organization score, compared to the relevant competition, on those factors that are most valued?
- What can you do to add value to the customer experience and provide a differentiated, "breakthrough" encounter?

Understanding the four keys to extraordinary value is only one competency of the high-performing enterprise. The next important proficiency is "retrofitting" your enterprise for the value decade by redesigning, or reengineering, the core business processes that make your organization "go."

TOUCHSTONE

2

Redesigning Business Processes

You can't make an omelet without breaking eggs.

French proverb

In the fiercely competitive and customer-driven environment of the 1990s, "functional hierarchies" are no longer the best way to organize your enterprise. Vertical organizational structures are crumbling fast, as companies seeking to compete more effectively and create value are scrambling to rebuild themselves "horizontally." The second critical competency that your enterprise must master is the ability to manage your core business processes. A business process is a series of steps designed to produce a product or service.

By its contribution to the creation or delivery of a product or service, each step in a process should add value to the preceding steps.

Inefficient and outmoded processes must be reengineered to achieve optimum value delivery.

CHANGES AT THE CORE

When Connecticut Mutual Life Insurance Company customers wanted to change the beneficiaries of their policies, the process used to take days. Someone would take the information by phone and fill out a handwritten form, then pass it down the line. Next, a clerk pulled a hard-copy version of

the file, filled out another handwritten form, and sent it out for word processing. The typists made numerous errors, so the form needed to be proof-
read and revised. Two final copies were prepared: one was for the file, and
one was mailed out to the policyholder. This paperwork-intensive, archaic,
totally inefficient process was reengineered (redesigned) to work like this:
Phone representatives now have individual workstations and make necessary
changes *on-line*, in a matter of minutes, as they are speaking with the policyholder. A confirmation of the transaction goes out in the mail to the policyholder in a matter of hours.

The reengineered process now operates with 13 percent less staff; one
supervisor can work with up to 30 people. Policyholders receive significantly better service. The price tag for this redesign effort? A hefty $5 mil-
lion, but Connecticut Mutual estimated that this investment would pay out
in two years. In fact, it paid out in 20 months—four months early!

Every organization is made up of a handful of core processes. Each
process consists of a set of interrelated activities, decisions, information,
and material flows, which together decide the competitive success of the
company. Core processes cut across functional, geographic, and business
units, and even company boundaries. The company of the future should
be viewed as:

> . . . a grouping of cross-functional core processes and not just a grouping
> of functions or business units—which can yield breakthrough levels of
> improvement.

"Business process excellence" seems to be the latest in a long list of strategies the Japanese have mastered, outperforming North American enterprises:

> Japanese manufacturers have come to realize that who invents a product idea
> is no longer very important. It is the company that can capitalize on the prod-
> uct idea and that has the highest quality, lowest cost, and quickest time to
> market with some form of legal copying (e.g., licensing) or legal patent
> "workaround" that often wins. Knowing this, they have traditionally put the
> bulk of their R&D effort into process improvement.

For example, a manufacturer might have four essential business processes: (1) new product and process design, (2) customer-order-to-delivery,
(3) materials management, and (4) estimating and contracting. A Ford Motor Company survey showed that 75 percent of a product's costs are fixed
by decisions made in the product design process, *not* in production. Yet,
most companies do not work to improve the way products are designed. In
other words, little attention is paid to the most important process that impacts cost.

Improving business processes means eliminating (1) anything that adds
cost but does not add value to the product (or service) or (2) anything that

negatively affects product quality or that adds time to the process. Possible waste areas might include excess overhead, lengthy manufacturing process travel distances, too many production locations, too many parts inspections, or an excessive number of engineering changes.

James Harrington writes in *The Journal of Business Strategy:*

> The single most important strategy for improving the quality of work life in the twenty-first century is reforming the business process itself. The inefficiency, bureaucracy, and complexity that have bogged down critical business activities, reducing productivity and competitiveness, have also greatly detracted from the satisfaction and pride that management and employees derive from their work.

Why Most Business Processes Are in Such Bad Shape

Most enterprises today are not configured to perform effectively and efficiently. They have the following six deficiencies:

1. Insufficient attention has been given to business processes through which value is generated and competitive advantage is obtained.
2. Most processes were originally designed for a less competitive environment than is the case in today's markets.
3. Extra processes have been added to the enterprise without a view to how they would affect existing processes.
4. Organizations are structured along functional lines, which cut across processes and create inefficiencies.
5. Functional management has led to individual department optimization rather than process optimization.
6. Attention has been given to some, but not all of the key value factors: quality, service, cost, and time.

When competitive pressures are low, process inefficiency is something you can live with. But today, to react more quickly to market changes and competitor attacks, radical change in your business processes is necessary.

Hallmark Cards, Inc. refers to its process redesign effort as "The Journey." It used to take Hallmark about three years to produce a new line of greeting cards, from initial idea to market. Incredible as it may sound, the company discovered that, for 90 percent of that time, work just lay dormant. Projects were usually sitting in somebody's in/out tray waiting to be worked on. In fact, from the time an idea was given to Hallmark's creative staff until the product was ready for production, it had been passed back and forth 25 times!

To remedy the problem, and to create a more stimulating environment for its creative staff, Hallmark reorganized its card development staff entirely. Departments formerly separated by work disciplines, departments, buildings, or floors, were brought together into multidisciplinary teams. The restructuring has proved to be worthwhile. Hallmark's teams of artists, writers, marketers, and production staffs now push brand new lines out the door within a year, cutting the concept-to-market process time by more than 50 percent.

FUNCTIONS VS. PROCESSES

What is the difference between a business process and a business function? Processes are the naturally occurring sets of activities comprising the business itself; functions are the logical structures used to decompose the processes into manageable chunks. As shown in Figure 2.1, business functions are organizational units with responsibility for activities such as ordering ("Materials"), handling accounts payable ("Finance"), and designing a new ad campaign ("Marketing").

Core processes usually cut across several functions. For example, acquiring raw materials involves the purchasing function (locating suppliers and executing orders), the accounting function (paying for orders and tracking payments), the warehousing function (unloading and storing

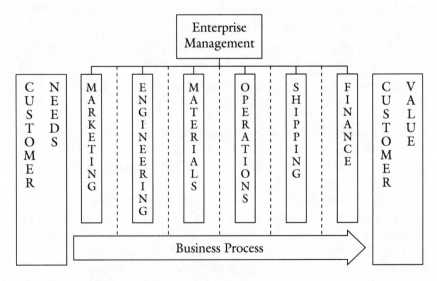

Figure 2.1   Creating value for customers.

materials), and the inventory control function (managing materials on hand).

The problem with a traditional functional view of the enterprise is that it promotes a "silo" mentality, which often pits one function against another. When this happens, each department tries to optimize its own performance. Individual managers may perceive other business functions as enemies rather than as partners in the battle against the real competition; departments build "walls" to exclude "foreign" departments. An enterprise should, instead, be viewed as a set of interrelated processes that share the common goal of providing efficient and effective response to customer needs.

> In small or new organizations, this vertical view is not a major problem because everybody in the organization knows each other and needs to understand other functions. However, as time passes and the organization becomes more complex as the environment changes and as technology becomes more complicated, this view of the organization becomes a liability.

Turf Wars

Kaoru Ishikawa, often considered the "father" of total quality control (TQC) in Japan, noticed the problems of turf battles in the early 1950s. Working to reduce defects in a steel mill, he discovered what he called "sectionalism," which is a lot like "siloism." He asked one department to talk to another about problems it was having because it was receiving poor raw materials from the group just before it in the production line. The workers refused because they did not want to talk to their "enemies."

Friction often becomes evident between "staff" and "line" functions. This stems from the fact that many staff departments operate on the erroneous assumption that they run (or should run) the entire company. They believe the role of the line functions is to carry out the tasks ordered by "head office." Ishikawa recommends that staff departments, such as top management, accounting, and engineering, should devote 70 percent of their time to their "true customer," the line departments and workers.

In other words, the staff group has services to perform for the line functions in order for the company to effectively serve its external customers. The role of the accounting department, for instance, is to provide data to the line departments to enhance their work methods, their profit generation, and their cost controls. The role of top management is to develop plans and programs that will lead the enterprise effectively into the future. Staff groups exist to give the line functions good service so that the line functions, in turn, can give good service to external customers.

MANAGING "HORIZONTALLY"

What activities are necessary to create and maintain a "horizontal" organization?

- *Creating shared values.* Shared decision premises and a common culture or set of business values are necessary. Philip Selznick says moving toward shared values ". . . involves transforming men and groups from neutral, technical units into participants who have a peculiar stamp, sensitivity and commitment."

- *Redefining managers' roles.* Managers must create, maintain, and defend an organizational context that promotes lateral decision making oriented toward the achievement of competitive advantage. They should influence decisions and actions more indirectly, referee situations, and facilitate lateral processes.

- *Assessing results.* Individual performance measurement traditionally rewards the local organization over the enterprise as a whole, and polarizes the company. Because of complex interdependencies, a horizontal organization cannot be run simply "by the numbers." The local general manager's task is to create a linkage among local actions, enterprise advantage, and overall results.

A horizontal organization is flatter, with fewer levels of management than the traditional structure. In *Horizontal Management: Beyond Total Customer Satisfaction,* author D. Keith Denton reminds us of Federal Express, a company with 70,000 employees and only five levels between the CEO and the operational levels. The traditional vertical organizational structure focuses employees' attention on the people above and below them rather than on the people who really matter: customers and suppliers.

There isn't any institution that is now practicing pure horizontal management. However, leading enterprises are moving toward this ideal. A powerful method for promoting improved horizontal linkages in your enterprise is through the motto of Next Operation as Customer (NOAC). The NOAC idea is that each department or individual within the enterprise is both an internal customer and a supplier to someone else.

Generally, identifying one's external customers is easy, but isolating internal customers and suppliers takes far more analysis. For example, some companies have internal advertising departments, complete with creative and production staffs. They may create marketing materials for an easily recognizable group of external customers. However, each copywriter, designer, and production manager should treat the company's marketing manager(s) as their internal clients. This means meeting deadlines and solving problems just as they would for a client using an outside advertising agency; in turn, each marketing manager must treat his or her creative and production staff as internal suppliers, working closely together to serve the external customer.

From a NOAC perspective, the overall business process begins when an external customer interacts with the "front line" of the enterprise (usually the salesperson), and continues by working backward through the various series of internal suppliers and customers. The customer transaction concludes when the external (paying) customer receives what he or she wanted. In short, NOAC means identifying the critical communication links and hand-offs that are necessary within the enterprise to satisfy the external customer.

Getting employee groups to see other departments as customers (maybe a better word is "client," reserving the term "customer" for the external user of goods and services) for their outputs may require changing your compensation system to promote the right kind of attitude. At Johnsonville Foods, for example, a new reward system has been devised to support the "serve the internal customer" philosophy. Johnsonville takes a portion of total monthly profit and divides it by the number of workers. The quotient equals one "share" in the profit pool. Each month, work teams meet with their internal customers to negotiate above-and-beyond target performance for the supplier team. At month-end, the customer uses the agreed-on criteria to evaluate the supplier team's performance on a scale of 1 to 10. A mediocre rating gives the team less than 100 percent of its share of the pool.

Company spokespeople recommend using caution in moving toward this approach: "This would not have succeeded early in the empowerment process at Johnsonville." Still, it is a good example of how to institutionalize the NOAC idea.

Another method is to borrow the notion of service guarantees used for external customers and apply them inside. Creative Professional Services (CPS) has taken this approach with good results. At CPS, a 135-employee company in Woburn, Massachusetts, many mistakes were happening "because procedures aren't defined." For example, there were problems between the sales department and the production people. Salespeople discussed ideas for direct-mail pieces with prospective clients and scribbled down details. They gave their notes to account managers who, in turn, gave the information to production. There were always mistakes that were hard to pin down, until a service guarantee was devised between the two departments. Now, the expectations of both parties are much clearer, and problems can be traced to failure to meet a specific criterion. The new system makes it easier to prevent the problem from happening again.

The components of CPS's internal service guarantee will provide good guidelines for anyone wanting to adopt this practice:

- *The promise.* It can be specific ("I will deliver *x* service by *x* date") or sweeping (the CPS salespeople pledge to account managers "all the information you need to do your job").

- *The payout.* "I fail to deliver, I give you *x.*" Here's where the internal guarantee differs from the classic consumer guarantee: money usually isn't appropriate in an internal guarantee, and the payout is designed not to punish offenders as much as to reward employees for invoking the guarantee. If the CPS salesperson delivers inaccurate or incomplete specifications, the account managers choose the payment: treat me to lunch, or do data-entry work on the job yourself.

- *The invocation procedure.* Activating the internal guarantee must be easy. CPS employees deliver a simple invocation form to the person who has erred. Some employees find it difficult to use the guarantee for fear of getting peers into trouble. This can be overcome if the department making the guarantee communicates its desire to get the feedback in order to improve performance.

CPS has achieved good results using internal service guarantees. Jim Hackett, Vice President of Sales, reports:

> Before, almost half for the order entries had some sort of error. Now, we're pulling about 10 percent a month, and the errors are real minutiae.

"BREAKING OUT" TO HIGH PERFORMANCE

If you're thinking about redesigning your organization's work processes, there are three choices. The first is *process improvement,* where core business processes are redesigned to improve efficiency and effectiveness. Productivity-style improvements such as these may be critical to a company's operation, but they are largely driven by internal factors, such as correcting process problems or meeting a budget. This level of process improvement doesn't deal with the strategic challenges facing the enterprise, however.

The second choice is *working to achieve parity with competitors,* where your company employs benchmarking techniques and customer research techniques to detect what buyers want, how well you perform compared to competitors, and how you can move to close the "performance" gap. This level of process improvement goes beyond mere efficiency and addresses performance improvement in the context of external factors.

The third choice is *going for the "breakouts" in performance*. Breakout process redesign includes both of the first two choices, then moves beyond them toward a final level—a breakout that can create market dominance. A breakout is a level of process improvement that results in a performance that goes beyond customer expectations and overwhelms competitors' ability to respond. With this choice, you are seeking to "break out" from the bounds of conventional thinking to achieve previously unheard-of levels of performance.

Medrad, a $60-million medical imaging company, employed this type of thinking to achieve a giant leap in performance. Formerly, the company used a variety of shippers for its disposable products. Preparing orders caused delays, and the company had virtually no ability to meet rush orders.

Medrad completely rethought its delivery process and took a radical step to simplify its approach. The company created a new partnership that saw most of its shipping needs met by one company. The shipping company supplied hardware and software to schedule and monitor shipments, which resulted in more open lines of communication. On-time delivery went from 86 percent to 100 percent in six months, and order processing costs were cut in half. Meanwhile, customer complaints went from 150 per month to zero per month.

In the early 1980s, the trade magazine *Farm Journal* faced bankruptcy because it couldn't deliver specialized audiences to its advertisers. To aggravate matters, as the number of farmers in the U.S. decreased, so did the *Farm Journal* base rate for print ads. The magazine was finding it difficult to compete with smaller, more specialized magazines and direct-mail distributions, which gave advertisers a cheaper way of targeting farms with certain characteristics such as a specific crop or type of livestock.

In 1984, the *Farm Journal* completely reengineered its production process using a new technology called selective binding. It now produces up to 5,000 customized versions of a single edition, a bonus for readers and advertisers alike. Each version provides exclusive editorial and advertising content to better meet the individual needs and interests of the one million farms in the United States. The redesign effort rescued the magazine from financial ruin.

The magazine also created a new revenue source through the creative use of its newly enhanced subscriber database. It now regularly conducts market research studies for farm product manufacturers. It has also been asked to maintain proprietary databases of sales and distribution information for agricultural supply giants such as John Deere, Pfizer, and Ciba-Geigy.

Another example of achieving dramatic performance improvement with a breakthrough strategy occurred at Dun & Bradstreet Information Services, which managed to halve the amount of time it took to turn around a customer-ordered investigation. Response time plummeted from seven to three days.

Thirty years ago, when the company first started offering D&B reports, customers were satisfied to receive these through the mail. In today's climate of quick response, this standard is no longer acceptable. The turnaround time of seven days was a source of constant irritation among customers. Buyers wrote complaint letters, customer surveys confirmed the problem, and customers were actually deserting the company over the issue. D&B found that its system actually *encouraged* delays. Backlogs were seen as insurance that employees would have something to do! The company mistook activity for productivity and quality.

D&B decided to go for a breakthrough in performance: a short, intensive effort, with high involvement of employees, to find a way to redesign the way work was done. A meeting was held, with 50 D&B employees attending. The challenge put to them was: Cut turnaround time in half, and do it in two months or less, without any increase in resources or decrease in quality.

The team, known as "The Greensboro Groundbreakers" (after the site of the meeting), set to work. Tal Phillips, Vice President of Eastern Operations, described what took place:

> The "order faucet" was shut off for several days, and orders diverted to the other 65 D&B locations. This allowed the Greensboro associates to clean up their backlogs. The team also analyzed all the steps in the investigation process. They looked at which steps added value to the customer, which did not, which were there because they'd always been there. They eliminated those that added no value or impeded the process. We always though that management could see the forest for the trees. But it was just the opposite. Our associates knew the steps that did not make sense in the process, and they quickly eliminated them.

The result of the effort was the cut in response time from seven days to three. Quality did not go down in a single area. Indeed, the company believes quality improved in many ways. More important, to associates, "customer" now was more than just a word. It became a person on the other end of a request, who needed a D&B product.

A Breakout Checklist

The following checklist will be helpful when you are deciding whether your company is in need of a breakout process redesign:

1. New product development is critical to your success, but competitors are getting products to market months or years before you do.

2. You employ many more people to do a job than the industry leader does.

3. You need to cut costs significantly and quickly because competitors offer the same products at lower prices.

4. You want to improve productivity by more than 50 percent within two years.

5. Customers demand faster delivery or processing and you don't know how to give it to them.

6. You can't meet your customer's fundamental needs for product and service quality at an affordable cost.

7. Your company's market share is shrinking substantially.

8. You want to be global in your market reach, but aren't competitive with offshore suppliers.

9. Government regulations require you to do business differently.

10. You've tried other methods (downsizing, TQM, automation) and they haven't produced the competitive leap you need.

11. Market change or shareholder dissatisfaction threatens your survival.

12. You're planning to introduce a major new information system or reengineer an existing system, to provide a competitive advantage.

Breakouts versus Continuous Improvement

If you're answering "yes" to some of the challenges on the checklist, you must distinguish between the need for continuous improvement or a complete business process reengineering (BPR) exercise.

A continuous improvement approach to process redesign attacks the problem incrementally. This approach is effective when the organization's current processes are reasonably close to delivering to customer requirements, and technology can be used incrementally to create small gains. You face little risk using this method because the impact is usually narrow. In the end, the cost of making a change seems almost "free"; performance improves steadily over time, and you gain increasing momentum.

On the other hand, BPR creates rapid, revolutionary change—an appropriate approach when existing processes are broken down or outmoded. The organization needs to challenge its fundamentals and view technology as a process transformer. There is more risk in taking a true reengineering approach because the impact is great, everyone in the organization is affected, and the cost of the change is often very high.

In BPR, outrageous levels of improvement are expected, not incremental increases in performance. "Andersen Consulting advocates the 'ten times' rule: in reengineering a business process, you should aim for shrinking the difference between your company's current performance and the best performance in the industry by a factor of ten." BPR seeks the achievement of breakthroughs in delivering better value to customers *beyond* the capability of competitors.

BUSINESS PROCESS REENGINEERING

Business process reengineering has enjoyed tremendous popularity in the 1990s. But many organizations, not fully comprehending its widespread implications, have oversimplified views of the idea. For example, some people believe BPR is simply about reducing costs.

> Reengineering . . . has been given a wide variety of names, including streamlining, transformation, and restructuring. However, regardless of the name, the goal is almost always the same: the increased ability to compete through cost reduction.

In answer, CSC Index's James Champy says that companies that try to compete simply by cutting costs and capacity miss the fact that markets are dramatically changing. When the economic downturn of the early 1990s ends, it is not going to be "business as usual." Companies such as Aetna, PepsiCo, Alcoa, and Herman Miller are redesigning themselves "for what promises to be a wildly unpredictable environment." Herman Miller CEO Kerm Campbell reports that the office furniture maker has moved to a more flexible, cross-functional, team strategy, and likens the future to ". . . permanent white water . . . constant turmoil."

The seductive appeal of BPR in today's slow-growth environment is that it promises to increase market share by serving customers better, identifying opportunities more adeptly, speeding-up new product development, *and* bringing costs down!

Skeptics claim that reengineering is simply another euphemism for "laying people off," much like "rightsizing." But author Michael Hammer, professor of computer science at MIT and credited with being one of the foremost popularizers of the concept, counters that reengineering is ". . . the fundamental rethinking and radical redesign of business processes to achieve dramatic improvements in critical, contemporary measures of performance, such as cost, quality, service, and speed."

Four key words are embedded in that definition: (1) fundamental, (2) radical, (3) dramatic, and (4) processes. Fundamental refers to the probing questions that must be asked about the business—questions such as: Why do we do this? Radical means getting to the root of things. Dramatic signifies achieving quantum leaps in performance. Processes refers to the collection of activities that take one or more kinds of input and create an output that is of value to the customer.

BPR: Latest Pet Rock or Critical Need?

One management pundit has called BPR ". . . the latest pet rock of management techniques." BPR appeals to "quick-fix" managers because it tears down existing structures and holds out the promise of "overnight" improvement.

The growing popularity of BPR is also the result of the perceived failure of previous "new age" business solutions, such as TQM, as discussed in Touchstone One. In "Lessons from the Veterans of TQM," published in the *Canadian Business Review,* Céline Bak reports that her research indicates many TQM efforts yielded no perceived business advantage. A 1991 survey in *Electronic Business* magazine indicated that only 13 percent of CEOs found their quality efforts paid off in higher operating income or profits. Another survey, performed by *TQM Magazine* and consultant A. T. Kearney, discovered that 80 percent of TQM initiatives ultimately fail.

Despite these gloomy reports, Bak nevertheless found that three-quarters of the companies surveyed are still nurturing or planning total quality improvement initiatives. TQM veterans are now discovering that there are certain success patterns you *can* benefit from. In companies with successful efforts, their TQM initiatives lasted three or more years. They also focus intently on improving business processes.

One example of this focus comes from north of the border. AMP of Canada Ltd. organizes around processes rather than functions. People cooperate in cross-functional teams that work toward one common goal: improving customer satisfaction. An "on-time delivery team" comprised of representatives from the quality department, the inside sales group, and the warehouse and inventory control departments achieved seven consecutive months of 98 to 99 percent delivery "as promised." Bak's investigation concluded:

> . . . processes, not functions or departments, produce the goods and services that delight your customers and satisfy your business requirements. Teams empowered to improve processes will succeed in their task if customer-driven corporate goals are clearly communicated and understood by all.

"Dumbsizing"

BPR is not just about cutting costs, although a more cost-efficient business process may be the outcome. Rather, BPR is a way to make sure enterprise downsizing doesn't become "dumbsizing." When a bloated, unfocused work force is the problem, cutting the work force just means you'll have fewer unfocused employees. A critical flaw in the methods organizations use to downsize lies in the fact that the workers may be streamlined but the work isn't. A study of 1,005 firms, conducted in 1991 by Wyatt & Company, found that 86 percent had downsized but only 36 percent took steps to eliminate low-value work in the aftermath.

Further difficulties arise from failure to educate employees about their place in the new structure. Front-liners and middle management often have little say in shaping the post-downsizing environment. There is also an over-reliance on early retirement programs, which means the loss of experienced employees. The results? Expect a cynical and exhausted work force, reduced productivity, and hit-or-miss customer service.

"Smartsizing"

"Reengineering is to quality improvement what gutting and rebuilding is to home renovation." Gabriel Paul, president of Juran International distinguishes two types of reengineering: (1) "business reengineering," which turns the whole organization upside-down, involving a change to the financial system, information management system, and human resources system; and (2) "process reengineering," which takes aim at the core processes one at a time. Paul calls process reengineering "the only sane choice for most companies." In other words, an approach that targets selected critical processes is preferable to either across-the-board staff cuts or enterprisewide reengineering.

THE FIVE PHASES OF REDESIGN

There are five key phases to a process redesign project, as shown in Figure 2.2.

Phase One

Phase One defines the core processes that will drive the competitive nature of the company for the years ahead. It addresses the major strategic directions and the key problems of competitiveness. All major processes and information flows affecting time, total cost, quality, and service should be included. Key activities that link to customers and suppliers must also be incorporated.

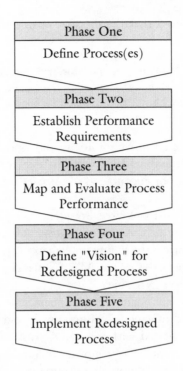

Figure 2.2   The five phases of business process redesign.

The processes should be defined at levels high enough for redesign to yield breakout improvements, but still low enough to be managed practically. The core process view should optimize the interdependent activities and functions within a core process while minimizing dependencies across core functions.

It's important to note, however, that the same processes are not "core" processes for every company. Most businesses have between five to ten core processes, for example: new product/service development, order acquisition, order fulfillment, supplier management and materials acquisition, customer service, customer invoicing and cash collections, the acquisition and management of financial resources, human resource acquisition and development, and competitive strategy development. In other words, companies will reengineer different processes because each identifies different areas needing improvement. The processes you choose to reengineer must be tied to strengthening the competitive position of the enterprise.

As an example, consider AT&T's Power Systems Division, created in 1988. Its product line includes switching power supplies, converters, linear power supplies, and uninterruptible power supplies.

AT&T soon discovered that the division wasn't performing up to customer expectations:

> The new division was losing millions per year, with product costs higher than competitors, lead times of months instead of days, and the time to prototype a customer's request took three to four months while the market was increasingly requiring prototype responses in weeks.

The division suffered from poor focus and poor accountability; employees operated in functional silos with little interfunctional contact or support. Workers were not encouraged to uncover the root causes of their problems.

Andy Guarriello, Divisional Vice President and General Manager, arrived on the scene to turn the division's fortunes around. He began a continuous improvement effort, including implementing just-in-time (JIT) and total quality management (TQM) at AT&T's plants in Dallas, Matamoros (Mexico), and New River (Virginia).

Guarriello removed redundant layers of management; nearly 40 percent of the supervision was "leaned out." Moreover, the old functional organizational structure was replaced with job-based units and a cross-functional structure. A product marketing group, devoted solely to power systems, was developed. The design engineering group was relocated from the Bell Laboratories in New Jersey to Dallas, a change that enabled the division to break away from the R&D functions at Bell Laboratories. Design engineers could work more single-mindedly on issues of manufacturability, quality, and short lead times rather than working in isolation with little concern for the end user.

By 1990, the changes helped deliver savings of $60 million, bringing the Power Systems Division back into the black. Guarriello hopes that the Power Systems Division will win the Deming Award for quality by 1994. In an effort to achieve this, he is attempting a second round of breaking down the business and rebuilding:

> As the BPR undertaking becomes more mature, he [Guarriello] feels that the incremental goals he sets must be higher for employees to continue having the sense that they are making great strides rather than plodding along and falling into an effort that is merely one of continuous improvements.

Phase Two

Phase Two involves establishing performance requirements. Redesign efforts should flow from an enterprise's strategic objectives, with each core process addressing one or two objectives for competitive success or sources of competitive differentiation. Performance requirements should be measures of key operating parameters such as throughput time, output quality, service levels, new product success rates, and total cost. The "gaps" between current and required performance should then be evaluated via feedback from customers and benchmarks set by best-of-class companies. This approach creates both the motivation for change and the basis for measuring success.

When Ford Motor Company planned to reduce its 500-person accounts payable department by 20 percent, it initially considered this goal a huge undertaking. Then, Ford learned that Mazda—a company with similar accounts payable needs—had a department consisting of only five people! Ford raised its sights considerably and decided to redesign the entire parts acquisition process to the point where it no longer needed to issue paper invoices. Now, Ford's suppliers all use electronic data interchange (EDI) systems. The end results were a 75 percent reduction in staff, a simplification of material control, and improved accuracy in financial reporting. The radical change and resulting performance improvement would not have been possible without setting an improvement goal that was a quantum leap beyond Ford's current ability.

Phase Three

Phase Three is dedicated to pinpointing problems and diagnosing the causes of performance gaps. Mapping of process and information flows is the first step. Next, the existing information and technical systems architecture should be analyzed.

The case of the IBM Credit Corporation is a frequently cited example. The "Big Blue" unit that arranges financing for the company's computers researched its loan approval process. The actual working time to process a loan was around 90 minutes, but in "real time" terms, it took six full days to complete documents moving, them from one specialist to another. This "down time" gave potential customers ample opportunity to research alternative forms of financing. Now, after the reengineering effort, a single person handles a financing request, from the beginning to the end of the process. He or she is supported by a new easy-to-use computer system that provides access to all data and tools specialists would use. Turnaround time has been slashed to just four hours, and the number of personnel once involved in loan approvals has been greatly reduced.

Phase Four

Phase Four involves developing a long-term redesign "vision" and establishing a set of specific change initiatives. A process redesign effort is carried out by a cross-functional team whose task is to analyze the current processes, diagnose problems, and develop the blueprint for an improved way of doing things. This involves defining performance requirements in terms of "stretch" targets, brainstorming possible solutions, developing a long-term redesign, evaluating alternatives, and developing an action plan with specific initiatives and time frames.

A decline in net earnings over the past decade pushed Kodak to reengineer its $11 billion Imaging Group's order management process. In the past, it took the Imaging Group 8 to 12 days to fulfill an order for a customer in Canada from its head office in Rochester, New York, which is only a three-hour drive away! The Group determined its need for—or, rather, its customers demanded—faster turnaround. The logistics department created a team that found a way to provide faster service at a reasonable cost. The analysis process, dubbed "Case For Action," involved answering these four questions in considerable detail:

1. Why reengineer order management?
2. What's in the way?
3. What do the benefits look like?
4. What's the future vision?

Kodak calculated that its present order management process cost $327 million annually. The process cost encompassed distribution expense, inventory carrying cost, accounts receivables carrying cost, and selling expense. Kodak wanted to cut costs and improve service at the same time. Management viewed Order Management as a cost center instead of a strategic tool, and managed its various processes in a reactive rather than a proactive way. Additionally, the Imaging Group needed to create win/win relationships with *all* customers, not just with the biggest buyers.

An important early step in the reengineering effort was segmenting customers into three groups and defining their critical requirements. The first group, *large customers,* such as Wal-Mart, K mart, and Eckerd Drugs, require a broad range of services and close integration with suppliers; these accounts expect Kodak to virtually manage inventory on their behalf.

The second group, *smaller customers* such as minilabs, require a different approach. The business process reengineering team discovered:

> Running a minilab is unforgiving. Competition is intense, they have to operate as leanly as possible. But the pricing and service is nowhere near that of Wal-Mart. So in some cases when a minilab runs out of our product they can get it faster by buying it from Wal-Mart rather from us, their major supplier . . . which doesn't make for satisfied customers!

The third group, *midsize dealers,* were being squeezed by mass merchandisers on one end of the market and by the minilabs on the other. These customers, some of Kodak's oldest, needed help figuring out how to keep their customers satisfied and how to remain profitable.

The Imaging Group then looked at operational issues and defined the need for reengineering. A high percentage of orders were exceptions, such as backorders, disputed invoices, returns, credit referrals, and expedited shipments. It developed a vision of providing "zero defect basic service" and doing business in a segmented way to meet the different needs of its three customer groups. It developed three order management service models: (1) self-service (flexible, no hassles, no frills) (2) partnership (helping customers to do business), and (3) category management (managing the customer's entire supply chain).

The process focus of reengineering, compared to the more traditional vertical organizational approach, will now allow Kodak to serve customers better. Manufacturing scheduling and resource allocation should dramatically improve, and Kodak's selling effort can focus on win/win customer partnerships.

However, while implementing the reengineering campaign, Kodak has encountered resistance from its employees: "People operate vertically, and don't think about what's to their left or right." Many employees didn't understand the current Order Management processes, or their role in it. So Kodak must address how to change employee attitudes in order for the new concepts to work. Despite some barriers to success, the estimated payoff for Kodak is $138 million in savings.

The Final Phase

Phase Five focuses on action: making it happen. In order for Phase Five to work, it's important to build the motivation necessary to make the redesign strategy stick. Strong leadership, cross-functional involvement, creativity, a rigorous approach, and a single point of accountability are also key elements.

MAKING THE "GREAT LEAP" FORWARD

How can you prepare your work force for the dramatic change that may result from a radical redesign of processes? In successful BPR, the highest executive in the organization must take a leadership role, and senior managers must play prominent parts. The company's "best and brightest" people must participate in BPR, and the project must include a cross-functional mix of the practical and technical perspectives required for developing a successful "new vision" for how the process should work.

Five factors must be managed successfully if you are to make the transition to a more horizontal enterprise structure:

1. The enterprise leader;
2. The business unit leader;
3. The new organization;
4. The transition organization;
5. The individual within the organization.

For successful change, the *enterprise leader* must develop and sustain a "new vision" of the business that is compelling and meaningful to employees. This usually means that the top executive of the enterprise demonstrates, by his or her personal behavior, a dedication to excellence that is credible to followers.

In studying the leaders of successful enterprise change efforts, Coopers & Lybrand management consultants concluded:

> All these leaders drove themselves to excellence, and that characteristic was infectious to their subordinates. In short, the leader of a large company that is striving toward process excellence has a vision coupled with values that include customer focus, doing right by suppliers and employees as shareholders, and the desire for all in the organization to strive for personal best performance.

Britain's Anita Roddick, owner of The Body Shop, has created a unique vision for her company in several areas; for example, the company is dedicated to stimulating commerce in the Third World through its "Trade Not Aid" slogan. Roddick, herself, travels all over the world looking for unique ingredients she can use that will stimulate commercial production in remote areas. She regularly conducts seminars for The Body Shop employees, educating them on the latest ingredients and the culture and history of the countries where the ingredients are found.

Roddick is an enterprise leader who has made her personal values the company's values. She is against testing cosmetics on animals; The Body Shop was the first cosmetic chain to speak out against this practice, and indicates on its labels that it does not do it. Roddick, an opponent of environmentally toxic cosmetics, made sure that her products were "green" even before "environmentally friendly" was popular.

She is also in favor of charity; every employee of The Body Shop must volunteer time once a month to a number of charities The Body Shop endorses. Several copycat competitors have tried to emulate the standards and values of The Body Shop. Roddick has successfully demonstrated a commitment to excellence by her personal example.

The *business unit leader* is the person who usually drives the process redesign effort. He or she must choose between the need for speed to the new way of doing business and the inevitable disruption of daily business that will result in the short term. Questions for the business unit leader include:

- Who are my customers, and what do I need to do to create superior value compared to the competition?
- Which of my core business processes have the most effect on my customers' perception of value?
- What will my business look like if its processes are pushed to breakthrough levels of value delivery?
- How much change to existing processes will be required?
- How much change can the enterprise successfully absorb?
- What are the risks if my business doesn't move at the pace required?

An enterprise organized horizontally around business processes will be quite different from the company's present organization. In the new organization, work will be done through process teams supported by small groups of functional specialists. Process teams will be more self-managing and won't have layers of supervisors and managers overseeing their efforts. They will, however, understand how their process fits into the larger enterprise. Teams will be measured on the contribution they make to creating superior value. Therefore, their measures of success will differ from today's and will comprise indicators of quality, service, cost, and speed.

Transition

The move from a functional structure to one that can manage a reengineered core process requires a special, temporary, *transition organization*. The transition structure includes:

- *The business unit leader.* Forms the steering committee and champions the change process, but remains focused on running day-to-day operations.
- *The steering committee.* Responsible for deciding the sequence in which core processes will be tackled, setting goals, pulling together the teams who will do the actual redesign, and establishing schedules to manage the overall sequence of tasks.
- *The task teams.* Carry out specific analyses, redesign of specific core processes, and revamp of the support structures necessary to enable

the new process to function effectively; for example, the performance appraisal system and compensation arrangements may require modification to promote behavior that is consistent with the redesigned process.

- *The program management committee.* The "middle management' of the transition period; coordinates and coaches the task teams and lobbies the steering committee on their behalf.

The transition structure may appear cumbersome at first, when overlaid on the existing enterprise, but it is intended to be temporary. Task teams are dismantled as their work is completed. As new process designs take hold, the permanent organizational structure begins to take the shape necessary to manage the revised work activities and flow.

The *individuals in the enterprise* are obviously greatly affected during the redesign of work processes. They have to live with the outcomes. They will likely need broadened work skills, better analytical abilities, and increased proficiency in working in team environments. The goals and progress of process redesign must be widely communicated, and the training needed to enable individuals to perform effectively in their new roles must be provided.

In summary, the delivery of superior value requires an understanding of the crucial business processes that enable an enterprise to compete. These core processes cross the functions of the business horizontally, and often have to be completely reengineered in order to substantially improve the level of enterprise performance. A reengineered organization will be flatter and organized differently from traditional forms. The next chapter discusses in detail the new enterprise "architectures" that are emerging as frameworks for the high-value-delivering enterprise.

3

The New Enterprise Architecture

When the building is about to fall down, the mice desert it.

Pliny the Elder

The ubiquitous Tom Peters predicts the imminent "disappearance of the organization as we know it." Is this a prescription for his brand of "liberation management" or a descent into chaos? One fact is certain: never before have so many enterprise leaders questioned the fundamental principles of traditional organization structures as during this turbulent period of the value decade. The pressure to become more customer-driven, and to manage horizontally with greater attention to core business processes, is creating the need to rethink the way we configure enterprises. New forms of "organizational architectures" are emerging that are fundamentally different from the "command-and-control" structures of the past. The third competency of the high-performing enterprise is to design an enterprise architecture that is consistent with the demands of becoming a superior value-delivering business.

An example of an enterprise that can cope with rapid change and that shows tremendous flexibility is Ross Perot's former company, Electronic Data Systems (EDS). EDS's goal is to "help define and exploit fast-changing markets." EDS is unique in that it is quite possibly the world's biggest and best professional service firm. What's different about EDS is an organizational structure that looks nothing like the typical corporate hierarchy that most people in the business world are used to. EDS considers itself to be in

59

the "knowledge extraction, integration and application business." It operates almost entirely on the basis of "projects." In other words, the company's 72,000 employees, in 28 countries, are organized primarily around the completion of client projects rather than into business functions.

In 1984, when the company became a wholly owned subsidiary of General Motors, it registered a profit of $71 million on $950 million in revenue. By 1991, the numbers were up to $548 million in profit derived from $7.1 billion in revenue. The rapid growth of the company is a reflection of the tremendous growth of information technology around the world. EDS "offers information systems consulting, total information systems development, information systems integration, and total information systems management for clients."

The company is divided into 38 strategic business units (SBUs), each responsible for its own profit; these are subdivided into 32 vertical industry units dealing with such sectors as finance, manufacturing, transportation, and communications. There are also six horizontal SBUs that deal with specific, across-the-board client information systems capabilities.

For each client project, EDS assigns 8 to 12 employees who work together for a time span that ranges between 9 and 18 months. Some members of the group work with the customer on a full-time basis. "Though the project's product/result is buttoned down, the formal structure of the project team is murky. . . . Who reports to whom is not critical. Getting the job done is."

However, there are usually three discernible "ranks" within project groups: (1) the individual performer, (2) the subproject team leader, and (3) the project manager. Individual performers will often become subproject leaders when their skills match certain requirements. Then they will return to performer status on subsequent projects. An individual performer will qualify for project manager status after displaying project management skills in his or her work. All of these designations are extremely informal in nature to everyone but the customer. "The ball, when it comes to on-time, on-budget results, is clearly in that leader's court, formal designation or not," says Barry Sullivan, EDS's marketing head:

> EDS is "loose and flexible," says one EDS executive—but damned disciplined. Accountability is unmistakable. If you're assigned a job, you're expected to get it done, even if nothing is written down, even if your "authority" doesn't come close to matching your "responsibility."

EDS demonstrates many of the characteristics of the new organizational structures of the future: customer-focused, team-based work units; temporary work assignments; high levels of employee autonomy based on demonstrated skill competencies; and a clear accountability to "get the job done."

BUREAUCRACY BUSTING

The traditional command-and-control model for organizational structure is giving way to a looser, flexible, and more free-wheeling style. The "adaptive" organization in the value decade:

> . . . will bust through bureaucracy to serve customers better and make the company more competitive. Instead of looking to the boss for direction and oversight, tomorrow's employee will be trained to look closely at the work process and to devise ways to improve upon it. . . .

Raymond Miles, management professor at the University of California, Berkeley, likens the adaptive organization to ". . . a network where managers work much as switchboard operators do, coordinating the activities of employees, suppliers, customers, and joint-venture partners."

Apple Computer takes this idea to extraordinary lengths through its "Spider" system. This network of personal computers, with a video-conferencing system and a database of Apple employee records, provides project team managers with a record of every employee's skills, location, and position, plus color photographs. When a manager wishes to form a team to get something done, he or she is able to access Spider to identify and select employees from around the world.

What will the enterprise of the future look like? Former Harvard economist and now Secretary of Labor Robert Reich believes that, in the future, ". . . every big company will be a confederation of small ones. All small organizations will be constantly in the process of linking up with big ones." Welcome to the world of "no boundaries," "shamrocks," and "clusters."

"Boundaryless"

The requirements of the value decade place a premium on enterprise innovation and change. Your task is to design a more flexible organization, to break down the internal boundaries that make the enterprise rigid and unresponsive. However, as traditional organizational boundaries crumble, a new set of "psychological boundaries" must be successfully managed. These new dimensions can be identified as "authority," "task," "political," and "identity" boundaries. Each is rooted in one of four dimensions common to all work experiences, and each poses a new set of managerial challenges in the new work environment.

1. *The authority boundary: "Who's in charge of what?"* Even in the most "boundaryless" company, some people lead and others follow; some provide direction and others are responsible for execution. When managers and employees take up these roles and act as superiors and subordinates,

they meet each other at the authority boundary and will want to know: "Who's in charge of what?" Traditionally structured organizations don't find this question difficult to answer, but more flexible organizations do. For example, the individual with the formal authority is not necessarily the one with the most up-to-date information about a business problem or customer need. In addition, to be an effective follower means that subordinates have to challenge their superiors, to push for the best solutions to business problems. When leaders and subordinates fail to communicate at the authority boundary, they can't work together to achieve common goals.

2. *The task boundary: "Who does what?"* Work in complex organizations requires a highly specialized division of labor. Yet, the more specialized the work becomes, the harder it is to give people a sense of a common goal. This contradiction between specialized tasks and the need for shared purpose helps explain why teams have become such a popular form of work organization in recent years. Teams provide a mechanism for bringing people with different but complementary skills together, and tying them to a single goal. If teams are to succeed, however, decisions have to be made to address "Who does what?" People at the task boundary divide up the work they share and then coordinate their separate efforts so that the resulting product or service has integrity. Again, in a traditional organization, "Who does what?" was an easy question to answer. In a more flexible environment, the old standby, "It's not my job," doesn't work anymore. To work effectively in teams, workers must take an interest not only in their own jobs but also in their coworkers'.

3. *The political boundary: "What's in it for us?"* Just because an organization does away with traditional boundaries, it doesn't mean that it's suddenly "one big, happy family." There will always be politics, because each group within the enterprise has different interests. This is normal and healthy because it ensures that all aspects of the enterprise are being "looked out for." For example, R&D has an interest in long-term research; manufacturing, in the producibility of a product; marketing, in customer acceptance; and so on. A director of a research lab who tries to protect his or her scientists from intrusions from marketing is engaged in a necessary political agenda. The only time the political boundary doesn't work is when negotiating and bargaining fail and people can't reach a mutually beneficial solution. This is the difference between a win/lose and a win/win situation.

4. *The identity boundary: "Who are we?"* When traditional functional or departmental boundaries are abandoned, a more common identity for all employees in the enterprise can be fostered. Having fewer boundaries helps to break down the "us against them" thinking that leads to conflicts

within the organization. However, when the identity boundary is strong, "team spirit" strengthens. Groups within the enterprise need to feel that "they are the best" without devaluing the potential contribution of other teams. When this seemingly paradoxical balance is achieved, people feel loyal to their own groups and also maintain a healthy respect for others. In other words, healthy pride prevails.

Shared Authority

A more fluid, boundaryless organization will create more blurred roles for workers, and will require new types of skills of the senior executives of the enterprise. Authority will have to be exercised in new ways.

> Authority in the corporation without boundaries is not about control but about containment—containment of the conflicts and anxieties that disrupt productive work. . . . In the corporation without boundaries . . . creating the right kind of relationships at the right time is the key to productivity, innovation, and effectiveness.

Here's an example of how one human resources executive exercised authority and leadership in the collaborative style that is becoming more common in the flexible organizations emerging in the 1990s. This vice president of a high-tech components manufacturer was faced with managing a massive downsizing and reorganization as a result of a shift in his company's strategic plan. He also had to figure out how his own department could best serve the company's new strategy while laying off 20 people—40 percent of the staff in the department.

He decided to ask his subordinates to help him design a new and smaller human resources department. By asking them to help plan the cutback, he felt the layoffs might feel less arbitrary and impersonal. Meanwhile, those who did leave could do so in dignity.

He divided eight people into two teams. He asked both teams to come up with a wide range of possible configurations for the new human resources department and to recruit some of their own subordinates as team members. The teams considered issues such as reporting relationships, spans of control, organizational structure, and new combinations of functions. At the same time, the new departments had to operate with 40 percent fewer people, while taking on additional responsibilities called for under the company's strategic plan. By asking each team to design several alternatives, he was able to avoid potentially explosive turf wars among team members, who, in essence, were designing themselves out of a job. The teams were encouraged to think through all options without becoming wedded to one solution.

The VP gave the teams less than a month to come up with their plans. This was done to create a sense of urgency and to establish a momentum to break free from the inertia of day-to-day activities. He also offered to meet with each participant privately, to discuss his or her own future in confidence. This allowed each team member to openly vent frustrations and connect personally to the VP. Every participant was given the opportunity to discuss how he or she might fit into the new organizational structure or even how the VP might help with the search for a new job.

Nine proposals were presented, and, although discussions were stormy, each team collaborator was committed to the task at hand—even if it meant supporting a plan that eliminated his or her job. In the end, the VP sketched-out a new organization that drew on elements from all nine plans.

The downsizing and implementation went smoothly for everyone involved. Each team member felt that all viewpoints had been heard and a fair and effective solution had been reached. The vice president never wavered from the goal of establishing a smaller department. However, he created a way in which conflicts could surface and be dealt with in a productive manner. He managed the "psychological boundaries" of the group effectively.

Shamrocks and Portfolio People

Besides enterprises "without boundaries," what other forms might an enterprise take in the value decade? Management observer Charles Handy proposes an unusual metaphor to illustrate his predicted organizational structure: the "shamrock," an enterprise that resembles a four-leaf clover.

The first leaf contains core workers—qualified professionals, technicians, and managers; people essential to the firm. The second leaf contains contract workers. Nonessential work is contracted out to people who specialize in one particular task and who did it well at low cost. The third leaf features the flexible work force, the part-time and temporary workers used as the organization expands and contracts its services to match customer requirements.

External customers form the fourth leaf. The customer is not viewed as separate from the organization, but as an integral part of the overall "shamrock."

The shamrock framework envisions relatively temporary links connecting everyone involved except the "professional core." As a consequence, Handy strongly believes that the worker of the future will have to be adaptive and flexible. The new worker won't have just a job, but a "work portfolio" made up of many different types of work. *Wage (salary)/fee work* will be done where money is paid for time expended or upon the completion of a particular job. *Homework* will include such things as cooking and cleaning. *Gift work* will be done for charity, for neighbors, or for the community. *Study work* will include the learning or training necessary to keep other work skills up-to-date and relevant.

Portfolio people will see themselves as "minibusinesses," continually contracting their skills where there is the greatest demand, then moving on when the assignment is finished.

Vineyards

D. Quinn Mills suggests, in his provocative book, *Rebirth of the Corporation,* the preferred architecture of the future will be "the cluster organization." He defines this concept as "a group of people so arranged as if growing on a common vine, like grapes." In business, the common vine is the vision; the employees are in groups arranged by the vision; and the vine and clusters together produce the wine of business success.

> Clusters succeed because they make it possible for a firm to hire the best people, develop an ongoing commitment to quality, be quickly responsive to shifts in the marketplace, and provide a process for rapid revitalization when performance declines.

In Mills's vision, people will be drawn from different disciplines to work together on a semipermanent basis. The six types of clusters are:

1. *A core team.* Comprised of top management; has the central leadership role and is akin to European management committee.
2. *Business units.* Clusters with customers external to the firm; they conduct their own business, deal directly with customers, and may be profit centers. Their flexibility, responsiveness, and autonomy allow a complex company to move at the same pace as far smaller firms.
3. *Staff units.* Clusters with customers internal to the firm, such as accounting, personnel, and legal. These units may price services to internal customers, and may evolve into business units with external customers.
4. *Project teams.* Assembled for a specific project. They lack the ongoing business orientation of the business unit, but projects may last a long time, and teams may appear semipermanent.
5. *Alliance teams.* Today's version of the joint venture. Teams involving participants from different corporations are becoming common in marketing, sales, and product development fields.
6. *Change teams.* Created for the purpose of reviewing and modifying broad aspects of firms' activities, their objectives are limited to achieving a specific end-result.

Even More Variations

Boundaryless enterprises, shamrock-shaped organizations, and companies that resemble clusters of grapes are only a few of the new forms of enterprise structures that are emerging. What other types of architecture might you consider for your company? The choice is wide, but the common denominator is a focus on flexibility and responsiveness.

- *Autonomous work teams.* These self-managed units are responsible for an entire piece of work or a complete segment of a work process. They provide their own supervision, cross-train and trade work tasks, and are empowered to take responsibility for the work process and results. They are used extensively in factories and will become more prevalent in knowledge-intensive work.

- *"Spinouts."* Rather than lose innovators who supply more opportunities than there is time to take advantage of, companies will "stake" entrepreneurs in the creation of new organizations in which they will retain equity. Spinouts may evolve into joint ventures, become fully independent companies, or continue to be associated with the parent, but will usually not end up fully integrated. In the future, there will be many "satellite" operations of this nature, with various degrees of coupling to the core business.

- *Networks.* Companies will evolve into a combination of wholly owned operations, alliances, joint ventures, spinouts, and acquired subsidiaries. These networks will be linked together through shared values, people, technology, financial resources, and operating styles.

TEAMS OF SPECIALISTS

The important components of the "new enterprise" architecture are: small task-oriented collections of people who carry out essential enterprise activities, using team-based structures as the "linchpin" for delivering value to a clearly defined customer group. Noted management writer Peter Drucker models the new organization after a soccer team or a doubles tennis team; team members have designated positions on the field of play, but they also have the mobility to move into another area if that will produce the optimum result. Drucker writes:

> Because the modern organization consists of knowledge specialists, it has to be an organization of equals, of colleagues and associates. No knowledge ranks higher than another; each is judged by its contribution to the common task rather than by any inherent superiority or inferiority. Therefore the

modern organization cannot be an organization of boss and subordinate. It must be organized as a team.

A highly skilled, more knowledgeable work force brings new pressures on an enterprise. Unless the environment in the organization fosters innovation, creativity, and flexibility, the "knowledge worker," who has transportable skills, can easily leave and find an organization better suited to his or her needs. Team-based organizations work well in satisfying the needs of knowledge workers and improving business process efficiency.

As discussed in Touchstone Two, Hallmark is a good example of how team-based organizational structures work to better harness the talents of specialized technicians and creative workers. Approximately 700 writers, artists, and designers are responsible for creating the 40,000 new cards and other items Hallmark produces each year. The company recently reexamined its organizational structure because, although it was happy with the cards being produced, it took too long to turn an initial idea into a salable item. The long gestation period was caused by the sequence of sketches, approvals, cost estimates, and proofs that had to be completed as the product ideas moved from one department to another.

Hallmark staff members are now assigned to separate "holiday and occasions" teams. A Valentine's Day team, for example, consists of artists, writers, designers, lithographers, merchandisers, and accountants. At the head office in Kansas City, team members have been relocated for a closer physical proximity that allows them to work more intimately as a unit. A single card can now move through the production stages faster. This new way of organizing the work at Hallmark has cut cycle times in half, saved money, and made the company more responsive to its customers' changing tastes.

Hired Help

As employees within the enterprise become more specialized, a trend to hire outside subcontractors is emerging. Leading organizations are investing heavily in the training and development of their core staff—in building core competencies. They then "buy in" the expertise and services of outside specialists who can perform noncore tasks more effectively than in-house staff. This approach improves organizational flexibility and drives down costs. But new skills are required to smoothly mesh the efforts of outsiders with full-time employees.

Xerox Canada's former Director, Communications, Monica Burg, made subcontracting an integral part of her department. She restructured Xerox's marketing department and explored nontraditional partnerships with advertising agencies and other suppliers, such as printers, graphics companies, and individual copywriters. In what she termed "best of breed, best of price," Burg handpicked a cross-section of experts and put them together in a Xerox "partnership." The result: competitors became collaborators. Burg even went to the extent of making an agreement with her advertising agency of record (Young & Rubicam) to have a few of the agency's employees work out of Xerox's offices and cross-train with Xerox staff. Xerox benefited from the expertise of dozens of companies instead of going to only one agency for every service. Burg therefore eliminated the problem of mediocre services at high prices. "For the same budget that gave us one commercial last year, I did six commercials, a corporate video and a national print campaign."

Subcontractors can be involved at all levels of the enterprise, including research and development. Apple Computer has maintained the lion's share of its "thinking function" at home, but utilizes software writers by the thousands, and hires independent contractors to help with its research and development.

It's important to treat your subcontractors as your own people. Train, share values, share information, and invite them to participate in your enterprise, just as Xerox Canada has. But there's a catch. Although outsiders must be given access to virtually all information, if "insiderization" becomes extreme, you lose the element of a fresh approach—the main purpose behind subcontracting in the first place. Innovation is imperative. Keep your enterprise "scouring the world for subs" who unexpectedly leapfrog your current partners' offerings.

Finally, don't "sub your soul." Determine what's special or unique about your organization, and make sure it doesn't get subcontracted out.

Self-Management

For core tasks that must be retained within your enterprise, how should the teams of employee specialists be governed? "Self-management" seems to be the answer for many innovative companies in the value decade. Self-management is not a new idea. For example, there are Procter & Gamble factories that have been worker-run since 1968, unbeknownst to competitors and even to some people at corporate headquarters!

Thomas A. Stewart predicts, in *The Search for the Organization of Tomorrow*, that the organization of the 21st century will be created through the convergence of three streams of reasoning:

1. A new emphasis on managing business processes rather than functional departments like purchasing and manufacturing;

2. The evolution of information technology to the point where knowledge, accountability, and results can be distributed rapidly throughout the organization;

3. "The high-involvement workplace" where self-managing teams and empowered employees are the rule.

A classic example of self-managed work teams that has received wide attention is Johnsonville Foods. Johnsonville, a family-owned sausage-making company, was growing rapidly in 1988, but CEO Ralph Stayer still thought something was wrong. He looked around and found that none of his employees was having any fun; they were simply carrying out his orders. This discovery led Stayer to launch a program where self-managed work teams have become the rule.

To better prepare them for self-management, Johnsonville workers were encouraged to broaden their skills in any way they wished, with the company picking up the tab. Workers could take drama courses, painting, or karate, or upgrade their personal computer skills. The choice didn't matter, so long as each worker felt enriched as an individual.

> Johnsonville workers are among the one percent or less in the United States who are encouraged, with company financial support, to study anything— job-related or not.

One Johnsonville "member" says:

> Look, anything you learn means you're using your head more. You're engaged. And if you're engaged, then the chances are you'll make a better sausage.

Self-management continues to be the backbone of Johnsonville Foods. As for the company's self-managed team formula, the following ingredients are included in Johnsonville's "recipe":

- Each team recruits, hires, evaluates, and fires its own people;
- Team workers regularly acquire new skills as the company sees fit, and train one another as necessary;
- Teams formulate, track, and adjust their own budget;
- Teams make capital investment proposals as needed after completing support analyses, visits to equipment vendors, and so on;
- Teams handle quality control, inspection, subsequent troubleshooting, and problem solving;
- Teams are constantly improving every process and product;
- Teams develop and monitor quantitative standards for productivity and quality;
- Teams suggest and develop prototypes of possible new products, packaging, and other components;

- Teams in the plant routinely work with their counterparts from sales, marketing, and product development;
- Teams participate in "corporate-level" strategic projects.

Johnsonville revenue has grown from around $7 million in 1981 to about $130 million in 1991. Stayer believes great results come about because "people want to be great." This CEO wants all of his employees to develop to their full potential, "to be the instrument of their own destiny. It is unconscionable for people not to have the chance to use their full talents."

Focus on Process

Organizing people around processes, as opposed to functions, permits greater self-management and allows companies to dismantle unneeded supervisory structures. This kind of structure also improves communication and eliminates the "crab grass" that often grows between departments, "Purchasing buys parts cheap, but manufacturing needs them strong. Shipping moves good in bulk, but sales promised them fast." Organizing around processes helps ensure that the overall goals of the enterprise are reached with greater ease.

Says Xerox's Richard Palermo, Vice President for Quality and Transition:

> If a problem has been bothering your company and your customer for years and won't yield, that problem is the result of a cross-functional dispute, where nobody has total control of the whole process; people who work in different functions hate each other.

Here are ten ideas for promoting a more horizontal structure:

1. Organize primarily around processes, not tasks;
2. Flatten the hierarchy by minimizing subdivision of processes;
3. Give senior leaders charge of processes and performances;
4. Link performance objectives and evaluation of all activities to customer satisfaction;
5. Make teams, not individuals, the focus of organizational performance and design;
6. Combine managerial and nonmanagerial activities as often as possible;
7. Emphasize that each employee should develop several competencies;
8. Inform and train people on a just-in-time, need-to perform basis;
9. Maximize supplier and customer contact with everyone in the organization;

10. Reward individual skill development and team performance instead of individual performance alone.

HIGH-PERFORMANCE WORK SYSTEMS

The work systems of superb value-delivering enterprises are designed for high performance. David A. Nadler, Marc S. Gerstein, and Robert B. Shaw define high-performance work systems (HPWS) as:

> An organizational architecture that brings together work, people, technology, and information in a manner that optimizes the congruence or "fit" among them in order to produce high performance in terms of effective response to customer requirements and other environmental demands and opportunities.

This sounds like a sensible idea, but what is the most superior configuration? There are two conflicting schools of thought about the "best" enterprise structure. Some observers promote the "melting pot" solution, which gives employee teams the freedom to organize themselves as they see fit; structure and hierarchy are secondary, if not irrelevant, to this view. Another group argues that somewhere "out there" is a perfect solution to your organizational problem. The solution can take any shape—hierarchical, matrix, parallel, team-based, or fashioned after a symphony orchestra. Whatever your own bias toward organizational design, keep these HPWS design principles in mind:

- Perfect structure is in the eye of the beholder.
- Complex problems sometimes demand complex solutions.
- In a turbulent world, structures must be flexible enough to allow "fleet-of-foot" responses to strategic opportunities and competitive challenges.
- Determining what does and doesn't work largely depends on the competency and attitude of leaders.
- Continuous assessment and improvement should be a way of life.
- The two key tests of an effective structure are: (1) the customer's needs are being met, and (2) the structure stimulates learning at all levels of the organization.
- There is a strong correlation between market responsiveness and flat structure.

The Zoological Society of San Diego illustrates the HPWS principles in action. Its management practices are as unique as the species it houses. With 1,200 year-round employees, $75 million in revenues, and

5 million visitors annually, the San Diego Zoo directly competes with amusement park heavyweights such as Disneyland. In addition to maintaining high technical standards, the zoo also champions environmentally sound business practices.

In 1988, the zoo remodeled its displays according to "bioclimatic zones." This was a radical change from its former method of display, which grouped types of animals together according to their species, such as primates and pachyderms. As a result of the new display philosophy, the zoo had to change its internal management structure as well. The old zoo was managed through 50 departments—animal keeping, horticulture, maintenance, food service, fund-raising, and so on; a traditional functional management structure was used. For example, if a groundsman, responsible for keeping paths clear of trash, was rushed or tired, he would sweep garbage under a bush, suddenly transforming his trash into the "gardener's problem."

After the Zoo's redesign, the departments became invisible. Each bioclimatic section is run by a team of mammal and bird specialists, horticulturists, and maintenance and construction workers. The team tracks its own budget on a separate personal computer that is not hooked up to the zoo's mainframe. Team members are jointly responsible for their displays and it's difficult to tell who is from which department. When, for example, the path in front of one of the buildings needed fixing one autumn, both the construction person and horticulturist did it. As team members learned one another's skills, teams have been gradually trimmed in size from 11 to 7. It became apparent, when some staff left the zoo, that it was not necessary to replace them.

Because the teams are self-managed, zoo executives, who were once burdened with petty managerial tasks, have much more free time to focus on increasing attendance. In 1991, although the Gulf War and the recession had depressed California tourism overall, the San Diego Zoo enjoyed a 20 percent increase in attendance. Management attributes this success to the employees' new sense of ownership and their effort to improve the zoo attractions for visitors.

"High-Performing TV"

Other interesting examples of high-performing design principles can be seen in the television industry.

When the Cable News Network (CNN) went on the air on June 1, 1980, it had secured access to only 1.7 million cable subscribers, far short of the 7.5 million "minimum" founder Ted Turner needed to cover 50 percent of operating costs. By 1992, the number had grown to almost 60 million in the U.S. alone.

Turner's dream was to revolutionize televised news programming by "delivering news on demand." Traditionally, newspapers and established TV networks delivered the news according to *their* schedules. Morning newspapers are delivered at about the same time each day regardless of when a major story breaks. Televised newscasts appear on air at exactly the same time each day and night, regardless of the events being covered. Only news announcements that have profound national or international consequences are aired immediately. Otherwise, it is rare for the major television networks to preempt regularly scheduled programming.

From the start, CNN was run contrary to established TV network practices. CNN's first president, Reese Schonfeld, advised everyone to "avoid slickness at all costs." Decisions that would take the major networks and newspapers hours to make were routinely handled by CNN executives in minutes. Furthermore, committees aren't part of the CNN decision-making process.

This formula continues. At CNN, the news is the "star," not the anchor persons. Unlike the major networks, which require an entire team of people for a remote news report, CNN operates leaner and meaner. CNN "video journalists" (VJs) will often write, direct, and report a story solo. A VJ may even be responsible for sound; the only other CNN team member may be the camera person. VJs may be required to be on air "live" for many hours on end when a major story breaks in their area. (This was the case for Bernard Shaw, who reported live from Baghdad during the Gulf War.)

Atlanta, Georgia, is the hub for all the network's activities, and CNN's key decision makers are found there. The staff at this highest level has been organized in an extremely flat structure, and each member of the core group is very familiar with the others. However, the structure of remote video journalists and assignment desks pushes the responsibility for the live stories away from the "core."

> CNN is a superb example of radical centralization and radical decentralization—at once. Everyone at CNN is encouraged to take the initiative for split-second decisions. People on or close to the firing line have extraordinary autonomy, yet they must buy into the vision and understand how their piece fits into the larger puzzle.

Turner's vision has become a reality and a money maker. By 1984, he had lost $77 million in launching CNN. In 1985, the organization was in the black for the first time, recording profits of $13 million on $123 million in revenue. In 1991, CNN generated $479 million in revenue and $167 million in profit.

Fashion Television

Another high-performance success story is found in the design of CITY TV, a television station in Toronto. The unique aspect of CITY TV is that the station operates with no studios. Cameras are not "hard-wired" to studios and control rooms. A network of 32 exposed "hydrants" connects audio, video, intercom and lights, and 90 miles of cable. Literally, any corner of the station can be on-air within minutes. All programming is casually broadcast from the desks and workspaces of CITY TV staff. CITY successfully creates live, interactive programming using workspaces, offices, or the station's lobby, roof, or parking lot as a living "set."

CITY TV's unorthodox and flexible organizational design has spawned several thriving "niche television magazines," the most successful of which is *Fashion Television* (FT). Although produced and edited locally in Toronto, the show uses the latest technology to combine and use "on-location" footage from all over the world. *Fashion Television* reports on sophisticated haute couture trends as well as on pop culture and other art forms. The flexible style of the show gives viewers the feeling they are "on the inside" with the latest fashion trends.

AN ARCHITECTURE THAT IS RIGHT FOR YOU

Where does all this leave your enterprise? Your task is to find the right framework—one that is responsive to the turbulence of the value decade. Four organizational components must be in fine working order if your organization is to achieve long-term success: (1) the work—the basic tasks to be done by the organization and its parts; (2) the people—the characteristics of individuals in the organization; (3) the formal organization—the various structures, processes, and methods created to get individuals to perform tasks; and (4) the informal organization—the emerging arrangements regarding structures, processes, and relationships. Here are some design tips for creating a high-performing enterprise:

1. *Customer-focused design.* The design should start from outside the organization, beginning with customers and their requirements and then moving back to the work and organizational processes. The core purpose is to enable sets of people working together to deliver products and services that meet customer requirements in a changing environment.

Xerox, formerly a traditional company—with separate vertical functions such as R&D, marketing, and sales—recently adopted a new, horizontal structure.

The new design creates nine businesses aimed at markets such as small businesses and individuals, office document systems, and engineering systems. Each business will have an income statement and a balance sheet, and an identical set of competitors.

"Each business will be run by teams with a strong emphasis on the customer. Says Paul Allaire, Xerox CEO, "We've given everyone in the company a direct line of sight to the customer."

2. *Empowered and autonomous units.* Organizational units should be designed around whole pieces of work—complete products, services, or processes. The goal is to maximize interdependence within the unit and minimize interdependence among units, and the aim is to create loosely coupled units that have the ability to manage their relationships with each other. Teams, rather than individuals, are the basic organizational building blocks.

3. *Clear direction and goals.* Great latitude should be given in how work is done, but there is a great need for clarity about the requirements of the output. A clear mission, defined output requirements, and agreed-on performance measures provide the necessary guidance.

4. *Control of variance at the source.* Work processes and units should be designed so that variances (errors) are detected at the source, not outside the unit; information and tools required for early detection must be built in.

5. *Sociotechnical integration.* Social and technical systems should be inexorably linked. The design's purpose is to achieve effective integration between the two.

6. *Accessible information flow.* Members of autonomous units need to have access to information about the market, their output, and the performance of their work processes. The flow of information must allow members to create, receive, and transmit information as needed.

7. *Enriched and shared jobs.* The strength of a group effort is fortified if people are cross-trained in a variety of skills. Broader jobs increase individual autonomy, learning, and internal motivation. The unit's ability to reconfigure is enhanced, as is people's ability to participate in the design and management of the entire work process. Learning becomes an important driver for individuals.

8. *Empowering human resources practices.* There should be practices consistent with autonomous, "empowered" work units, such as locally controlled staff selection, skill-based pay, peer feedback, team bonuses, and minimization of rank and hierarchy.

Ralph Heath, President of Ovation Marketing Inc., of La Crosse, Wisconsin, discovered that the path to "empowerment" isn't always easy. In the past, purchase requisitions and travel budgets had to be approved by both middle management and himself. This was time-consuming for Heath in particular. Heath made a decision: employees were told to approve their own expenses.

Two weeks later, however, Heath was still being swamped with purchases and expenses submitted to him for approval. Heath realized that his employees weren't comfortable with this responsibility and didn't trust that he was willing to let them operate without constant approvals. So, he called a meeting and explained again that requisitions were now an individual responsibility. He then set fire to his stack of purchase orders to prove how serious he was!

Not only hasn't he received any more purchase orders or expenses for approval, but six months later, Ovation's travel expenses were down 70 percent; entertainment expenses dropped 39 percent; car mileage dropped 46 percent; and office supply expenses dropped 18 percent. Ovation's profits went up 16 percent in 1991, compared to profits a year earlier. The "empowerment" of employees has paid off.

9. *Empowering management structure, process, and culture.* Ensure that the larger "host" system is supportive of the empowered autonomous unit. There will be different approaches in each unit to planning and budgeting, modes of decision making, management styles, types of information systems, and management processes. These differences should be acknowledged and accepted.

10. *Capacity to reconfigure.* The enterprise should be designed to anticipate and respond to changes quickly. Work units need the ability to act on their learning, either through continuous improvement or through large leaps of design.

Organizations in the future will clearly be flatter. The high-performing enterprise will be comprised of small units, linked together into networks. The team will be the basic building block of the firm, and the most prized enterprise skill will be effective collaboration. Above all, the high involvement of all members of the work force will be critical to success in the value decade. The ways to achieve the high-involvement workplace are prescribed next.

TOUCHSTONE
4

The High-Involvement Workplace

Management is 85 percent of the problem.

W. Edwards Deming

We saw in Touchstone Three that the ultimate competitive advantage may be an enterprise's ability to organize and manage people. Today's flexible networks of specialized-knowledge workers demand a different style of management compared to the command-and-control methods of the past. Fostering a culture that promotes teamwork and self-management is an important enabler of the horizontal management architectures that characterize the high-performing enterprise. The fourth critical competency is therefore high-involvement management.

OLD WINE IN NEW BOTTLES?

The concept of high involvement or participatory management has been around a long time; the ideas were originally developed about 40 years ago. This style of management has been particularly popular in Europe, where it has been legislated into law in some places. Why is the concept only now reemerging in North America? Experts, like University of Southern California's Edward Lawler III, feel that the reason can be summed up in one word: *dissatisfaction.*

I think the best and simplest explanation is that people only change their basic paradigm when there's an overwhelming amount of dissatisfaction with the

77

existing one and a lot of evidence that refutes it, and where there also exists a more attractive alternative . . . . By now, I think we've reached the point where most major U.S. businesses have suffered enough setbacks to begin to question the effectiveness of the way they operate.

• • •

Certainly, the ideas behind participatory management are not new. But there are two good reasons why it's being practiced more today, and will be even more so in the future. First, the competitive arena has changed dramatically, and performance levels have been raised tremendously—not just in terms of cost-effectiveness, but also in terms such as speed, quality, ability to innovate, and bringing new products to market. What used to be good enough performance is no longer good enough.

Control versus High Involvement

Approaches to employee management can be divided into two categories: (1) control and (2) high involvement. The fundamental difference between the two is in how they deal with the organization and management of work at the lowest levels of the enterprise. In the high-involvement approach, work is designed to be challenging, interesting, and motivating. Employees are encouraged to self-manage and are given enough power to influence decisions that affect their jobs.

The control-oriented approach to management forces employees into a specific set of corporate tasks predetermined by their supervisory structure; they are to do what they are told. The high-involvement management style encourages employees to make suggestions that could potentially improve the workplace and/or the work process.

> The key assumption in the involvement-oriented approach is that if individuals are given challenging work that gives them a customer to serve and a business to operate, they can and will control their own behavior.

The high-involvement style assumes that new employees will need supervision initially, but will be able to govern themselves eventually. This philosophy also presumes that each employee, once given the freedom to become more involved in the work process, will be able to add value to a product by using his or her head, not just his or her hands.

The Bottom Line

Does the high-involvement enterprise produce better business results? A growing body of evidence points to a resounding "yes!" For example, Catharine G. Johnston and Carolyn R. Farquhar, of the Conference Board of Canada, studied seven leading Canadian companies to learn about the impact of employee involvement programs. Johnston and Farquhar found that the key reason for adopting a high-involvement style in each of the companies was simple but powerful: capitalizing on the creative abilities of all their employees. No organization has the capability to compete successfully through the efforts of just a handful of top decision makers. Enterprises need to learn to link the roles and responsibilities of every employee to maximize customer satisfaction. Dick Medel, senior plant manager at Chrysler Canada, recommends:

> Eliminate fear, create an environment where people are truly unafraid to participate and where people become part of the solution.

Each of the seven companies Johnston and Farquhar studied had achieved measurable improvements as a direct result of employee involvement and empowerment methods of managing the work force:

- *Chrysler Minivan Plant.* A 45 percent improvement in outgoing product quality from 1985 to 1991; grievances reduced 55 percent from 1990 to 1991; 1990 union–management contract signed without a strike for the first time ever; warranty conditions per hundred declined 44 percent.

- *GE Canada Inc.* An 8 to 9 percent increase in productivity every year; absenteeism currently less than 3 percent; employee turnover is currently less than 1 percent.

- *IBM Canada Ltd.* Quality up four to ten times on various products from 1982 to 1989, and up another four to ten times from 1989 to 1991; manufacturing cycle time reduced by 75 percent and material costs by 58 percent on a one-million-bit memory module; rework is currently less than 1 percent; employee job satisfaction increased by 45 percent from 1982 to 1992; employee morale index is 83 percent, highest in IBM in North America, third or fourth in IBM worldwide.

- *Linamar Machine Limited.* Sales per employee improved 32 percent in one year; 15 percent reduction in scrap; 80 percent reduction in customer returns.

- *Milliken Industries of Canada Ltd.* Total improvement of 65 percent in off-quality production from 1986 to 1989; improvement of 51 percent in plant throughput time from 1986 to 1989.

- *Pratt & Whitney Canada Inc.* Throughput (raw material plus added value) improved 64 percent in 1991; throughput over operating expenses advanced 57 percent in 1991; cost of nonquality over throughput improved 37 percent in 1991.

- *Wireless Systems Calgary, Northern Telecom Ltd.* A 200-fold improvement in defects in the manufacturing process in 6 years: from 6,000 defects per million to 31 defects per million in 1991.

In addition to improvements in product and process quality, the companies studied reported their high-involvement efforts resulted in more positive employee attitudes.

Another study, by Edward E. Lawler III, Susan Albers Mohrman, and Gerald E. Ledford, Jr., confirms the benefits of participatory management. In 1987 and 1990, the authors sent out surveys to Fortune 1000 companies, asking them about their employee involvement efforts. They found that American companies were more competitive and productive when their employees were involved in decisions about jobs, work environment, and the business overall.

To produce effective results, however, employees must be provided with the power, information, knowledge, and rewards necessary to become fully involved with the organization. Appropriate reward and incentive programs are particularly important in the high-involvement approach to management. The emphasis should be placed on common goals that employees can work toward as a team.

> Individual incentive plans are usually not particularly supportive of employee involvement. They focus on individuals and do not tie the individual in to the overall success of the business; moreover, they can interfere with teamwork and problem solving.

"Open-Book" Management

Some companies are taking information sharing with employees to entirely new levels. The notion of "open-book management" is growing in popularity. The idea is that management "opens the books" to everyone in the company, making available full information about the enterprise's results and challenges. In this way, employees can better see how their role contributes to the success of the company and their own standard of living.

John Schuster, President of Capital Connections, a consulting firm in Kansas City, Missouri, says open-book management is not a strategy for the faint of heart because employees are given the information needed to question management decisions.

SMC (Springfield Manufacturing Corporation) CEO Jack Stack launched a program that taught every employee the language of accounting.

> We developed a process to tell employees how they affect the income and profitability of the company and how they generate cash and what they can do

with the cash they generate. What we basically try to do is let everybody have a part in the decision-making process.

SMC then initiated an employee stock ownership program (ESOP). The stock has gone up in value by 18,200 percent in eight years and sales growth exceeds 30 percent per year. Says Stack: "Because our work force understands the big picture, they see these efforts as tools for achieving bigger and better things."

Here's another example of how sharing financial information with employees promotes a better understanding of the problems and opportunities facing an enterprise. Owens-Illinois, a diversified manufacturer of glass and plastic containers in Toledo, Ohio, wanted to renegotiate its health care plan with union representatives. In November 1991, management proposed more individual cost sharing, in an effort to help offset the spiraling health care costs. Through their 44 representatives, the 9,000 Owens-Illinois employees voted the proposal down 44 to 0!

Management then decided to open the books, to provide the employees with the hard facts and figures of health care costs. A program was developed to increase employees' level of understanding by showing them the company's accounts and allowing them to see for themselves how health care costs for the company had gone out of control. Says James Hysong, the company's Vice President and Director of Human Resources:

> We presented the information—such as the increase in price for even basic health care, and what the company had to do to recoup those costs—and asked them to use their intelligence and draw their own conclusions, instead of telling them what their conclusions should be. It was a powerful difference.

After communicating its position more effectively and educating the employees and their representatives, the company held another vote. This time, employees voted 44 to 0 in favor of the cost-sharing plan!

The "Dark Side"

As participatory, high-involvement management styles become more widely adopted, they will bring tremendous changes to employees in the work force:

- More sophisticated training will continue throughout employees' careers;
- Cross-disciplinary organizations, such as work teams, will have extensive decision-making powers;
- Hiring policies will select recruits based on their adaptability to change;
- An unprecedented emphasis will be put on retraining existing employees in a shrinking labor pool;

- Unions (where they still exist) and management will enter into different, mutually dependent relationships;
- The traditional notion of career will be redefined, and there will be more lateral movement within the enterprise rather than vertical promotion within the hierarchy.

The hazardous element about empowering individuals in the workplace is that not all employees will respond favorably. Any employee who does not want to be challenged by his or her work will not react well to a work situation that is suddenly made more complex. In addition, the high-involvement approach revolves around teams of employees working together to improve their work processes. Effective teamwork requires a certain set of skills not found in all employees.

As a general rule, employees who lack self-discipline will not do well in a high-involvement culture. It has been widely documented that some employees find the high-involvement approach stressful because of increased responsibilities, the pressures of continuous learning, and the demands of having to work in teams.

Furthermore, the high-involvement workplace may be best suited for only certain types of businesses. In the manufacturing sector, the biggest successes have been in capital-intensive process industries, such as chemicals, food processing, and paper making. On the other hand, toll booth operators would not benefit from high-involvement management. The nature of the work depends on a reliable (not creative) person to staff a booth; problem-solving skills simply aren't necessary.

People who desire complex and challenging work, enjoy social interaction, value social rewards, and embrace continuous learning make the best staff for a highly participative style of executive leadership. They must also have well-developed interpersonal and group decision-making skills.

> The high-involvement approach requires that individuals are selected based upon their ability to grow and develop as a member of the organization and, of course, to be a contributor to the culture and management style of the organization.

The ability "to do the job" is no longer of prime importance in an organization that tries to make the work *more* than just a job.

CREATING THE HIGH-INVOLVEMENT WORKPLACE

Numerous elements are needed for successful implementation of the high-involvement philosophy. The three most important factors are: (1) creating team-based organizational structures; (2) encouraging a high volume of employee suggestions and ideas, and (3) recognizing and rewarding employees for their active participation in improving the enterprise.

Self-Managed Teams—Again!

In 1911, Frederick Winslow Taylor, originator of the "scientific management" theory, argued that the productivity of workers could be increased greatly by measuring, in minute detail, the activities of workers, and then standardizing and accelerating those tasks. Managers who followed Taylor's advice soon discovered they had a conflict on their hands: workers resented being "timed" and equally despised the idea of being "watched over" by engineers with stopwatches.

> "Taylorism" is now vilified as the epitome of a hierarchical, authoritarian style of management which caused decades of labor strife. No right-thinking manager today would describe himself as a disciple of Taylor.

One aspect of Taylor's theory that didn't receive as much notoriety or attention was his belief that a willing partnership among workers and managers was also necessary to create improved productivity.

Paul Adler reports in the *Harvard Business Review* that some 80 years later, Taylorism is making a comeback. The New United Motor Manufacturing Inc. (NUMMI) factory—jointly run by General Motors (GM) and Toyota—is bringing "Taylorlike" systems to Fremont, California.

The former GM plant was previously blighted with drug abuse, alcoholism, absenteeism, and union–management conflicts. These factors contributed to the closure of the plant in 1982. In 1984, NUMMI reopened the plant and rehired 85 percent of the previous workers. By 1986, plant productivity was higher than any GM plant, and twice as high as the highest point reached as a GM plant. In fact, plant productivity almost equaled Toyota's Japanese plants.

What does the stopwatch have to do with high involvement? Under GM's previous management, 80 industrial engineers walked the plant floor, designing jobs and setting performance levels that workers were bullied into reaching. Under Toyota's direction, the work force was divided into 350 teams, each consisting of five to seven employees. Team members designed their own jobs, then studied them, timed each other with stopwatches, and explored ways of improving performance. The performance of work teams was judged against that of teams performing the same tasks, but on different shifts.

Once the tasks were fully analyzed, the workers were encouraged to participate in decisions that would make each task more efficient. White-collar staff played only a supporting role. Adler writes:

The reason that this method has produced such startling results, is that Toyota has persuaded workers that they are the key element in the factory's success. A no lay-off policy, extensive training and constant consultation with the workers have earned their trust. Most convincing of all, this lets them control the assembly line.

Chrysler has employed similar team-based structures to achieve higher levels of performance. In the development of its "supercar," the Dodge Viper, Chrysler formed a "platform" team of more than 40 of its best designers, engineers, manufacturing specialists, and managers. Liberated from the company's existing hierarchies and given the freedom to draw on all of the company's resources, the team created a vehicle that has vastly improved the company's image. The cross-functional team employed "concurrent engineering": different elements of the final product are designed and created at the same time. In other words, the talents of everyone involved in the product were pooled together, from design engineers and manufacturing specialists to marketers and salespeople.

GM's Saturn plant calls its version of self-managed teams "work units." These are integrated groups containing between 6 and 15 team members performing up to 30 different functions. Each unit plans its own work, makes hiring decisions, and performs repairs.

To support this style of employee teamwork, each team member receives 92 hours of training per year; there are 20 large training rooms in the manufacturing plant and 24 rooms in nearby locations. Training effectiveness is measured by surveys, pre- and postinventories, and performance checklists.

Results are impressive. The 6,000 Saturn employees and their 200 robots accomplish an output equivalent to six or seven traditional GM plants.

The success of Saturn is fully dependent on its people and this joint effort. From the very start of the Saturn project, management and the union recognized the necessity of developing a cooperative problem-solving relationship if a competitive world-class vehicle was to be manufactured in the United States.

Mining for "Golden" Ideas

The very heart of high-involvement management is to capitalize on the creativity and resourcefulness of every individual in the organization. Effective employee suggestion and idea-gathering processes are critical. New methods are now emerging to "mine" the best ideas from the enterprise.

Each year, about 25,000 General Electric (GE) employees attend "work outs," which resemble town meetings, to discuss a cross-section of business-related issues. Individuals are picked from all levels of the organization. The purpose of these meetings is to solicit divergent viewpoints and, through discussion, eliminate or simplify the most bureaucratic and non-productive aspects of how GE is now managed.

The meetings can appear truly "wild" to the uninitiated. Anything can be discussed, and managers are required to make decisions on many suggestions on-the-spot: "Yes or no?" Follow-up meetings are held to allow GE employees to voice their opinions on how well their suggestions were implemented.

Incentive magazine reports that the success of concepts such as total quality management, just-in-time, and business process reengineering all depend on a steady flow of employee suggestions. Enterprises that consistently inspire on-target employee suggestions have the following characteristics:

1. *Their employees know what is important to corporate success.* Communicating a clear enterprise vision ensures better suggestions.

2. *All their employees know where they fit in the system, and how they can contribute to it.* Workers are provided with flow charts that display how their task can affect the entire work flow.

3. *Their employees maintain customer contact.* Employees routinely visit their internal customers—the people next in line in the work flow—to gain a better understanding of the entire process. Periodic visits to outside customers are also arranged.

4. *They invest a large amount of money in training.* High performers spend as much as 5 percent of operational costs on employee training; instruction in job skills and cross-training add depth and insight to a worker's ability.

5. *They employ teamwork.* Well-trained teams generate many ideas and help employees to focus on the ideas that have the highest payoff.

6. *They value "quality of work life" suggestions.* Suggestions such as more parking spaces, or different food in the cafeteria, may have a relation to safety, productivity, and efficiency that's not readily apparent but is of great importance to the quality of life of those who do the job every day.

7. *They train employees to make suggestions.* Employees should learn to recognize opportunities for improvement, not just know how to fill out suggestion slips.

8. *They turn suggestions around quickly.* High performers act on nearly all suggestions in a matter of days because managers and line supervisors have the authority to approve most ideas. This is crucial because it shows the workers that their ideas are valued and receive immediate attention.

9. *They give recognition and rewards.* Frequent use of noncash awards—coffee mugs, pins, T-shirts, dinner with the boss, or ceremonies where employees talk about how they came up with ideas—are all excellent ways to recognize and reward simultaneously.

10. *They place emphasis on volume.* The average Japanese company accepts about 17 ideas per employee per year versus 0.4 idea per American employee per year.

11. *They have tracking systems that monitor the suggestion program's performance.* They ensure that no suggestions are lost in the shuffle; attention is paid to each idea.

The High-Reliability Program (HRP) at Fujitsu's Oyama, Japan, facility promotes both group improvement projects and individual suggestions. Steven Miller, Director of Manufacturing at Fujitsu Network Transmission, Inc., of Richardson, Texas, spent 30 months in the management apprenticeship program at Oyama.

Miller reports that an improvement project at Fujitsu usually involves 5 to 10 group members and typically requires two to five months to complete. The Japanese plant completes about 1,000 of these group projects per year! Fujitsu's 4,000 employees make some 35,000 suggestions per year, with all suggestions documented, logged, and taken into serious consideration.

The floor-level staff is empowered to evaluate and follow up on suggestions, turning them into actual improvements. Miller believes that the plant's high performance is a direct result of employee suggestions, which allow all staff to continuously improve in their own areas.

To ensure that employees have a clear sense of the organization's overall goals, each department is provided with planning information that lays out the plant's priorities for reliability and improvement for the coming year.

A group that implements a good improvement project is acknowledged through a recognition ceremony and receives special acclaim from the plant manager, a top manager of the product group, or a top manager of the entire corporation. For especially significant improvement projects, the President of Fujitsu hands out certificates of recognition.

Rewards and Recognition

How do you keep the ideas and suggestions flowing? You must carefully think through the best ways to reward and recognize employees for their creative participation in making the enterprise better.

Harris Corporation's Communications Systems Division needed a reward system that supported the company's efforts to promote total quality management (TQM) and higher levels of worker involvement: "a program flexible enough to recognize deserving behaviour regardless of work assignment, yet uniform throughout the division."

Rachel Waters, Harris's administrator of total quality management, led a group that developed the "Wall of Fame" program to recognize people "who consistently seek to positively influence their environments by contributing improvement ideas, implementing innovative initiatives, and promoting team spirit and cohesiveness."

Harris set up nine separate awards, each with its own set of criteria:

1. *Customer Service Award.* Rewards employees who provide something "extra" in exceeding customer expectations, maintaining open lines of communication, fostering cooperation between individuals and organization, or exemplifying highest standards in business dealings.

2. *Above and Beyond Award.* Rewards positive team-player attitudes: employees who take responsibility when it's not required, take leadership roles, or take initiative and accept risks.

3. *Reuse Award.* Rewards the reuse of engineering designs, cost histories, proposals, approved parts, data, technical publications, and recyclable materials.

4. *Innovation Award.* Rewards employees who develop or suggest ideas that are adopted and result in reduced cost, shortened schedule, improved productivity, eliminated waste, or a new product or service.

5. *Excellence through Teamwork Award.* Rewards team recommendations that result in improving productivity.

6. *Program/Team Award.* Rewards employees who make an outstanding contribution in performance against team goals (milestones, cost, performance, schedule, and so on).

7. *Exemplary Leader Award.* Rewards an employee who sets direction, vision, and strategies; communicates, directs, empowers, and develops leadership culture; achieves company vision through motivation, inspiration, feedback, coaching, and role modeling.

8. *Total Quality Individual Award.* Rewards the employee who consistently produces a high-quality product or service; acknowledges those who apply the key principles of TQM in performance of their jobs.

9. *Total Quality Management Award.* Rewards an employee who exhibits management leadership in multiple areas; fosters excellence within the organization; participates in process mapping and benchmarking activities; uses recognition programs; achieves above-average percentage of department participation on teams;

exhibits support for appropriate training for employees in TQM programs and processes.

Harris's approach to recognition may be too comprehensive for many companies, but it shows the wide range of methods available to reward employees for their creative involvement in improving an enterprise.

Money Works Too!

Cold hard cash is often the best reward you can give an employee, because it's something he or she can actually use! Infiniti, the luxury car division of Nissan Motor Company, wanted to create a strong incentive for its dealers to provide excellent customer service—something that helps distinguish Infiniti from its competitors. Infiniti awards a $100,000 annual bonus to dealerships that provide excellent service, based on customer satisfaction surveys and reports from "mystery shoppers" (market research staff who visit dealers posing as customers).

Whenever a customer buys a car or has a vehicle serviced, he or she is surveyed by the factory. Infiniti dealerships that meet or exceed Infiniti's high customer service standards are rewarded with cash payments of up to $25,000 per quarter.

Chrysler Corporation embarked on a similar incentive program with its dealers. The dealers' Customer Satisfaction Index (CSI) ratings are based on responses from car buyers immediately after purchase, after two months of ownership, and after a year. High CSI ratings translate into cash rebates to the dealer of $50 to $500 for every car sold. The dealership owners can then pass along the money to customers in the form of rebates, or to employees in the form of bonuses.

Another example of the effect of monetary rewards on employee suggestions is the experience of two manufacturers that are working together to build a better car. CAMI Automotive Inc., located in Ingersoll, Ontario, is a joint venture between Suzuki and General Motors. One of its strategies to boost productivity and quality has been to implement an employee suggestion program, supported by a strong reward system.

Employees accumulate points for each suggestion they make, then redeem the points to purchase goods through a Consumers Distributing catalog. (Consumers Distributing is a large retailer of housewares.) Once an employee has accumulated 55 points, he or she is eligible to receive $10 worth of merchandise. Year-end awards have been put in place as well, with prizes worth up to $1,000.

In 1991, 17 percent of all CAMI employees qualified for an award. The incentive program has paid off: each employee comes up with 4.8 suggestions per month, compared to 3 per month in Suzuki's plant in Hamamatsu, Japan. New suggestions are implemented quickly by workers. In fact, almost 90 percent of all suggestions are implemented by hourly-rated team leaders, eliminating the frustration of waiting for executive approval.

Guidelines for Success

There are six principles to consider when redesigning your reward and recognition systems:

1. *Appreciation.* People want to know that someone notices and cares about their work.

2. *Contribution.* No one wants to feel that his or her work is menial and pointless; people need reassurance that they add value to the enterprise.

3. *Nonmanipulation.* People know when acknowledgment or appreciation is insincere; they should be treated as knowledgable adults who contribute to the enterprise.

4. *Repetition.* People are more likely to repeat or exceed earlier accomplishments after they've been rewarded consistently for that behavior.

5. *Participation.* When people are involved in the design of the recognition and reward systems, the processes will be more effective.

6. *Celebration.* When work is done properly, improvements are made, customers are satisfied, costs are reduced, and the bottom line is strengthened. Don't forget to celebrate and reward your employees for all those results.

The Baxter organization makes employee involvement a way of life at the Baxter Credit Union. The credit union is a full-service, not-for-profit financial organization that serves Baxter employees and their relatives. Sponsored by Baxter Health Care Corporation, the credit union has enjoyed tremendous growth. Chartered in 1981, it is currently the third largest of the more than 800 credit unions in Illinois, and is in the top 150 of the 14,000 credit unions in the United States. The successful organization has 66,000 members and assets of more than $240 million. The 102 full-time and seven part-time employees benefit from a compensation package, with incentives, that ranks in the top 10 percent of all credit unions. A key reason for the institution's success is its competitive products and rates, but equally important is Baxter's focus on employee incentives.

The Baxter incentive program began in 1988. Three-quarters of Baxter employees are eligible to receive incentives and bonuses. Those who aren't eligible but have earned recognition are rewarded in other ways, such as a dinner out on the company's expense account.

Incentives are paid based on achievement of department goals or authorship of suggestions to improve procedures. For example, in the Collection Department, each employee is measured in three ways: (1) reduction of customers' loan delinquency, (2) reduction of accounts over two months delinquent, and (3) staying within their "charge-off budgets." Each collector is responsible for a group of accounts based on the letter of the alphabet of the account's last name. They work on an account from the time it becomes overdue until it's either "charged off" or paid up. This system eliminates finger-pointing; accountability is clearly assigned. For every target area where collectors are on target each month, they earn $150; if they're on target in all three areas, they earn $450. Managers receive rewards when all their employees are on target, and the Collector of the Year Award entitles the winner to a free trip.

Other awards at Baxter include the Service Excellence Award and the Thomas Edison Award. The Edison Award is for the best idea to reduce or eliminate waste from processes and/or bring value to a process. The winner is presented with the "light bulb" trophy, has lunch with the President, and gets a day off with pay. In 1991, Baxter paid out $141,000 in incentives, but the net increase in earnings over budget was $613,000.

RECRUITING AND TRAINING THE BEST

The high-involvement workplace needs the "best" types of employees. The superior way to build a solid foundation for a participatory style of management is (1) choose the right people to begin with and (2) train them intensively in the necessary skills for contributing to the high-performance enterprise. A. William Wiggenhorn, Vice-President, Motorola, predicts:

> The 1980s was the decade of improving the quality of our product. The 1990s will be the decade of improving the quality of our people.

Finding the "Gems"

Specific characteristics define the "high-performing" employee. Recruit for the following attributes and you stand a better chance of success:

1. *Ability to learn.* Learning encompasses continuous acquisition of new information, different insights and perspectives, and basic skills; an ability to analyze problems; an understanding of cause-and-effect relationships; and utilization of sound logic.

2. *Technical knowledge.* Look for competence in one or more technical disciplines, such as computer literacy and applications software, as well as proficiency in written and verbal communication and basic mathematical skills.

3. *People skills.* High performers must be able to communicate with individuals at all levels of the enterprise. The necessary skills include: public speaking, collaboration, negotiation, participation, and listening abilities.

4. *Emotional literacy.* Find people who have insight into the human condition as well as their own personal relationships; they will relate effectively and productively on the job. Recruiting for this skill will help eliminate bigotry, harassment, sexism, and power struggles, and will promote acceptance and tolerance in the workplace.

5. *Intuitive abilities.* Confidence in their "gut feelings" provides high performers with the skills necessary for risk taking. These are crucial for breakthrough improvements in performance as well as for reaching creative solutions.

6. *Personal management.* Being in control of one's life is a critical skill for a self-managed employee. An ability to set specific, challenging goals and to combat the pressures, stresses, and strains that sometimes threaten performance is part of managing oneself.

Polishing the Gems

Good employee "raw material" is obviously important to your success, but new staff must be given the proper tools and training if they are to succeed. Motorola, with record sales of $13.3 billion in 1992, spent $120 million on employee education, equivalent to 3.6 percent of its payroll. Motorola calculates that every dollar spent on training delivers $30 in productivity gains within three years. Since 1987, it has cut costs by $3.3 billion, without having to downsize.

The company's training effort, known as "Motorola U," offers employees classes in everything from communications and cooperation to fractional fractal experiments. The company credits training as an important factor in the company's success. Sales per employee have doubled in the past five years, and profits have increased 47 percent over the same period.

Combining effective recruiting and training has been one of the keys to the success of Rosenbluth Travel. In 15 years, Rosenbluth revenues have soared from $20 million to $1.5 billion annually. Along the way, the company achieved above-average profitability for its industry. Rosenbluth Travel also boasts a client retention rate of 96 percent.

The reason why it's so successful? The company lavishes attention on its employees, so employees can focus on the customers. Each Monday and Thursday, a New Associate Orientation program begins at Rosenbluth's Philadelphia head office. New employees, regardless of position, department, level, location, or line of business are required to attend these sessions before they report to work for even a single day. On the morning of the first day, recruits get acquainted and become immersed in the company's corporate philosophy and values. In the afternoon, they learn about teamwork, perception, and listening skills. On the second day, the focus is on service, customer expectations, and clients' needs.

During these orientation sessions, groups of four or five discuss the "worst travel service experience imaginable." The story is embellished until it resembles a one-way "ticket to hell." The teams then get up on stage and act out the episode. Afterward, they turn the experience around by identifying where service could have been improved or problems avoided. Finally, they act out the now-positive story and think of ways the good service experience could be turned into a superior service encounter.

After this exercise, new employees tour Rosenbluth's Resource and Development Center and corporate headquarters. Here, they get a surprise: the recruits are served afternoon tea by Rosenbluth's top officers to show what "beyond exceptional service" really means.

To determine its employees' impressions of the work environment, Rosenbluth instituted a unique employee involvement program. A letter was sent to 100 associates along with construction paper and a box of crayons; they were asked to draw "what the company means to me." Management discovered that each person had a different impression of Rosenbluth Travel.

Most of the pictures were positive in nature, but five weren't. To Hal Rosenbluth, this was where the value of the exercise was realized. One picture, entitled "Before," showed a happy environment filled with color: a family sitting around a fire, children at play with kittens and puppies. The same artist drew a "Now" picture, in pencil, showing a person alone and shivering: the fire was out, the family departed, the room empty.

Rosenbluth discovered that this associate worked in an office that had just learned that some of its work was being transferred to another office. What the people weren't told was that they were going to be trained for a new function that was slated for that office. The drawing exercise revealed that a serious breakdown in communication had caused the associates of the office to become terrified of being laid off.

The method proved so worthwhile, Rosenbluth decided to do the same thing with his clients. Again, the company sent out 100 letters and packages of drawing supplies to a random list of clients. And again, the company obtained insights into clients' perceptions of service that had never before surfaced. Since the initial program, Rosenbluth has repeated the exercise four more times. Now, the company receives unsolicited drawings from clients and associates who prefer this form of communication!

Rosenbluth believes that companies are fooling themselves with the standard, the-customer-comes-first message.

> We're not saying choose your people over your customers. We're saying focus on your people because of your customers. That way everybody wins.

Staff recognition is also an important part of Rosenbluth Travel. With the creation of the "Associate of the Day" program, anyone within the company can now spend a day with a senior executive, doing everything he or she does, taking calls, attending meetings, and so on. This provides visible recognition for high-performing individuals and gives them insights into how the company is managed. Initially, the only executive involved was Hal Rosenbluth himself, who held the program once a week. But the program proved so popular that it has been expanded to include all the leadership positions and is held three days a week—sometimes with two associates per day. Through this program, associates learn more about their company and gain a greater understanding of what it takes to fill a leadership role.

Hal Rosenbluth's approach to human resource issues is both refreshing and insightful:

> All too often companies bring stress, fear and frustration to their people— feelings they bring home with them each night. This creates problems at home which people bring back to work in the morning. The cycle is both terrible and typical, but not what most companies would want as their legacy.

CREATING CHAMPIONS

Your job, as a leader in a high-performing enterprise, is not only to provide direction, but also to empower your team in these turbulent times. Wes Rydell, who either owns or has an interest in ten car dealerships (GMC, Chevrolet, GEO, Saturn) in the upper Midwestern United States, comments on empowerment and leadership:

> You hear the word empowerment a lot. To me that means equipping people to use their brains, to make better decisions and make them on their own. That doesn't happen automatically. They need more guidance to do a more complex job. They need more clarity of purpose, more understanding of what you and your store need to accomplish for everyone to be successful. They need a better, clearer vision of what a "job well done" looks like. That's pretty practical, down-to-earth, money-making stuff to me.

How well do you stack up against this list of leadership requirements for creating champions in your enterprise?

- Developing and communicating to employees a corporate vision and specific goals.

- Creating a positive atmosphere for employees, so they feel good about going to work. An average employee spends three-quarters of his or her conscious life preparing for work, going to work, and physically working. Anyone who dedicates that much of his or her life to your company deserve to enjoy it.

- Building good teams of people, with a cross-section of interdisciplinary skills.

- Listening to your employees—just as you would listen to your customers.

- "Sharing the wealth" and making recognition and praise a way of life.

- Delegating authority and responsibility.

- Appraising your staff fairly; promoting only those deserving promotion, and not holding back the advancement of the most capable.

- Reinforcing the importance of customer satisfaction to ensure long-term enterprise success, and training your people in the skills they need to keep customers happy.

A unique example of these ideas in action is DeMar Plumbing, a Clovis, California, plumbing, heating, and air-conditioning company. The company trains its employees three days a week, offers unlimited income based on commissions, puts staff through Dale Carnegie courses, and has a profit-sharing plan.

DeMar is open 24 hours a day, 365 days a year, which translates into some long hours for workers, or "service advisers," as they're called. But service advisers are encouraged to take responsibility for their work and are treated like independent business owners—almost like DeMar franchisees. The loyalty that results is phenomenal: all DeMar service advisers conform to the company's conservative grooming code; virtually everyone works from about 5:30 A.M. until 10:30 P.M.; employees show up for Wednesday (6:00 A.M.) training sessions, where awards are handed out, problems are aired, and customer compliments are read aloud.

Exceptional customer service is so important to DeMar's President, Larry Harmon, that, in 1991, 50 percent of service advisers hired at DeMar were asked to leave the company within the first year because they couldn't meet the high standards required. Because of the autonomy DeMar employees have, some people took advantage of the company. But if employees are loyal to DeMar, DeMar is loyal and gives rewards in return.

To reward service advisers for delivering the level of service expected, DeMar has a unique system. DeMar employees earn points for exhibiting the desired service qualities. At the end of the month, the three "winners" earn sales commissions that are 50 percent higher than the standard rate. The "losers" are either let go or retrained.

In the DeMar point system, customer perception is the determining input; 250 points are awarded for a positive phone call, and 500 points for a positive letter. When a customer requests a particular service adviser for a return service call, he or she receives 1,000 points. When negative feedback is received, the advisers lose points accordingly. Demerits of 250 points are logged for each customer complaint, and arriving late for an appointment, without notifying the customer, costs the service adviser 500 points.

Service advisers can earn points in other ways. They receive 3,000 points for working on a holiday and 1,000 points for selling a twice-yearly service contract. Selling a service contract to a neighbor of a customer earns a service advisor 3,000 points, and a perfect score on a ten-question follow-up survey of the customer translates into 1,000 points. The message: When good work is rewarded and appreciated, employees tend to continue to do good work and to strive for even more rewards and higher recognition.

Blowing-Off Steam

Employers who think that employee stress is none of their business are wrong: it can radically affect the bottom line. A Gallup poll suggests that one in four workers suffers stress-related problems, and absentee rates among these employees are three times higher than among others.

Business Week estimates that stress-related problems and mental illness cost $150 billion annually in health insurance, disability claims, lost productivity, and other expenses. In addition, high job stress causes low morale, high turnover, and an inability to attract top employees. Meanwhile, employees who do stay are disinterested, passive, and inefficient. Their workdays are characterized by late arrivals, personal phone conversations, long lunches and coffee breaks, early departure, and a high rate of absenteeism. Other negative consequences may include drug abuse, employee sabotage, theft, moonlighting, high workers' compensation claims, and higher health care expenses.

Researchers at Northwestern National Life Insurance Company (NWNL) have devised a ten-point plan you can use to help employees deal with workplace stress:

1. *Allow employees to talk freely with one another.* People thrive in an atmosphere where they can consult with colleagues and defuse stress with humor.

2. *Reduce personal conflicts on the job.* Resolve problems through "open communication, negotiation, and respect"; treat employees fairly and clearly define job expectations.

3. *Give employees more autonomy.* People are less stressed when they have greater flexibility on the job.

4. *Ensure adequate staffing and expense budgets.* Give people realistic budgets with which to successfully complete their projects. Don't create more stress by forcing them to work miracles with nonexistent financial resources.

5. *Talk openly with employees.* Keep them informed about good and bad news, and give them the opportunity to air their concerns.

6. *Support employees' efforts.* Ask for feedback, listen to answers, and address issues of concern.

7. *Provide competitive personal and vacation benefits.* Workers need time to relax and recharge their energies in order to perform well.

8. *Maintain current levels of employee benefits.* Cuts in health insurance, vacations, benefits, sick leaves, and other perks, promote stress; employers can't overlook the high cost of "burnout."

9. *Reduce the amount of red tape for employees.* Don't waste workers' time on unnecessary paperwork and procedures.

10. *Recognize and reward employees.* A pat on the back, public praise, a bonus, and similar recognition, can pay off in higher morale and productivity.

SOFTENING THE BLOW OF DOWNSIZING

Authors Tom Peters and Charles Handy predict a future workplace that is made up of "networks" of independent businesses and individual knowledge workers. Although large corporate hierarchies are now unpopular, they did have advantages: they enabled firms to reward outstanding employees with promotions to higher-paid positions; to promise job security; to demand a lot more from long-term employees, who may have been relocated, with their families, at company expense every few years; and to offer a clear path and direction for loyal employees.

Job security used to be one of the main reasons why many people worked for big American or European firms. But as a result of severe staff cutbacks that even "untouchable" companies (Eastman Kodak, Siemens, Phillips, and IBM, to name a few) can't avoid, the days of a lifetime career with one organization are over. The brutal competitive realities of the value decade present a paradox: "How do I foster a highly committed work force, when, at the same time, I may have to downsize to remain competitive?"

Here are some ideas for successfully negotiating a work force downsizing and for transforming a negative situation, such as a plant closing, into a more positive experience for all who might be affected: displaced employees, survivors, customers, suppliers, politicians, and the media:

1. *Organize an intensive management-team planning period.* Delegate responsibilities; identify potential "hot buttons" and deal with them openly. Make sure your people know what they're supposed to be doing, whom they should be ignoring or acknowledging as authority figures, and where they should be during the crisis. Infighting and confusion are at their highest points during these times.

2. *Let your employees know where they stand and how the crisis will affect them.* The sooner and more fully you communicate this information, the better for everyone involved. Whose jobs and reputations are on the line? Make sure everyone knows the risks. Fear and paranoia can destroy the fabric of an enterprise during a downsizing crisis.

3. *Treat your employees as generously as your financial means allow.* When it's time to let people go, try to provide for them and their families as much as possible. Don't just cut them off as though they mean nothing to you as individuals. Devise generous compensation or severance packages.

4. *Offer free relocation counseling, which can be a valuable part of the termination process for all employees, not just management.* Make sure your laid-off staff have the emotional support they'll need to face unemployment and the tough times ahead.

5. *Carefully prepare your reasons for the action you are announcing, and explain them repeatedly.* Identify hot issues in advance and have answers ready. Be prepared to stand by your decision, but back it up with numbers and real facts. Don't give vague explanations about your downsizing efforts. People understand that staying in business can mean hard decisions, and they will appreciate your frankness.

6. *Be sure to consider the needs of the media at a time of crisis.* Professional media consultants can be a definite asset. They can keep a negative press at bay and can arrange press conferences at your convenience, not the reporters'.

7. *Keep various levels of government informed.* Be assertive; don't wait for municipal, state/provincial, or federal government bodies to come to you, inquiring about the implications of your downsizing in terms of job loss and similar effects. Waiting until they call you is a passive, unproductive move that risks letting the downsizing become a political issue.

8. *Inform your customers immediately, and, as with employees, explain specifically how your decision will affect them.* Use different methods, depending on the importance of each customer. Will the downsizing improve products, services, or prices? Is the sacrifice going to benefit customers, or does it create risks?

9. *Make a real effort to relocate displaced employees within your organization if possible.* Try to hang on to as many people as you can. A relocated employee is a grateful, more productive employee, and you'll be doing the right thing.

10. *Be absolutely certain to spend at least as much time explaining your corporate decision and its impact to survivors as to displaced employees.* Employee morale must be a major consideration at times of crisis. Promptly and clearly, communicate where the remaining people stand and what is expected of them.

MANAGING DIVERSITY

By the year 2050, 50 percent of the U.S. population will consist of African Americans, Hispanic Americans, Native Americans, and Asian Americans. A more diverse work force is a fact of life in your enterprise's future. Companies that don't know how to lead and manage people with radically different cultures and backgrounds won't prosper. Similarly, companies that refrain from hiring minority employees because of xenophobic hiring practices will lose the respect of customers and suppliers.

Canada's Honeywell Ltd., the Scarborough, Ontario, makers of heating, cooling, and ventilation controls, has been tackling the issue of diversity head-on. The company has been trying to implement new ideas in the factory, such as just-in-time inventory management, total quality management, and self-directed work teams. But, for these new programs to work, enterprisewide communication was necessary. The problem Honeywell faced was how to bridge a culturally diverse work force; many of Honeywell's employees speak only foreign languages—Greek, Chinese, or Eastern European languages. These employees punched in, did their job, and went home without speaking to their coworkers because they couldn't communicate with one another.

The company developed an education program called "Learning for Life," in which employees take courses, on their own time, in English, math, computers, and communications. Honeywell's investment of $300,000 in training is aimed at making its work force more competitive on a global scale. About 60 percent of the 450 employees have taken at least one course, and employees can upgrade themselves in whatever areas they wish.

For example, an employee who may be an excellent computer programmer may not be able to speak English at an acceptable level. A North American-born employee may have an excellent command of English, but may be computer-illiterate. Executives may be excellent verbal communicators but poor writers, or they may have weak computer skills, and so on. The program works because it allows each employee to improve individual skills and, by extension, his or her job performance.

You can use some specific strategies to help your organization prosper with a more diverse work force:

- Conduct and support multicultural events within the company and community, and encourage employees to attend;
- Make certain all training programs and systems related to developing managerial and supervisory skills address respecting, valuing, and appreciating a diverse work force;
- Require all employees to attend workshops that deal with issues such as racism, sexism, and so on;
- Conduct on-site and off-site educational courses that teach about different cultures, and make attendance a requirement for promotion opportunities;
- Sponsor foreign language courses, accent reduction lessons, and accent listening courses;
- Require higher-level managers to become mentors and sponsors to women and minorities;
- Hire more people who have studied liberal arts, especially foreign cultures, for managerial positions;
- Devise ways to utilize and maintain the dynamism of an aging work force, such as phased retirement and permanent part-time;
- Require all managers to become involved in community service;
- Sponsor company discount tours to various parts of the United States and foreign countries, with the purpose of helping people to understand, respect, value, and appreciate differences;
- Try to locate plants and facilities in a wide variety of communities;
- Develop a comprehensive family care program focusing on child, aged, and disabled care.

Disabled persons require sensitive attention in your enterprise. They represent an underutilized talent pool. Carolina Fine Snacks (CFS) of Greensboro, North Carolina, hired its first disabled worker in 1989. David Bruton, one of many challenged adults seeking employment, was hired despite the fact that he had a learning disability. Bruton was hired as a packer and shipper and soon proved that he could perform his tasks at a much higher level than some of his fellow employees. Since that time, Bruton has been promoted twice and now works as a production assistant in charge of shipping.

Prior to Bruton's employment, the company never exceeded $500,000 in annual revenues, and faced an 80 percent employee turnover every six months. Bruton's high productivity and job performance were so impressive that CFS decided to hire more disabled workers. Now, 8 out of 19 CFS employees are disabled; handicaps range from severe learning disabilities and cerebral palsy to deafness. No physical changes to the plant were necessary and the company's insurance costs remained the same; every employee has the same benefit plan.

To reduce the stress that disabled workers can experience in unfamiliar surroundings, CFS holds weekly staff meetings in which workers are educated about different jobs. The personnel manager has learned sign language to communicate more effectively with the hearing-impaired, and able-bodied workers help train disabled staff in all aspects of company functions.

The disabled employees also have direct contact with clients, who are often taken inside the plant on special guided tours; in others words, the disabled are not "hidden" from clients. Instead, clients have an opportunity to witness the unique employee diversity of the company and to expand their own sensitivities. Overall production has gone from 60 percent of capacity in 1989 to 95 percent in 1992, and employee turnover is down to 5 percent.

The high-involvement workplace requires new thinking and behavior by executives who may be accustomed to a traditional command-and-control management style. There is growing evidence that a participatory, collaborative approach contributes directly to increased productivity and improved morale. The challenges posed by the value decade are too difficult not to capitalize on the best ideas of everyone in the organization. Indeed, the high-involvement approach is proving to be just as important to managing relations outside the enterprise. Partnerships for prosperity are the next topic.

TOUCHSTONE
5

Partnerships
for Prosperity

The way to have a friend is to be one.
Ralph Waldo Emerson

The world of commerce is increasingly becoming a network of interconnected and sometimes fleeting enterprise relationships. The rapid pace of change in the value decade is causing businesses to reconsider how to effectively collaborate with outside organizations: customers, suppliers, even competitors. Relationships that make sense today may no longer be useful in a changed future. Linkages that are inconceivable now may become crucial as a response to rapid changes in customer requirements or emerging competitive threats.

Temporary alliances are often the quickest way to enter new markets or to bring new technology to commercial readiness. Business partnering, the ability to quickly and effectively enter into collaborations with outside organizations, is the fifth critical competency of the high-performing enterprise.

An Ernst & Young study, published in a 1993 *Futureletter,* indicated that 89 percent of American electronics firms have struck up alliances or joint ventures with other companies. In addition, 38 percent of these firms collaborated with competitors! The study indicated these partnerships were formed to improve marketing and distribution while allowing greater access to domestic and foreign markets.

For most global businesses, the days of flat-out, predatory competition are over. The traditional drive to pit one company against the rest of an industry, to pit supplier against supplier, distributor against distributor, on and on through every aspect of a business, no longer guarantees the lowest cost, best products or services, or highest profits for winners of this Darwinian game.

Far-sighted enterprise leaders are reevaluating their traditional "go-it-alone" philosophy in favor of a more open attitude toward cooperative relationships with third parties. These new relationships can come in a variety of forms, from simple customer–supplier agreements to the establishment of complex new business alliances. Small companies that used to contract out aspects of a project will now form alliances and create temporary organizations.

Business partnering may be defined as:

> The creation of cooperative business alliances between constituencies within an organization and between an organization and its suppliers and customers. Business partnering occurs through a pooling of resources in a trusting atmosphere focused on continuous, mutual improvement. The alliances formed allow the involved parties to establish and sustain a competitive advantage over similar entities.

The term "virtual corporation" has been coined to reflect the new enterprise alliances that are emerging. The name is adapted from the computer industry's "virtual computer," which allows a computer to act as if it has more memory and capacity than it actually does. The virtual corporation has more "memory" and skill as well, and it promises to create new products or services faster, cheaper, and better than any of its lone competitors.

The film industry is perhaps the best known and oldest example of virtual corporations. For each individual film production, independent companies come together to produce the film and then go their separate ways when the project is completed.

Partnering often refers to strategic alliances, short-term arrangements designed to achieve specific marketplace advantage. For example, in the mid-1980s, British pharmaceutical giant GLAXO teamed up with Swiss competitor Hoffman La Roche to take on American giant SmithKline Beecham in the ulcer medicine market. GLAXO's highly competitive new medicine, when married to Hoffmann La Roche's 5,000-person sales force, proved to be more than a match for the Americans. This arrangement set the stage for those that followed—some 8,000 to 10,000 alliances now at work worldwide, according to Wharton Business School professor Jordan Lewis.

Partnering also means getting "closer to the customer" in new ways. Harvard Business School professor Theodore Levitt used to describe the buyer–seller relationship as a form of dating: wining, dining, and dancing, followed by a sale. Today, he advises picturing it as a marriage, with the relationship only beginning after the sale is made. "If the new partnering is about anything, it is about relationships that, like a good marriage, both last and grow." Partnership advice covers much the same ground as marriage advice. Experts advise business partners to communicate openly, share feelings and fears, forgive, show mutual respect, celebrate successes, and learn from failures.

The pace of change in the computer industry, combined with the fact that the change is occurring in so many areas at once, means that this industry is one where business partnering can be seen in full bloom.

> The multilayered structure of the new computer industry and the large number of firms it now contains, mean that any single firm, no matter how powerful, must work closely with many others. Often this is in order to obtain access to technology or manufacturing expertise. A web of thousands of joint ventures, cross-equity holdings and marketing pacts now entangles every firm in the industry.

Even firms with a revolutionary new product—developed wholly in-house—need to create a "community" of other firms to fully exploit that new product. Business partnerships in the computer industry are particularly tricky because few alliances are exclusive or restrictive. For example, Apple and IBM have joined forces to develop new chips, operating systems, and multimedia products. Yet they remain fierce competitors.

Microsoft and IBM spent two years and hundreds of millions of dollars in developing the OS/2 operating system to replace MS-DOS. When OS/2 debuted in 1990, it sold poorly. Microsoft consequently pulled out of that agreement and threw its resources behind its own Windows operating system. IBM has since gone on to sign marketing agreements with Microsoft's rivals, Novell and Lotus.

In the 1980s, Compaq used a unique agreement with Intel to gain a considerable piece of the assembled PC market; Intel provided early supplies of its latest microprocessors to the assembler. But when the RISC microprocessor, designed by Sun, and others appeared to leave Intel's chips far behind, Compaq jumped ship to hook up with Sun.

Nineteen other firms depending on Intel's chips formed the consortium ACE to search for an alternative to Intel. In response to this marketplace emergency, Intel rushed a new generation of microprocessors out, and the members of ACE stayed on board.

Similarly, Lotus predicted that IBM's OS/2 would succeed, so it developed its 1-2-3 spreadsheet program to work with that operating system. When Windows proved to be the market darling, Lotus did not have a Windows version of 1-2-3. As a result, Microsoft's own spreadsheet program, Excel, became the more popular program.

The volatile relationships in the computer industry merely highlight the degree of skill and flexibility necessary to achieve successful business partnering. The range of partnering arrangements is diverse; it includes joint ventures, alliances, comarketing arrangements, co-op research and development, employee exchange programs, and technology agreements.

Regardless of form, the three most important partnering arrangements your enterprise is likely to have are those with (1) customers, (2) suppliers, and (3) business allies with whom you work to exploit commercial opportunities.

THE CUSTOMER AS PARTNER

Your enterprise's most important partner for achieving high performance is your customer. In Touchstone Two, we established that creating value for customers is the enterprise success strategy for the 1990s. Customer partnerships are based on trust, and trust is created through open communication. One of the best examples of this kind of open communication can be seen in a "symbiotic relationship," where deep communication enables both parties in the relationship to anticipate and meet one another's needs.

Every time a Childress Buick (of Phoenix, Arizona) is sold or brought in for service, the customer service representative makes a follow-up call to the customer. On every car sold each year, the dealership also follows up—for five years—to make sure it's running smoothly. This intense interest in building relationships has helped make Childress Buick one of the top 50 of 3,000 Buick dealers, in terms of profitability and sales.

The dealership's 14 salespeople earn commissions based on gross sales and bonuses based on a customer follow-up survey that rates the individual and the company. Employees who are not salespeople receive $50 for cars sold through their referral; the person with the most referrals receives a $500 bonus.

In addition, all employees receive ongoing training and personalized business cards. Salespeople and service advisers are teamed up in pairs; both are cross-trained to do the other's job in case filling-in is required. Both are trained to handle their customers' every request. Every prospective buyer is given a tour of the dealership and meets everyone from the service reps to the car washers. Human Resources Director Susan Mack says: "Customers are amazed to see how well we cooperate with one another—they see us fill in for one another." The results are impressive: auto dealers in the United States average 12 percent repeat service; Childress retains 70 percent of its service customers.

The Ritz-Carlton Hotel Company also works hard to deliver "symbiotic" service for its customers. This 1992 winner of the Malcolm Baldrige National Quality Award emphasizes highly personalized, genuinely caring service. The hotel company spent nine years developing a system to deliver premium service to meet and exceed the expectations of more than 240,000 customers.

According to the Ritz-Carlton's own satisfaction research, 97 percent of its customers had their expectations met and received a "memorable" experience. An outside survey research company, Gallup Surveys, confirms that the hotel group was the first choice of its customers in 1991 and 1992. The survey gave Ritz-Carlton a 94 percent satisfaction rating; the second-place hotel group posted only a 57 percent satisfaction rating. It's not surprising that the Ritz-Carlton won 121 quality-related awards in 1991 alone.

The Ritz-Carlton believes that in order to provide complete customer satisfaction, the needs and expectations of the customer must first be fully understood. The hotel gathers information on its customers from a number of sources: extensive research by travel industry associations and publications; focus groups with different market segments; surveys of customers who have just used the company's services; and briefings from employees who come in contact with customers daily.

An information system allows Ritz-Carlton employees to enter data on customer preferences into a computer. This information then becomes part of the company's on-line "repeat guest history program." When a repeat customer calls the central reservations number to book a room, the agent can retrieve the individual's preference information directly from the on-line system. This information is sent to the specific location where the room is booked, and the hotel outputs the data in a daily guest recognition and preference report, which is circulated to all staff. With this system, the staff can anticipate a particular guest's breakfast habits, newspaper choices, and room preferences.

The Ritz-Carlton's employees are well trained, to ensure that they are able to respond to the customers' needs. As part of the customer management system, the first employee who becomes aware of a customer complaint becomes responsible for resolving the problem quickly and completely. Each employee can reverse a transaction up to $2,000, without prior approval—if necessary—to keep a customer satisfied.

Aftermarketing: "Together Forever"

The companies described above practice a critical form of customer partnership building: aftermarketing. It's no longer sufficient to focus attention on customer acquisition strategies alone. Slow market growth and intense competition require working intensely to hold on to hard-won customers. Customer retention is at least as important as new customer conquests.

Aftermarketing is the process of providing continuing satisfaction and reinforcement to individuals or organizations that are past or current customers. Customers must be identified, acknowledged, communicated with, audited for satisfaction, and responded to. The goal of aftermarketing is to build lasting relationships with all customers.

• • •

Customers have a distinct life with an organization, from their first purchase to their last. The problem is that, although a first purchase is easily identified, a customer' last purchase is not as evident. But a customer will at some time stop purchasing a company's products or services. Whatever the reason— receiving poor service, purchasing a defective product, moving out of the trading area, and so on—there comes a time when every customer stops buying from a firm.

The trick, of course, is to delay for as long as possible that time when the customer stops buying. Witness the turnaround that took place at Xerox Corporation, beginning in the early 1980s, when it was spurred to action by the threat of Japanese companies such as Canon—competitors that were stealing market share at an alarming rate.

[Xerox] developed and implemented a far-reaching quality improvement strategy called Leadership Through Quality. Company managers defined quality as meeting customer requirements and, in 1987, declared customer satisfaction the top corporate priority—higher than profits and market share.

Since that time, the measurable improvements recorded have included: a tenfold improvement in manufacturing quality, a 50 percent reduction in manufacturing costs, and the recovery of vital market share. In 1990, the Xerox copier line was named most outstanding of the year by a leading independent office-product testing laboratory, Buyers Laboratory Inc.

Incorporating the customers' suggestions and responses is an excellent way to improve performance. This philosophy also creates a stronger customer–supplier bond, which gives customers the ability to collaborate with suppliers and leads to higher customer satisfaction. Xerox President and CEO Paul A. Allaire agrees: "In the 1990s, . . . successful companies will empower their customers to be codesigners of their solutions and coproducers of their service."

In 1990, Xerox established the Total Satisfaction Guarantee, a three-year guarantee that gives customers the power to decide their level of satisfaction; if they're not happy with the product, they can replace it free of charge. This type of arrangement achieves two key objectives: (1) it virtually ensures complete customer satisfaction, and (2) it promotes trust between the customer and the supplier.

The Xerox Customer Satisfaction Measurement System allows 40,000 surveyed customers to evaluate the company in the areas of product quality, sales, administration, and service. The monthly reports of the survey are posted internally for all staff to see for every product and every market segment.

At Xerox, a second database has also been developed from (1) information gathered through personal contacts (in person, on the phone, or by mail) with customers and (2) information gleaned by Xerox executives during their quarterly visits to major customers.

Xerox's corporate policy dictates that a solution to a customer complaint must be reached within five days of receipt of a survey, letter, or phone call. The complaint must be resolved within 30 days.

The company's 99,000 employees worldwide are taught the importance of customer satisfaction from day one. They're also given a tangible reason to make customers their top priority: employee compensation and promotion criteria are—in part—based on customer satisfaction levels.

Plugging the Leaking Barrel

In the past, when markets were growing strongly and there were plenty of customers to go around for every supplier, a company could afford to practice "leaky barrel" marketing. The term means giving top priority to capturing new customers: pouring them in at the top of the "barrel"—the total customer base. As long as the level in the barrel was rising, the company was probably happy.

However, the level may have been ebbing, despite frantic efforts to fill up the barrel with new customers. Why? Because the customer barrel most likely had leaks: poor quality, indifferent service, inadequate guarantees, and misunderstanding of customer needs. Precious customers were leaking out of the barrel faster than new ones could be poured in. The remedy is to turn attention to plugging the holes. Customer retention strategies have a huge potential for boosting an enterprise's bottom line.

Glen DeSouza, President of Strategic Quality Systems Inc., writes that the concept of customer retention is easily understood by most decision makers, yet it's also frequently overlooked. Market share figures are common knowledge for marketing managers, but customer retention rates are not widely known.

DeSouza refers to a Bain & Company study, which found that customer retention has a greater effect on profits than market share, scale economies, and other traditional variables associated with competitive advantage. The study determined that reducing customer defections by 5 percent translated into a boost in profits of between 25 and 85 percent. There are a number of logical reasons behind these percentages. Marketing costs decrease with increased customer retention because finding new customers to replace lost customers costs money. Furthermore, loyal customers often refer associates to the company they're loyal to, further reducing the expenditures necessary to attract new customers. DeSouza writes: "The true cost of losing a customer is the amount that person could have spent while involved in a business relationship with the company over a lifetime."

To avoid customer "defections," design a successful customer retention strategy. These are the four steps involved:

1. *Measure customer retention.* If customer retention is not measured, it cannot be managed. The *gross retention rate* treats every customer loss as equivalent; it measures the absolute percentage of customers who are retained. The *weighted retention rate* charts customers according to the amount they buy. A customer who used to spend a greater-than-average amount of money is a more costly loss than a customer who usually spent a less-than-average amount of money. A *customer penetration index* indicates whether sales to retained customers are growing as fast as overall market growth would predict. A customer may stay in the fold, but something is still wrong if he or she is buying less than before.

2. *Interview former customers.* Writing off lost customers is a huge mistake. "One can learn a great deal by talking to former customers, either directly or through a consultant. There is no need to guess why customers leave when you can ask them. The information they provide is likely to be more specific and actionable than usual market research."

In 1992, Air Canada surveyed 2,500 frequent fliers to find out why they became infrequent, reducing their business with the airline by some 20 percent between 1990 and 1991. The airline then matched flying patterns of defectors with their reasons for leaving, and used that information to estimate the cost of each service failure. Walter Garrett, Air Canada's manager of consumer intelligence says:

> This is what senior managers want to hear—something like unfriendly flight attendants between Vancouver and Toronto drove away X number of passengers who would have flown X number of times, adding X dollars to our revenues.

Lost customers generally fall into one of the following categories:

- *Price defectors* are those who switch to a lower-priced competitor. For example, in 1981, People Express flights between Boston and Newark cost half as much as comparable flights on Eastern Airlines. The upstart airline successfully attracted students, tourists, and other discretionary travelers through this lower-cost option. By 1984, People Express was the fastest growing airline in the history of aviation. Later, when the airline moved away from this low-price strategy, it failed miserably.

- *Product defectors* switch to a competitor that offers a superior product. These types of defectors are often lost for good. Any company that offers a noticeably better product will always find a market for that product.

- *Service defectors* leave because of poor customer service. When People Express stretched its resources too thin, it started to lose luggage, mess up reservations, overbook and delay flights, and, ultimately, lose customers. As soon as the major carriers were able to selectively match People's low airfares, customers began to leave in droves. In 1986, People Express was forced to sell out to Continental Airlines.

- *Market defectors* are customers who are lost but not to a competitor. These customers may have gone out of business or moved out of the market area. In the early 1980s, many drilling equipment companies lost their oil-drilling customers to bankruptcy after oil prices dropped off.

- *Technological defectors* convert to a product offered by companies from outside the industry. For example, typewriter manufacturers lost customers to word processor manufacturers at the start of the personal computer revolution.

- *Organizational defectors* are customers lost because of internal or external political considerations. For example, Boeing encountered problems when selling to state-owned airlines in the developing world. These airlines often receive financial aid from European governments, providing they purchase from Airbus.

3. *Analyze complaint and service data.* Although customer complaints can be a nuisance to deal with, ". . . complaint data can be a gold mine for the analyst who wants to identify problems that cause customer defections. After all, for every customer who complains, there are possibly ten others who did not voice their complaints."

Paying attention to customer complaints and then "making it right" can go a long way toward retaining the otherwise silent and unhappy customer. For example, in 1977, Procter & Gamble became the first large consumer packaged-goods company to print a toll-free telephone number on all its products. This action greatly increased the number of customer contacts, thereby escalating the amount of information Procter & Gamble had at its disposal to analyze customer perception.

Complaint analysis has achieved a high profile: it is now recognized by the judges of the Malcolm Baldrige National Quality Award as a critical element in a quality management strategy. Judges examine how customer complaints are analyzed, how they are resolved, and how they are used to bring about improvements in product or service quality.

Once complaint data have been gathered, they must be classified—for example, by problem, product model, product year, registration number, and dealer. Statistical analysis is then used to determine which elements of the product are at fault. Sometimes, complete product redesign is necessary.

Polaroid received complaints that an early model of its Instamatic Camera was poorly conceived. When customers tried to pull the film out of the camera, the pictures would rip. In designing its next model, Polaroid kept this information in mind, and incorporated an automatic ejection feature for the film.

Service data differ from complaint data in that they track technical problems that are uncovered during service calls or when customers bring in their products for regular maintenance. An example is when a new car buyer is required to bring in his or her car for service at regular intervals. If certain service problems keep recurring, the company is alerted that changes have to be made. This is what happens when automobile manufacturers recall certain models after discovering a potentially annoying, or dangerous, pattern.

4. *Identify switching barriers.* Analyzing defections and complaints is a good start for a company seeking to improve its customer retention rate, but ". . . a good retention strategy must move beyond problem resolution. It should identify barriers that will prevent a customer from switching to a competitor, even one who is perceived as offering a better product at a lower price."

Lotus Development Corporation competes against companies that sell cheaper and, in some ways, more advanced software—and Lotus wins. It does so by creating a Lotus infrastructure of millions of users, countless applications and macros, and many special-purpose user groups. This infrastructure makes it more difficult for the Lotus customer to switch to a merely cheaper or better featured competitor.

Electronic Data Interchange (EDI), discussed in Touchstone Six, is an example of how information technology can be used to create very effective switching barriers. With EDI, the company and its customer share data. A department store that sells a certain product, and is linked to the product manufacturer through EDI, can keep track of how much stock is remaining, and save money by keeping far less inventory on hand. The cost savings to the store creates for the manufacturer a more loyal customer. The two parties are bound together through the technology link.

Strategic bundling is another method of reducing customer defections. "A bundle is a group of products or services offered as a single cost-saving and convenient package." A banking bundle would include such products and services as a credit card, checking and savings accounts, cash flow statements, and loans. "A customer who buys a bundle is less likely to defect if someone offers a better deal on one of the items in the bundle."

Perhaps the most important strategy to retain customers is to make sure employee job design, training, and performance appraisal support the importance of customer retention. Cadet Uniform Services of Toronto has a "controllable" customer retention rate of 99 percent (not including the loss of customers through outside forces such as bankruptcy). This high rate is due, in large part, to the way Cadet employees are paid. The uniform rental company has 35 delivery drivers, called customer service representatives (CSRs), who are hired after successfully completing about seven separate interviews. The CSRs are trained for three months and spend an additional nine months riding alongside qualified CSRs. After this first year, the new CSR is given a solo route.

Says Arnold Gedmintas, Executive Vice President of Cadet: "Our compensation plan says that if you keep customers, you're going to make a lot of money." Once accounts are assigned to CSRs, they're responsible for retaining those accounts. If a CSR's customer defects from the company for "controllable reasons," the driver loses income. About 50 to 60 percent of employees' pay is based on customer retention. Gedmintas adds: "To put it in perspective, if a CSR's retention rate drops down to 96 percent, he can't afford to work here because the pay drop is so dramatic."

An additional 28 percent of pay is based on face-to-face interviews conducted with customers by five full-time Cadet team members. The team asks over 30 questions about the level of service provided to individual accounts.

The industry average salary for drivers is $25,000 to $30,000; at Cadet, salaries of $45,000 are not unusual. The investment in training and customer focusing has paid off for the company. Cadet drivers typically service twice as many customers as drivers for other companies. Employee turnover is close to zero, as is customer turnover. Cadet's average growth for the past 18 years has been 22 to 23 percent annually. Gedmintas says: "You have to love your customers to death. And you have to listen to them intently and with genuine interest."

SUPPLIER PARTNERING

The second most important group of partners for an enterprise is the suppliers. Supplier alliances can take many forms: joint research and development projects, quality improvement programs, and cross-organizational problem-solving teams. The old-fashioned attitude of buying on the basis of lowest-price-only is disappearing quickly. Cost-effectiveness is still important, but collaborative relationships with suppliers can uncover hidden burdens, which cost both sides money. The cost of poor supplier quality often shows up in "soft" terms, such as customers that don't return, or lower satisfaction ratings. In "hard" terms, poor quality translates into wasted staff time, discarded materials, wasted hours, and rework.

> Supplier partnerships are a competitive imperative. A critical component of your long-term strategy to deliver quality product and service to your customers is your strategy for doing business with your suppliers. Your suppliers have the power to move you forward or leave you behind: a glitch in your supplier's production schedule, a lack of understanding of your time lines, or even a clerical error can seriously interfere with your service excellence goals. You need to take control so that you and your suppliers understand what is required from each other.

• • •

> One of the more challenging realities of business is the reality that the service you give your customers is a reflection of the service your suppliers give you. If you receive deliveries late, incomplete or inaccurate, your service to your own customers will inevitably suffer. Your customers will not make allowances for your difficulties with your suppliers. They will simply take their business elsewhere—probably to your competitor.

Like any relationship, successful supplier partnerships require certain conditions:

- The role of each partner is collaborative, not adversarial;
- Requirements or standards are clearly defined and are compatible with suppliers' capabilities;
- Communication is two-way and frequent enough to reflect changing needs, expectations, and business practices of both organizations;
- Both organizations understand that it is mutually beneficial to have high-quality service standards on both sides;
- The purchaser assists suppliers in meeting its requirements; both organizations are of service to each other.

Sears has developed a program that spans North America and is designed ". . . to help suppliers meet the standards Sears has set to best meet the needs of its customers." Sears launched its quality program in 1985, beginning with action planning teams that included people from every level of the company, from the president to the front-line staff. The common goal was to discover ways to increase customer satisfaction and reduce costs.

Early on, the action teams determined that a large number of catalog sales returns were due to poor quality; this disturbing pattern was costing Sears heavily. Any improvement in product quality would immediately show up in the bottom line. The challenge was to convince suppliers to improve their products, while at the same time allowing Sears to price competitively.

In 1987, 24 suppliers in Canada were invited to become part of the Sears Supplier Quality Partnership; senior executives were given an overview of the program and were encouraged to participate. All 24 agreed. A Sears Quality Control Manager visited the suppliers' plants for a full day, after which an assessment was presented to the supplier management team. The program has since evolved to mirror the ISO 9000 program, a set of internationally recognized quality standards.

Each supplier is given guidance on the requirements of the Sears assessment system prior to the plant visit. More than 20 pages of information are filled out by the Sears auditor. A score of 91 percent or higher means the supplier will be considered for recognition as a Sears Certified Quality Supplier. Currently, one-third of Sears's purchases are from certified suppliers, with the others originating from either suppliers coming up for certification or off-shore vendors not yet in the program.

Following an assessment, Sears will suggest general improvements a supplier might make and will recommend experienced consultants to help with those directions. Six months after the initial assessment, Sears returns for a follow-up assessment, and submits another report to the supplier's management.

Howard Tremaine, a member of the original Sears assessment team, sums up the attraction of the program: "By bringing assistance to our suppliers, we are helping them to survive in an increasingly competitive environment."

"Genetically Engineered" Suppliers

Successful supplier–buyer relationships can't be left to chance. The high-performing enterprise has a well-developed set of skills for selecting and managing those few vital supplier partnerships that are crucial to success.

Cummins/Onan Corporation's Huntsville operation does exactly that. The company manufactures one- and two-cylinder gas engines for generator sets, turf, and welding applications; and three-, four-, and six-cylinder diesel engines for industrial and automotive generator sets and marine applications. Believing that total quality is the key to surviving global competition, the company devised a scientific supplier selection plan to evaluate suppliers objectively.

As part of the plan, the company designed a supplier selection matrix that divides assessment criteria into six categories, one for each of its departments:

(1) purchasing, (2) material control, (3) design engineering, (4) receiving, (5) inspection, and (6) quality assurance. The horizontal axis of the matrix lists selection criteria; the vertical axis lists the names of parts manufactured by suppliers.

The company rates its suppliers in each of the six categories and computes the averages. The results produce a "ranking" score: suppliers are ranked from "worst" to "best." High-ranking suppliers are perceived as candidates for "supplier certification"; they are then considered for a more exclusive partnership with the company. Meanwhile, low-ranking suppliers are considered for an "improvement plan"—being told how to become a higher ranking supplier with the company—or are simply deleted from the list for future purchases. The results are used to help suppliers improve their service, while enabling the company to choose the best supplier for each job.

Growing Pains

In the value decade, business partnering with suppliers requires new patterns of thinking. Moving to a deeper relationship with vendors will take some getting used to; new bonds of trust must be developed. These are some of the new ideas that must be adopted:

- Supplier evaluation and selection are examined to ensure sources are "supply-friendly" to the entire buying organization; suppliers should be willing to work out improvements in the supplied product or service that go beyond the question of price.

- Bidding practices should be challenged to ensure a price-only philosophy does not predominate.

- Quality must be fully guaranteed by an ongoing quality management process that is ingrained in the processes of the supplier; incoming inspection of goods should be unnecessary, and the supply of services must meet customer satisfaction demands.

- Concepts of just-in-time must be understood and practiced, including quick setups, small lot sizes, on-time delivery, correct quantities, and close-to-zero inventories.

- Electronic data interchange is needed to reduce paperwork and inherent errors as much as possible.

As in any relationship, establishing strong bonds with suppliers takes time and effort. You can, however, anticipate the typical evolution of a supplier relationship toward the ideal of true collaboration. Does your enterprise have the maturity to move through the following growth stages of the supplier partnering alliance?

Stage 1: Uncertainty and cultural inhibitions. In the beginning, each party is uncertain about how honest the negotiation effort will be and how each will mutually benefit; individuals in the buyer's organization may be accustomed to dealing with existing vendors and have no history with the prospective partner.

Stage 2: Short-term pressures. The buyer is under pressure to hold the line on costs or to meet some cost-improvement objective; the seller will be pressured to meet the always-budgeted increase in volume.

Stage 3: Negotiating a new paradigm. The buyer exercises a position of controlling orders in exchange for transfer of existing costs to the supplier; the seller is anxious to secure preferred business because of an investment in time, preparation costs, and effort.

Stage 4: Paradigm change. Both sides exercise their learning and dedication to forge a different, mutually beneficial relationship; testing is necessary to prove the validity of the emerging principles that will eventually create the new alliance.

Stage 5: Mutual awareness. The buyer and seller who want to build a meaningful, long-term alliance must shift from self-interest and independence to trust, sharing, and partnering.

Stage 6: New values. Values are discussed, tested, reviewed, modified, and solidified; joint analysis, problem solving, investment in equipment, focused facilities, continuous improvement, and the importance of the alliance for competitive advantage become major points of dialogue.

Stage 7: Partnering at last. Consistent quality, faster response time, flexible manufacturing, lower inventories, shorter cycle times, and innovative enhancements for the buyer are achieved by the buyer through partnering; the seller gets larger orders, better forecasts, specification changes that positively affect productivity, and added margins through shared savings.

When a successful supplier partnership is established, the supplier aligns its goals with the purchaser's objectives. An outstanding example is Toronto-based Padulo Advertising, which supplies creative services and promotional strategy to large retail clients across Canada. The agency has enjoyed one of the hottest winning streaks ever recorded in Canadian advertising history.

Padulo's secret is not that complicated; it provides its clients with a partnership-oriented approach. Instead of leaving it to the clients to "close the sale" for their products, Padulo Advertising gets just as involved with selling as its client's sales staff does. Says Richard Padulo, President:

> We have a mandate, and it's a condition of our employment, to be just as responsible for our client's bottom lines as they are. One of the problems with the agencies is that they say, "Come on, we gave you great creative and won lots of awards. We did our job—you didn't do yours!"

Padulo Advertising makes sure that it gets involved both behind the scenes and "on stage." It doesn't stay within the confines of its own building, producing nice little ads and promotions for its clients. Instead, it gets involved on-site as a promotions "consultant," merging its creative staff and resources with the client's in-house communications departments. For example, Padulo guides the client on store layouts, pricing posture, and product packaging; creates incentive programs and cross-promotions programs; and, rather than concentrating on just producing "breakthrough creative," focuses on growing communications vehicles, such as database and relationship marketing.

Bonnie Shore, director of marketing for Fairweather's, one of Padulo's retailer chain clients, recalls that when she came to Fairweather's she started a search for a new advertising agency. She gave each agency a fact sheet outlining the critical issues and challenges facing Fairweather's if it was to be successful in this decade.

> Padulo won hands down. They were the most creative, most retail realistic and most interactive to understand our goals and mandate. . . . We see Padulo as partners. They're always working with us to come up with new and fresh ideas, but it's up to us to educate them. An agency is as good as you educate them to be. Padulo's been very responsive and proactive. They act as a true partner and run as fast as we do.

Rules to Live By

If closer supplier links are in your future, follow these guidelines for getting the most out of the relationship:

- *Review and update your criteria for selecting suppliers.* Are there guidelines? Is there a formal selection process? Is there a list of factors, such as reliability, credibility, responsiveness, competence, accountability, courtesy, security, access? Has each factor been evaluated on the cost/benefit scale?

- *Meet with your suppliers to discuss what you are doing and to ask for their input and support.* Offer to talk to their people to show them what you're doing and why. Tell them about the importance of "total quality and service" in your company, and explain the key role of suppliers.

- *Review the input that comes from staff regarding the competence of the specific suppliers.* Devise ways to regularly canvas the opinion of everyone who comes in contact with suppliers.

- *Develop a performance report on suppliers.* Aim to bring suppliers up to your standards and to provide them with regular performance documentation.

- *Develop a clear course of action upon completion of each report.* Define who receives the report internally and externally; what action will be taken, by you and your suppliers, as a result of the performance report; the penalty for poor performance; what level of performance is acceptable.

- *Communicate with your suppliers.* Find out what barriers within your company may prevent you from receiving excellent products and service from your suppliers.

- *Assure all your suppliers that this is a partnership approach.* Emphasize that you're *both* in the business of making quality products and service an integral part of doing business with each other.

STRATEGIC ALLIANCES

High-performing enterprises are wide open to establishing with third-party organizations any form of collaboration that will deliver more value for their customers. This is why "strategic alliances" are fast becoming the way of the future. As we saw at the beginning of this chapter, the computer industry offers the most visible examples of this new trend.

In the early 1980s, Microsoft used its alliance with IBM to create the MS-DOS operating system, thereby launching itself to the top of the computer software industry. In 1984, Apple Computer and Adobe Systems combined forces to create the tools of desktop publishing, a major advance in the marketplace.

Perhaps most spectacularly, in July 1991, IBM and Apple forged a strategic alliance to share previously proprietary technologies. Through this alliance:

. . . IBM expands its influence into certain classes of personal computers, which it would be unlikely to achieve through internal development, and Apple Computer obtains improved connectivity to mainstream corporate computing.

A warning, however:

Despite their potential contribution, co-marketing alliances pose significant management challenges. The potential for serious conflict is always present as partners often compete with each other in other product lines and, on occasion, in those directly covered by the co-marketing agreement. The potential for opportunism is high as partners may use the alliance only as a means to gain market position at the expense of a partner or to build technological skills from exposure to the partner's intellectual property.

Strategic alliances cover a broad range of potential coalitions for meeting mutual objectives. Partners can include customers, suppliers, competitors, distributors, universities, and even firms in other industries. The first place most companies look when seeking out allies is among their suppliers. You need to be creative, however, in seeing new possibilities.

Motorola is widely known for the strong working partnerships it forms with components suppliers. It has taken this concept a couple of steps further, forming partnerships with hotels, banks, and data processing companies that provide it with other services.

> The most successful manufacturers, or any successful company for that matter, are successful because they are run from the shop floor more often than from the front offices. They are collaborating, cooperating, and celebrating the successes of the people who add value to products and eliminate waste from production operations.

Some experts argue, however, that the reason American manufacturers' performance can't catch up to that of their Japanese competitors is that the United States is ". . . a country of independent-minded achievers acculturated to feel the greatest joy in beating the pants off competitors." The Japanese, on the other hand, ". . . teach their citizens to cooperate unremittingly to the point of copying the best way to do something."

World-class manufacturers such as Eli Lilly have risen to the top, in part, because of this open and cooperative attitude. The Lilly Tippecanoe pharmaceutical plant, outside Indianapolis, Indiana, posted yearly performance improvements. But specialists at the plant knew that the time it took to convert equipment from manufacturing one product to the next—one week or more—was unacceptably long. To arrive at a faster solution, Eli Lilly turned to its suppliers for help.

When a changeover was needed, Lilly faced a complicated process that required adjusting and changing hundreds of nuts and bolts, and rerouting thousands of feet of pipe. To remedy the problem, the plant workers installed changeover stations that had permanent piping routed to the backsides and permitted the attachment of various supply systems to the front sides. Instead of using nuts and bolts to secure the supply systems, specialists worked on finding a one-turn cam clamp setup that would keep the toxic solvents flowing. Previous experience with one-turn cam clamps had not been successful; Eli Lilly couldn't find a supplier capable of producing a perfectly safe and problem-free unit.

Specialists at Eli Lilly worked side-by-side with the best suppliers to develop the necessary clamps:

> Engineers, line specialists, and production workers cooperated with their counterparts at the supplier's shop to design and develop the needed cam clamp. Cooperation and relationship building overcame competitive fear in the interest of improvement.

Indeed, the role of supplier and customer is becoming blurred as more and more enterprises link up to serve a joint user base. For example, through a partnership with IBM, Lexus uses a national computer network to track every car sold, giving every dealership in America access to each car's maintenance history. In this way, if a Lexus owner experiences car trouble, he or she will receive the same level of service at any Lexus dealership.

Commodore Business Machines decided to create a partnership with Business Logistics Services, a division of Federal Express, in order to better meet its customers' needs. Under this arrangement, Fed Ex staffs a 24-hour consumer help-line for Commodore customers. A computer in need of repair is picked up from the customer by a Fed Ex delivery person, a replacement computer is dropped off, and the broken unit is taken away to be fixed.

These new types of alliances create win win situations. Companies boost their customer retention through a better offering, and farm out various business functions to their supplier partners. In an integrated relationship, instead of pitting suppliers against one another to get the best price, purchasing agents work closely with a few select suppliers to reduce the total cost of the relationship, which makes everyone more competitive. Often, as in the arrangement between Fed Ex and Commodore, it is difficult to define the boundary between supplier and customer.

Supply Chain Management

The evolution of interconnected supplier, distributor, and end-user relationships has given rise to the idea of "total supply chain management." The goal of this approach is to optimize the flow of goods and information throughout the distribution system in a way that benefits everyone involved. In the health care business, for example, manufacturers, distributors, and providers traditionally have managed their businesses with the goal of maximizing the benefit of their individual participation in the supply chain. Becton Dickinson, a medical supplies manufacturer, has been a leader in forging a new set of relationships to manage the supply chain in an integrated way that profits all players in the system.

Becton Dickinson started down the supply chain management road by first defining a "partnership vision":

> Becton Dickinson is committed to developing a partnership with its distributors and customers with the purpose of creating an integrated supply pipeline that will deliver the best products and services at the lowest total system cost.

The company then created a supply chain management group. The group was led by a Group President who reported directly to the CEO. An important part of the reorganization was to bring the company's information technology department into the supply chain management structure. Integrated information flows were to form an important part of the strategy.

> It focused on creating an extensive electronic data interchange (EDI) system capable of providing the following services automatically to distributors: order entry, advanced shipment notification, electronic invoicing, electronic contract notification, electronic rebates, net billing, and ultimately, automatic replenishment.

These features support both Becton Dickinson and its distributors. The amount of inventory in the supply chain is reduced. The data links improve planning processes to produce product more efficiently, create fewer spikes in demand patterns, and facilitate a smoother delivery process. The improved information flow simplifies the ordering process for distributors and reduces the time for reconciliation of contracts and rebate agreements from hours to minutes. The distributor doesn't have to dedicate staff time to tracking shipments; the system does much of this work automatically.

The integrated supply chain benefits the health care provider through fewer stockouts, reduced cycle time, and an ability to ask for scheduled/ guaranteed deliveries. As confidence grows in a "stockless Just-in-Time supply chain," hospitals can begin turning unproductive supplies-storage space into hospital-bed areas or other uses that generate revenue. Lower inventory requirements allow providers to reduce the costs of their investment in inventory.

Better Together

A successful alliance is one that opens corporate horizons without destroying corporate culture. In the most common type of strategic alliance, two enterprises join forces to exploit commercial opportunities that neither could tackle alone. These types of arrangements in the computer industry (discussed earlier) are easily recognizable. Sometimes, the combined strength of the two parties is so unique that an alliance is the only way a venture can be initiated.

Corning's joint venture with Siemens to produce fiber-optic cable was successful *because* it was an alliance. The "Siecor" joint venture, which started in 1977, worked because it brought together complementary skills and capabilities. Corning had developed and patented processes to manufacture high-quality optical fibers. Siemens had capital, scale, and worldwide distribution of telecommunications cable. It also had the manufacturing technology and equipment necessary to produce cable from fiber. The alliance allowed both companies to focus on commercializing fiber-optic cable while relieving some of the financial pressure by dividing the investment.

Crédit Suisse–First Boston was a joint venture formed in 1978 to expand both companies' positions in the Eurobond market. First Boston provided access to U.S. corporate issuers of bonds and possessed the skills for structuring new financial vehicles like convertible Eurobonds. Meanwhile, Crédit Suisse was able to place issues with investors in Europe. This combination allowed the joint venture to assume a leading role in the rapidly growing Eurobond markets in the early 1980s.

It's crucial in strategic alliances that partners have an equal footing. McKinsey & Company, in a study that examined 49 alliances in detail, found that two-thirds of those between equally matched partners succeeded, and 60 percent of those between unequal partners failed. Partnerships with 50–50 ownership had the highest rate of success. The study also revealed:

- Acquisitions work well for expanding core businesses in geographic areas already served; alliances are better for edging into related businesses or new geographic areas.

- Successful alliances must be able to evolve beyond initial expectations and objectives; this requires autonomy for the venture and flexibility from the parents.

- Ownerships that are a 50–50 split are more likely to succeed than partnerships in which one partner holds a majority interest.

- More than 75 percent of alliances that terminated ended with an acquisition by one of the parents.

- Alliances between weak and strong companies rarely work; they don't provide the missing skills needed for growth, and they lead to mediocre performance.

A lop-sided joint venture was formed between a U.S. pharmaceutical company and a Japanese player. The U.S. company had a large share in its domestic market, a good portfolio of drugs, and strong R&D facilities. When it expanded its position in Japan, instead of looking for an equally strong counterpart, such as a leading Japanese pharmaceutical company, it joined forces with a second-tier company that had a large sales force.

The joint venture failed. Not only was the Japanese sales force poorly managed, but it was unable to meet its distribution targets. Worse, the Japanese partner was simply unable to push through Japan's development and approval process drugs that had been successful in other markets. It lacked insider contacts to guide the approval process, management resources, and the capital needed to invest in commercialization. The U.S. partner was stronger, but it wasn't able to hold the Japanese partner up.

Making the Marriage Work

Successful collaboration takes skill and a great deal of energy. In fact, a "U.N. level" of negotiating savvy is often necessary:

> Companies are just beginning to learn what nations have always known: In a complex, uncertain world filled with dangerous opponents, it is best not to go it alone.

Two heads really are better than one in the value decade. Here are ten points to keep in mind in managing effective strategic alliances:

1. Treat the collaboration as a personal commitment; *people* make partnerships work.

2. Anticipate that management time and budget will have to be expended.

3. Mutual trust and respect are essential.

4. Both partners must get something (especially money) out of the deal; mutual benefit will require mutual sacrifice.

5. Every alliance needs a tight legal contract and early resolution of unpleasant issues; once the contract is signed, file it away.

6. During the course of the collaboration, circumstances and markets will change; recognize each other's problems and be flexible.

7. Both partners should have clear expectations of the arrangement, including a time line that defines major milestones to be achieved together.

8. Get to know your opposite numbers socially; friends take longer to fall out.

9. Appreciate the different corporate and geographic cultures of the two parties; don't predict a partner's response based on your response.

10. Recognize your partner's interests and independence.

"Going it alone" can be the recipe for quick obsolescence in the volatile value decade. The high-performing enterprise knows how to create value through teamwork within the organization and collaboration with third-party firms. Shifting "network organizations" are becoming more common as the 1990s unfold. To permit the interenterprise "connectivity" necessary to work with strategic partners, you will need to understand the critical role of information technology, the enterprise competency discussed next.

TOUCHSTONE
6

Transforming through Technology

The new electronic interdependence recreates the world in the image of the global village.

Marshall McLuhan

The much heralded "information age" has arrived with a swiftness that seemed unimaginable only a few short years ago. Its arrival has positioned many enterprises on the verge of exciting new possibilities, but it has left many more struggling to reinvent themselves, trying to cope with the turmoil wrought by industry restructuring in the wake of "infotech"— emerging information technology.

Pierre Ducros, Chairman and CEO of the DMR Group Inc. and Chairman of the Information Technology Association of Canada, writes:

> Information technology is altering our world faster than it has ever been changed before. This industry, comprising computer and telecommunications products and services, is realigning our social, political and economic order. In such a boiling environment, new openings and opportunities seethe in profuse numbers. These new openings, and infotech's ability to enable managers to exploit them, give management its special transformative power. Management today is posed at an almost unique moment—a hinge in history. We are swinging open a new door, to a new age.

The decisions you make about infotech can make or break your quest to become a superior value-delivering organization. The sixth critical competency of the high-performing enterprise is to master the use of infotech as

124

the ultimate "enabler" for implementing the "new enterprise" ideas outlined in earlier chapters. This means using infotech to enable core business processes to work more efficiently, create closer links with customers, and enhance external partnerships that are crucial to competing in a fast-changing marketplace. New approaches to infotech support the high-involvement workplace; open networks and greater access to information by employees within the enterprise are key elements. Indeed, the very way we organize work and the relationships between employees and management are being fundamentally altered by infotech.

TECHNOLOGY TRANSFORMATION

The trends of the infotech revolution are well established and easily recognizable. The "new age" is characterized by:

- *A shift to knowledge.* World trade is growing two to five times faster in knowledge-intensive goods and services—such as engineering and robotics—than in resource-intensive goods and services.

  For example, in the past, housing starts and auto sales were used to gauge economic strength. Today, in the United States, more Americans make computers than cars; in Canada, more Canadians work in infotech than in pulp and paper and transportation combined.

- *Smaller hierarchies.* More knowledge power is available to more people, thereby eroding the power of large hierarchies.

- *A surge in networking.* In the past 20 years, the volume of telephone traffic in North America has increased 30 times.

- *Huge growth in infotech.* Twenty years ago, there were 50,000 personal computers installed worldwide; now 50,000 are installed each day; infotech is a trillion-dollar industry and is expected to double again within 10 years; International Data Corporation reports that infotech is the world's largest industry.

- *Shift in employee capabilities.* Richard Crawford, in his book, *In the Era of Human Capital,* predicts that within 10 to 15 years, almost all employment growth will be in knowledge-economy areas.

- *"No country is an island."* Infotech is dissolving borders and creating a global, knowledge-based marketplace.

How Infotech Creates Value

Infotech is a key enabler for the high-performing enterprise intent on creating the most value for its customers. The consulting firm, Arthur D. Little, identifies a number of specific ways in which infotech contributes to value creation:

1. *Streamlining the business.* Universal, easy-to-use data communications, electronic mail, electronic conferencing, and databases will permit instantaneous dissemination of information as well as more effective control of geographically separate workers. The number of middle-management layers and information-collection groups can be reduced.

Corporations such as General Electric and Du Pont have used information technology to form a closer link with geographically isolated offices. Through these integrated networks, teams of employees can be formed from employees who are located all over the world but are only a keyboard touch apart. This link not only promotes cross-functional work projects, but fosters a more tightly knit corporate entity. Meanwhile, team members are encouraged to stretch themselves beyond their narrow specialties.

> As information spreads throughout the enterprise in distributed databases, electronic mail, and universal file sharing, each part of the corporation more easily sees the inner workings of the others. In this way, each worker becomes more reachable and more able to reach.

2. *Responding rapidly to changing market conditions.* Closer communications-based interactions with customers and suppliers, coupled with more complete integration of marketing and production control systems, will permit faster ramp-ups and ramp-downs of the production line and less buffer stock in the warehouse. Such tightly coupled relationships will also facilitate the rapid identification of fast- and slow-moving items, thus allowing companies to revise their product mix in time to adjust to market trends.

In Tokyo, Coke machines automatically inform the distributor when they are running low. Teleterminal, a radio wave transmission system, monitors 62,000 vending machines in order to speed up the ordering process. Because buying patterns and seasonal fluctuations make product demand hard to predict, having dispatching trucks swing by to check stock and refill machines is pretty much an inefficient guessing game. With Teleterminal, the guesswork has been eliminated, and vending machines are restocked on a just-in-time basis. Data from these machines are also used to gauge the effectiveness of marketing programs and to determine production demands. The technology has been responsible for overcoming a labor shortage, raising operational efficiency, and improving service to retailers.

3. *Responding more rapidly to customer requests.* For an estimated 95 percent of the time between their receipt and fulfillment, customer requests

simply move from one individual to another. Document image processing systems and other automated processes can cut this wasted time to a minimum.

One major American trucking firm (6,000 vehicles in two fleets in 100 hubs) has developed a system that can take a customer order, commit to a delivery date while the customer is still on the phone, and quantify costs against delivery date tradeoffs. The system dispatches pick-ups from customers, consolidates them into truckloads (including en route consolidations), assigns trucks to the consolidated orders, and plans the routing based on various commitments.

The goal is to do all of this in "real time"—to minimize "deadhead" travel, to maximize truck utilization, and to minimize travel time. The system was built by analyzing the trucking company's business processes, identifying all of its activities, and simulating the business using automated models. Using real business data, and taking into account randomly generated environmental events, the simulation experiments indicated a potential increase in profitability of 15 percent.

4. *Using resources more flexibly and economically.* Computer-based conferencing, standardized electronic information formats, and universally accessible databases will allow ad hoc project teams to form and function with a minimum of travel. These teams—which can consist of sales, engineering, and industry-specialized marketing support personnel—might coalesce around a small, specific proposal or a large, broader project. They can cooperate via electronic media to get the job done without having to suspend their current assignments in order to travel.

5. *Innovating more quickly.* Teams of marketing, engineering, and manufacturing personnel, working in parallel on the same sets of electronic files and documents, will make dramatic improvements in time-to-market for most products. Every stage—product conception, design, development, and manufacturing—will be accelerated through the use of electronic communication and approval facilities. In addition, new computer-based tools, such as significantly enhanced workstations, will improve the productivity of engineers and reduce the span of time required to produce new designs.

6. *Expanding breadth of product line.* Increased ease of data communication among a corporation's operating units encourages product-line offerings that incorporate components and/or services from multiple divisions. This ability will permit companies to strengthen existing product lines or add new ones, which a single operating unit would not be able to develop and/or support on its own. Easy data communications and computer-based conferencing between customers and the vendor's personnel will permit more rapid and economical development of customized products. In addition, a vendor's

relationship with its customers will strengthen, leading to increased volume and, often, profitability.

7. *Improving total product quality.* The concept of building "quality" into the corporate processes involved in making a product has gained currency over the past decade. Computer-based aids ranging from statistical manufacturing control to standardization of data definitions using a corporate or divisional data dictionary go a long way toward improving consistent quality results.

8. *Competing for and serving customers on a global basis.* Competing worldwide requires coordination among geographically scattered personnel. The infotech of the mid-1990s will allow timely, cost-effective communications. A design project being worked on in New York can be transmitted at the end of the day to a team in Tokyo, where the sun is rising. Neither group wastes any of its crucial work hours waiting for responses from the other.

Only now are the changes in the business environment brought about by infotech's increasing presence being felt. Although the potential for improvements in quality, service, cost, and time are great, one recent study points out that the greatest barriers to the use of infotech are organizational, not technical.

> While many complex and significant technical issues must be overcome, the research showed that the main difficulties were not in the area of technology. Rather, the organizational structures for managing computing, along with the knowledge, skills, resource base, approaches to systems planning, and even organizational culture, were being challenged by the new era. Moreover, the basic nature of business operations which have been essentially unchanged for decades needed to be questioned.

INFOTECH AND COST CUTTING

The first objective you are likely to pursue through the application of infotech is reduced costs through improved business efficiencies. The intense interest in business process redesign, discussed in Touchstone Two, is closely linked to the understanding that new approaches to infotech can dramatically improve work performance.

For example, Cigna RE Corporation, an arm of Cigna Corporation, undertook a major business process reengineering effort in 1988, to share information with customers. It developed an integrated client management database to be accessed by sales and marketing staff for client leads. In launching the database, Cigna was able to replace 85 percent of its existing information systems, reducing the number from 17 to 5. Cigna moved from a central mainframe/terminal-based system to a PC-based, advanced network. At the same time, the structure of the organization was rearranged to include more self-managed work teams. The results were that Cigna cut in half its overall work force and reduced by 90 percent turnaround time for processing most documents. Operating costs were cut by as much as 40 percent.

Information technology can improve the efficiency and effectiveness of business processes in a number of ways:

- *Increasing speed.* Decreasing the elapsed time on critical path of a process, which may have a "domino effect" on other processes, increasing them as well.

- *Storage and retrieval.* With the touch of a button, files and other crucial information can be retrieved at a speed that even the fastest worker can't match.

- *Communicating.* Data and information can be instantly moved from one point in a process to another, in a variety of forms.

- *Controlling process tasks and improving quality.* Automated equipment can provide much finer measurement and manufacturing control than a person can. Human error is eliminated.

- *Monitoring.* Technology can use a set of standards as a measure of what is being done; immediate problems can be reported, corrected, and retested; and statistics regarding quality, performance, use of supplies, and process results can also be monitored.

- *Supporting decision making.* Data required to make decisions can be gathered and used to help staff make better or automatic decisions.

- *Fabricating, manufacturing, and delivering services.* Often, crucial information necessary to complete these services is held up by human error; infotech, on the other hand, can speed up all these functions.

- *Supporting process work functions.* It is often possible for automation to reduce the cost of an effort simply by being less expensive than labor.

The "Paperless" Enterprise

One of the biggest cost savings through infotech is reducing the torrent of paper that floods through the typical enterprise. Imaging technology is fast emerging as a way to handle information exchange among companies, customers, and suppliers, as well as between internal departments within the enterprise.

Imaging technology is a process in which paper documents are scanned by machines that convert information into electronic files. These electronic files are then stored in large computer databases and can be instantly accessed as needed. Imaging technology is leading companies toward that idyllic goal known as the "paperless office."

Essentially, imaging does the same thing as a fax machine: it converts a paper document into electronic images. Facsimilie machines take a picture of the document, change it into an electronic image, send the image along phone lines, and reconstitute it as a document on the other end. The key difference between imaging and faxing is that imaging has no end document printed on paper. High-speed scanners store electronic images into computers, fix them onto 12-inch optical disks (similar to compact disks) capable of storing 60,000 multiple-page documents per disk, or five filing cabinets' worth of paper.

> Many experts doubt corporate America will ever become totally paperless. Even those with paperless systems have some paper floating around. But the trend is powered by enhanced computer capability. And corporations, inspired by competition and the recession, are intent on improving customer service, getting better use of their work force, and pushing decision making to the lower ranks. Imaging can help accomplish all three.

Proponents of imaging technology point to the following advantages: workers can respond to customer inquiries in minutes instead of days and weeks; managers can get up-to-the-minute data on how much work is processed and discover any delays in processing customer requests; and work flow can be gauged and work rerouted for better efficiency. In addition, clerical workers can spend less time filing documents, which gives them more time for customers and performing more meaningful tasks.

To better appreciate the impact of imaging technology on business process efficiency, take the case of the United Service Automobile Association (USAA). When CEO Robert F. McDermott first arrived in 1969, the USAA was flooded with letters and calls complaining about the poor service. Luckily, USAA was able to retain customers by offering low premiums.

At least part of the reason for USAA's poor performance, McDermott figured, was the fact that the company was drowning under a tidal wave of paper—files, claim forms, applications, and correspondence. So many insurance documents were being lost in the shuffle, USAA had to hire 200 to 300 college students to work nights searching employees' desks for lost files!

Witnessing this mess all around him, McDermott vowed to create the "paperless office" and decided to use infotech to meet this goal. Twenty-three years later, the company is a leader in technologies such as an automated policy-writing system and the world's largest Automatic Call Distribution system. These systems have helped USAA become the country's fifth largest car insurer and fourth largest home insurer. Since 1985, it has increased its assets by 230 percent.

In 1988, in partnership with IBM, USAA installed the Automated Insurance Environment With Imaging Plus, a system that reduces to a five-minute phone call a process that used to take 55 separate steps. The elimination of piles of paper, filing time, and space has saved the company close to $5 million annually.

USAA is also the largest direct-mail company in the United States; 150,000 pieces are received each day. These days, much of the mail is scanned into the computer and stored in customer files. In this way, sales reps, who have an imaging system at their desks, are able to call up customer information and can answer questions on the spot. The system also enables incoming mail to be classified according to when it arrived and the line of business it's concerned with, such as special handling, renewal, or fire referral. Because priority numbers are assigned to each piece of mail, time-sensitive business is dealt with first when the service representative (SR) logs on to the computer.

Jack Church, USAA Policy Service Area Manager for Southwest Texas, says:

> When a call comes in, the SR asks for the member's number or name, and uses it to call up on the computer screen the member's policy information. The member's file shows any calls he's made or any correspondence sent from him or generated by USAA. It will also show which SR has worked on the account, what was done and when.

While speaking on the phone, a sales representative can access a customer's policy and make the customer's desired changes on the spot. As soon as the call is completed, the new coverage is active. All changes keyed in during the day are sent to the communications center at night and mailed the following morning.

Gerald L. Gass, USAA's Director of Quality Measurement and Improvement, says: "We see imaging and technology in general as a means of empowering our employees, because it's freeing them to deal with our members."

Look Before You Leap

In 1992, worldwide shipment of imaging equipment more than doubled, according to Dataquest Inc., a San Jose market research and consulting firm. But the switch to imaging technology can be costly and time-consuming. At

Twentieth Century Investments Inc., the changeover took four years. Desktop versions of imaging systems can cost as little as $10,000, but large systems can run up to $18 million. And, experts note, if the computer's down, you can't work.

Before you deploy infotech to improve your work processes, here are some critical steps to take:

- Assess current information services support and office technology related to the processes being studied;
- Find tasks and subprocesses that have an especially high critical requirement for information and information technology;
- Make sure you know what you need before you make a purchase; too often, the wrong infotech is purchased because prior to the acquisition no analysis was done regarding how it would improve work processes.

CAN INFOTECH CREATE HAPPIER CUSTOMERS?

Some observers predict that the rise of infotech will trigger the rebirth of customer service. Here are three ways in which infotech can be used to improve the service value perceived by your customers:

1. *Personalized service.* Frequent shopper programs, or pharmacies that track potentially dangerous combinations of drugs for specific customers, can use names instead of identification numbers to recognize customers. Or, infotech can help monitor store traffic patterns and redeploy sales personnel where they are most needed.

K mart Corporation's new ShopperTrak system—developed by Datatec Industries of Fairfield, New Jersey—is a sophisticated motion detector that counts the number of customers in the store. By accessing the store computer, managers can get up-to-the-minute traffic information and alert employees if they're needed at the checkout counter or on the floor.

Craig Mangold, K mart's manager of corporate information systems/research and development, says that the system can and will be used to determine average shopping time and to anticipate how many cash registers will be needed in, for example, 10 minutes' time. In this way, the system helps to schedule employees according to the busiest times of the week. This ensures that customers are never left wandering around looking for assistance and employees are never wandering around looking for something to do.

2. *Augmented service.* A product or service is enhanced by providing the customer with additional support related to the acquisition or use of the product.

United Parcel Service (UPS) has increased its information systems budget from $40 million to $300 million over the past five years in response to customer demand, increasing competition, and UPS's own long-term goal to become a paperless enterprise. The new technology includes a delivery information acquisition device (DIAD), an 11 × 14-inch handheld computer that allows delivery drivers to collect delivery information and customer signatures, which are then stored for printout later. Each unit costs about $1,300.

There's more. UPS has an onboard computerized system that allows clear, constant communication between drivers and dispatchers; radar technology can track the vehicles within one-tenth of a mile. Meanwhile, its UPSnet system, a $14 million worldwide telecommunications network, provides fast and efficient transmission of voice, facsimile, video, and still images among UPS's distribution centers. All this helps improve service to selected classes of customers by enabling them to know precisely where their computer-tracked packages are and when they will be delivered.

Ironically, UPS's investment in technology still isn't enough for some customers. George Moskoff, a managing partner of the Adderly Page Group Ltd., a consulting firm in Batavia, Illinois, says that these investments are necessary, but perhaps not enough. UPS's technology is new, but can be considered only "competitive-parity technology, not leapfrogging technology." In other words, the systems enable UPS to catch up to its competitors, not jump ahead of them. Industry leader Federal Express already has comparable information systems in place and is looking for the next big advances.

3. *Transformed service.* New info-tech intensive business practices that are developed that better satisfy customer needs and create business differentiation.

> Today, sophisticated information systems are taking us back to an era of made-to-order goods. Few industries will remain unaffected over the next decade. Children's books, greeting cards, and even birthday cakes are already being manufactured at the point-of-purchase with details tailored by the computer system for each recipient.

Examples of how high-technology systems have improved customer service are all around us. National, the car rental company, has a program in place called Emerald Aisle, which eliminates the lengthy, time-consuming rental agreement. Emerald Club members provide National with the necessary billing information only once; the information is encoded on a "smart" credit card. Club members then go directly from the airport to the rental lot, where their smart card is run through an electronic reader by an employee in a booth. Customers are then given the keys and drive away.

Another National innovation for frequent customers is Smart Key. With this system, customers select a rental car from a computer terminal. Once the customer has expressed his or her preference, the contract is printed out and the car keys are spat out from an on-the-spot dispenser. These innovations not only provide heightened customer service, but allow National to build a valuable customer database.

Rival company Hertz has used technology in a similar way. Frequent renters can hop on the Hertz bus at the terminal and travel directly to the lot; their cars are gassed up, running, and ready to go. When the renters return the cars, they give the lot attendant their mileage and a receipt is printed out immediately from a handheld printer.

A Canadian daily newspaper, *The Toronto Star*, uses technology to its utmost in order to provide excellent customer service. If, for some reason, a *Star* customer fails to receive a daily newspaper, the customer merely dials the *Star*'s customer service hotline to reach a computerized directory, enters his or her telephone number, and answers a question regarding the correct street number. The computer finds the customer's name and reports that a newspaper will be delivered shortly. Total time spent in the *Star*'s phone system is 26 seconds. Through e-mail, a message requesting an urgent delivery is delivered to the customer's area dispatcher. *Fourteen minutes later,* a newspaper is delivered to the customer's front door!

"Dialing for Dollars"

Toll-free 800-number call centers offer cost-effective ways to provide better customer service using fewer employees. Whirlpool, the home appliance manufacturing giant, has implemented a new Consumer Assistance Center (CAC) network with the goal of getting more customers to complain! Research showed Whirlpool that only about 6 percent of consumers ever bother to complain. The remaining 94 percent don't say anything; they just quietly take their business elsewhere. The company's response to this finding has been to recruit good customer service representatives, then give them the tools necessary to get the job done. The centers' vision is: "To be indisputably the world's best provider of services to consumers."

Walter J. Coleman, Vice President of Consumer Service Operations, says that before the centers were established, customers called more than 30 different field-office numbers for help or information. A high percentage of callers were placed on hold or asked to call back. Many were then referred to other departments, sometimes requiring another call. Under this archaic system, Whirlpool received 4 million calls per year. In 1992, the CAC network fielded 2.8 million calls. Its goal is to be able to handle 9 million calls by 1997.

The CAC "one-call system," Coleman says, was designed "to provide leading-edge technology that supports Consumer Assistance Center employees to assist consumers and customers quickly, efficiently, exceeding their expectations, in one telephone contact." When a consumer dials Whirlpool's 800 number, he or she is directed to the nearest CAC location. An automatic number identification system channels the incoming call and pulls up the customer profile on-screen for the customer service rep answering the call.

Using image retrieval, the Whirlpool rep can "call up use-and-care information, service bulletins, parts breakdowns, wiring diagrams, any information that is available on a given product." Over 250,000 pieces of paper are contained within this image-retrieval system. If the problem can be easily repaired by the customer following company guidelines, the rep can automatically fax the customer those guidelines from his or her workstation. If a service technician is required, the rep can ask the customer questions regarding the problem, and relay the pertinent information (such as which tools will be needed) to the assigned service technician.

According to Cynthia Grimm, director of the St. Louis office of Technical Assistance Research Programs (TARP), there is strong evidence that consolidating customer service operations in one central location is a solid business strategy. TARP, in conjunction with the Society of Consumer Professionals (SOCAP), conducted a study that revealed three major advantages in adopting this strategy: (1) an increase of 30 to 40 percent in overall satisfaction ratings by customers being served by centralized operations versus decentralized operations; (2) an improved ability to capture and review data on service performance, enabling better root-cause analysis of problems; and (3) decreased customer service costs, with fewer people giving the same number of customers better service.

Grimm advises that customer service is too important to be taken lightly. She warns that companies too often assign customer service tasks to people who have other duties, in an attempt to cut costs. Their thinking is that service can be handled "on the side."

Grimm reports, for example, that a financial services company was handling 8 million calls from customers. Many of the calls were the result of customers' having to be connected more than once to get in touch with the person they wanted to reach originally. The consequences were high customer dissatisfaction and a waste of corporate resources.

After implementing a highly visible, centralized 800 number, the total number of calls dropped by more than 2 million (due to less ping-ponging throughout the company), corporate resources for customer service were decreased by the equivalent of more than 100 full-time jobs, and customer satisfaction and loyalty actually increased.

According to the 1992 TARP/SOCAP study, these are the ingredients that contribute to the successful operation of centralized service call centers:

- They should attempt to resolve inquiries or complaints in one contact, resulting in increased customer satisfaction. Companies should concentrate on empowering employees to resolve situations, rather than on answering the phone just quickly.

- Written and formalized response guidelines should be developed for customers' "top 20" questions/problems, for difficult-to-handle problems, and for possible cross-sell opportunities. TARP research indicates that "employee knowledge" is a key driver of customer satisfaction, and that customers often rate companies the lowest on this attribute.

- The 800 number and individual employees should be evaluated on both process measures (number of calls handled) and outcome measures (customer satisfaction).

- Calls should be distributed evenly throughout the call center with systems such as automatic call distributors (ACD); TARP research shows reps using such systems are 200 percent more productive than those not using them.

- If the number of calls exceeds 500 per week, computer support database integration, word processing, and report generation software are needed.

GETTING TO KNOW YOU

Information technology can enable your enterprise to identify and track individual customers, monitor service levels by company representatives, and assist customers in specifying, acquiring, fixing, or returning products. This level of personalized service is precisely what consumers in the future will demand.

In the highly competitive global markets of the 1990s—markets in which the middle-aged baby boomers are increasingly asserting their rights—it is short-sighted and risky for sellers to estrange themselves from their customers and to alienate their primary source of revenues and profits.

• • •

Progress in information technology permits a return to an earlier era of hometown service, when customers were treated as individuals, products were often tailored to personal needs, and customer support was provided throughout the product's life cycle.

Beyond the Rolodex

Marketers are now beginning to recognize the power of fully automated customer databases and are extending them beyond mere electronic Rolodexes, mailing lists, and surveys. Databases can be used to get to know customers intimately and to help companies design products and marketing programs that will best meet the needs of specific target groups and reward repeat buyers.

For example, American Airlines first noticed in the early 1980s that two-thirds of its revenue came from business travelers. American devised its AAdvantage frequent-flier program, to keep these travelers coming back. Competitors, retail chains, banks, automakers, and countless other marketers now try to find ways to capture on a database everything from names and addresses to the data of a client's last oil change. The reasoning is this: a small percentage of customers accounts for a huge proportion of sales. Therefore, knowing who these customers are, and getting them to buy more, makes sense.

Even Atlantic City casinos are using database information for individualized marketing. Many Atlantic City-bound tourists line up at exit 38A of New Jersey's Garden State Parkway. College students, posted at the side of the road, with binoculars and notepads, jot down the license-plate numbers of each vehicle. The plate numbers are then matched against lists purchased from various states' motor vehicles departments, to obtain the names and addresses of their owners. The resulting list is cross-checked against a database of casino customers. Anyone not already a registered hotel/casino guest receives coupons from a variety of service-owners, inviting them to stop in for food, entertainment, and gambling activities.

Building Customer Relationships

Databases can help your enterprise deepen relationships with customers through "aftermarketing" programs. Walden Books runs a Preferred Reader Program in which customers are offered a discount on their current and future purchases for a fee of five dollars. This offer is partly aimed at creating an incentive for repeat purchases; more importantly, it tracks the names, addresses, and book purchases of Preferred Readers. Walden Books tailors special promotions and mail-order catalogs to its customers' interests. If their interests are geared toward cookbooks and gardening, they wont' be sent business books or computer books. Similarly, computer buffs won't be offered any cookbooks—unless it's software for cooking!

Journey's End hotels discovered, through an analysis of its customer database information, that the number-one customer concern was breakfast.

There wasn't any at Journey's End locations! Company management devised a more detailed survey that concentrated solely on breakfast. What did customers like to eat? Would a free breakfast they didn't like be better than an inexpensive one they did like? What would they pay to eat the breakfast they liked? And so on.

The typical "Continental breakfast" served by most hotels—a danish, juice, and coffee—was not the favorite breakfast. (Only 10 percent of those surveyed liked danishes—one of the most costly breakfast foods.) Nor did customers want big, hot breakfasts. The breakfast preferred by most customers was a muffin (30 percent chose this) or toast (60 percent liked this), served with coffee or juice.

Within a couple of months of the original survey, Journey's End began offering a two-dollar breakfast buffet. Although the results are still being tallied as of this writing, Journey's End's occupancy rates have risen 9.3 percent while the industry-wide occupancy rate has declined 2.6 percent. The breakfast response is a good example of a precisely tailored response to a customer need, based on targeted dialogue with buyers.

Let's Talk

Your customer database can be the next best thing to having a conversation with your patrons, but the database will be only as good as the information you have extracted. Here are some guidelines to setting up good customer databases:

- *Set clear objectives.* Decide what you want your database to do. Do you want to build customer loyalty? Recruit new customers? Determine best-selling products and top locations? If you know why you want the information, you'll know how to ask the right questions and how to interpret the answers.

- *Decide what information you need to achieve your goals.* Names, addresses, and telephone numbers give basic contact information, but think of what else may help you identify key customer segments: age, gender, income, credit cards, complaints, items purchased, dollars spent, dates or times of purchase. Well-planned surveys can capture even more data: attitudes, receptiveness to new products, and life-style habits.

- *Decide whether to build or buy.* You have two choices in creating a database: do it yourself or bring in a consultant. Building it in-house costs less and you own the data. However, you will probably need to modify and maintain off-the-shelf software.

- *Feed it.* Databases can't be left starving. You need to constantly feed them with information and continuous updating. They can be fed from a variety of information sources: service and help calls to an 800 number; individual sales calls updated on-line; fill-in coupons included in advertising; questionnaires; club newsletters; and compatible lists. You can offer incentives to initiate customer contacts; a research study is a good place to start. Build on the list by encouraging a response at every opportunity. Product promotions should encourage a reply through separate 800 numbers or bar codes that identify where or when the promotion ran.

"INTERENTERPRISE COMPUTING"

In addition to strengthening links with customers, infotech can be used to strengthen relationships with suppliers and with some competitors; this is the essence of "interenterprise" computing. Electronic and human links among companies are creating a uniquely North American response to the Japanese corporate tradition of *keiretsu,* which ties banks, subcomponent suppliers, and huge electronics and auto firms together through cross-ownership.

"EDI or Die"

One of the important technologies that facilitates interenterprise computing is electronic data interchange (EDI). The phrase "EDI or die" has been coined by one Canadian publication:

> Think of EDI as the telephone for the year 2000, the invention that will transform business in the next century in exactly the same way as the telephone did in the 20th. For the year 1992, think of it as a strategy for grabbing a competitive advantage—but only if you get in early.

EDI is having a particularly profound effect on the retailing industry. Eaton's, the Canadian department store giant, is a prime example of EDI in action. The store decided it didn't want to carry inventory for bulky goods such as mattresses; it simply wanted to use its floor samples to sell to shoppers. Eaton's is working in conjunction with suppliers such as Bedford Furniture, Simmons, and Serta, to have EDI replace all paper transactions between stores and manufacturers. Using EDI, an order placed electronically at 7:00 A.M. can be ready by the end of the day. Customer orders are routed directly to suppliers, and the system gets rid of invoices, bills of lading, shipment notices, and receipt notices. Once the goods are received at the Eaton's warehouse, they are sent off to the correct store and the money for the goods is placed in the Eaton's client's account.

K mart Corporation, the retailing giant, has recently linked its computer systems with its top 200 suppliers to provide warehouse and sales information on-line in return for faster, more frequent deliveries. With this arrangement, suppliers are able to better forecast demand for their products. At the same time, K mart is able to reduce costly inventory, improve product availability, and strengthen its supply network. When information is shared among companies, the lines between companies are blurred and an increased sense of interdependency is created.

American Airlines' Sabre reservation network and American Hospital Supply's customer order system (which provides customers with direct access to its computer systems) were among the very first systems to display this emerging trend. "Frequent customer" programs—most commonly associated with airlines—are now present in the hospitality, retail, and rental car industries. These programs demonstrate how EDI is being used to forge closer links with customers.

Close business relationships are becoming one of the keys to staying competitive:

> When companies do not forge such technology-driven partnerships, they risk being squeezed out of the competitive picture. That has implications for . . . economic renewal. Every study of . . . competitiveness points to the lack of business partnerships required to compete in the new global economy. Information technology can be the factor enabling these alliances to develop.

The economic impact of these new alliances is being felt particularly by apparel manufacturers. In fact, these alliances are helping to keep "rag trade" jobs in North America. Many low-cost factories in Asia now face a formidable barrier because they cannot compete with a faster and more flexible North American supplier who is joined closely to a North American retailer. Conversely, North American suppliers who aren't using EDI are being shut out. By adopting the kind of integration pioneered by automakers in the mid-1980s, retailers are building the same technological links with suppliers.

Grand National Apparel, a profitable family-owned business, manufactures menswear at a factory in Toronto. Instead of doing business "the old way," where department store buyers come into the factory and pick through various suits, ordering what they like, Grand National supplies its wares electronically to a large department store chain. The retailer orders from Grand National electronically. Its "autoreplenishment" software automatically reorders goods as they are sold, to fill a "model" inventory that takes into account seasonal swings in buying patterns. For example, if a particular store sold 20 pairs of Haggar khaki shorts in the first week of May last year and 30 pairs the following week, the computer will order 40 pairs for the second week of May the next year, if the pattern is repeated.

In the past, all information between Grand National and the retailer was channeled through only a menswear buyer and a Grand National sales rep. If invoicing conflicts arose, Grand National's accountant would have to phone the sales rep, who in turn would phone the menswear buyer, who in turn would phone the retailer's accountant to try to find the person who could sort out the conflict. Now, Grand National and the customer have formed "cross-functional teams." Grand National's accountant can go directly to his or her counterpart at the retailer and straighten out the problem.

Wal-Mart Stores Inc. is generally considered the model for EDI links with suppliers. Wal-Mart was one of the first major retailers to establish complete point-of-sale EDI linkups with its manufacturing community. In many cases, it has placed the responsibility for managing store inventory directly onto its suppliers. Procter & Gamble Company is said to have more than 70 employees working at Wal-Mart headquarters in Bentonville, Arkansas!

Procter & Gamble began looking at EDI partnerships with transportation carriers in late 1989. In Ontario, for example, the company successfully tracks more than 20 percent of its shipments through an EDI application that monitors the exact status of any customer order in the hands of a carrier. Using EDI, the carrier can inform Procter & Gamble when each shipment is loaded, en route, expected to be delivered, and actually delivered.

Perhaps the most significant change EDI has made in retailing is in the role of the sales representative. Sales reps are spending less time handling annoyances such as finance, systems, and shipping complaints, and more time in the stores—working with managers and salespeople on the floor.

How does all this benefit the retail customer? Closer integration through the retail supply chain, better inventory control, and a structured way to drive costs from the system all translate into better selection, service, and value! EDI prevents retailers from selling out popular items or cluttering up their stores with bins full of discounted items that nobody wants. (Remember, an important part of the value equation is giving all of what the customer wants and *none* of what he or she doesn't want.)

INFOTECH AND THE "HORIZONTAL" ENTERPRISE

Author Ken Copeland, President of Digital Equipment of Canada Ltd., believes that infotech is "one of the key ingredients in the calculation determining organization shape and size" but that it is also "among the least understood ingredients of the organizational equation."

Copeland writes:

Information technology—or infotech, as it is now known—can impact an organization in two ways. Infotech creates pressure for change within the organization. Its presence shifts the power relationships and the organizational structure through information access, empowerment and control. Second, infotech operates as an external force, changing the competitive environment and putting new "evolutionary" demands on a manager's organization.

As a result of the growing influence of infotech, managers, by necessity, have had to redefine their roles—or have them redefined for them.

The internal focus on a self-sufficient hierarchical organization, so important in the industrial age organization, can no longer claim a manager's sole attention. Instead, there is more pressure on managers to pay more heed to the external alliances; to operate as diplomats, company flag-bearers and visionaries.

New technologies are therefore creating a new kind of leader. The role changes associated with the new leader include enhanced responsibility, with more decision-making information under the manager's control; supervision of smaller, more autonomous units; closer contact with and attention to the consumer; more responsibility for developing relationships with outside organizations; and expanded networking duties and targets.

With "infotech-supported" managers looking at more external factors that affect the enterprise, the internal leadership role will be passed along to the people who were once called "subordinates."

In the information age, the organization chart is likely to cease looking like the industrial-era hierarchy. It could instead be visualised as the serrated edge of a saw blade, with hundreds of decision makers at the tips of hundreds of information-enabled opportunity centres. This kind of company has the potential to become immensely more flexible, immensely faster. And if decision makers are in smaller units closer to the consumer, the entire product introduction cycle is apt to come under pressure to be more responsive.

Flattening the Pyramid

A wide range of infotech applications can help transform traditional "vertical" structures into the flatter workplace architectures that characterize today's high-performing enterprise. Here are 20 infotech applications:

1. *Data entry* captures data for collection and logging purposes. Simple handheld units can incorporate scanners to speed up entry and reduce error. For example, retailers and supermarkets now use scanners to speed up the checkout and bagging process. Former President Bush first discovered this "amazing" device during his 1992

campaign. (He hadn't been inside a modern supermarket in years, we assume!)

2. *Transaction processing* captures, processes, and stores information, and allows on-line interactive exchange of previously captured data. The use of modems and of fax cards is an example of transaction processing.

3. *Inquiry processing* supports business activities requiring interactive selection, extraction, and presentation of stored information from files and databases. Some software allows selection of only certain information from stored files. Libraries use this kind of infotech to do a variety of searches via topic, title, or author. Many video stores also have this infotech capacity.

4. *Decision support* provides interactive modeling and simulation tools that allow the user to analyze the effects of alternative decisions.

5. *Expert systems* use a type of artificial intelligence that takes or recommends actions based on presented situations and past "experience." They augment human decision-making processes where the expertise or thought processes of the decision maker can be described using rules, such as risk assessment. Medical schools have installed expert systems to teach surgical or diagnostic skills. The program plays out a certain situation, and the student must select the appropriate response. The program then continues based on the student's selection.

6. *Real-time control* supports event-driven processing for monitoring and actuating physical processes. Sensor-based systems and sophisticated alarm systems work with real-time control.

7. *Document processing* includes text and graphics composition capabilities to produce high-quality documents and presentations, with advanced formatting, styling, spell-checking, and color production. Any kind of in-house communications/publishing department of any enterprise would need this system, as would advertising, marketing, and promotions professionals.

8. *Electronic publishing* extends document creation and production tools to provide formal publishing capabilities, including photographic-quality images and color graphics and advanced formatting and style features. Publishing, communications, marketing, and promotions companies need some form of electronic publishing.

9. *Document storage and retrieval* is used to retain large volumes of stored information in document formats. Optical storage technologies allow for storage of scanned or computer-produced documents

using digital storage techniques like those of CDs. One CD-ROM (read only memory) disk can contain an entire encyclopedia collection. This is a crucial technology for researchers, libraries, or any professional, such as a lawyer or doctor, who needs to update information and research frequently.

10. *Graphics processing* supports creation and manipulation of complex drawing applications such as CADD (computer-aided drafting and design) and has the ability to rotate objects into three dimensions. Engineers and architects would use this type of infotech.

11. *Image processing* manipulates information in image format. CAT scanning, aerial photos, fingerprint identification, and aging of facial photos are among its best known uses.

12. *Sound processing* includes voice recognition, interactive voice response, and speech or sound synthesis. It is used for voice-activated computer interaction and for audio output editing.

13. *Video processing* is used to create video productions for TV or workstation display or for training sessions and other group presentations. It incorporates video images, graphics, animation, and simulation.

14. *Hypermedia processing* combines multiple forms of information into a workstation context. Users "navigate" through information displayed in the most appropriate form for their needs, and they follow whatever relationship best suits them.

15. *Electronic mail* (e-mail) distributes messages, documents, and files electronically among "mailboxes"; a fax capacity is sometimes integrated with the e-mail system.

16. *Voice mail* captures messages from callers who are unable to connect. Ideally, voice mail should be integrated with e-mail.

17. *Enhanced telephony* describes a computer-based phone that includes caller identification, call waiting, and call forwarding.

18. *Shared-screen conferencing* connects workstations via communications facilities and provides concurrent display of information and interaction between two or more users. When combined with voice conferencing, it provides low-cost "presentation" conferencing.

19. *Videoconferencing* provides limited or full-motion video between work sites and allows for personal interaction on a "face-to-face" basis.

20. *Broadcasting* allows private-use television for broadcasting to selected audiences.

Telecommuting

A specific application of infotech, telecommuting, promises to radically change how the high-performing enterprise organizes its "workplace." The workplace can now be anyplace that is linked to necessary resources or terminals by new technologies.

LINK Resources, a market research company based in New York, estimates that there were 6.6 million full- or part-time American telecommuters in 1992. That figure represents an increase of 20 percent over the 5.5 million telecommuters in 1991. In Canada, HomeBusiness Institute Inc. reported 500,000 telecommuters in 1992, up from 308,000 in 1991. Another study, by Toronto's Ryerson Polytechnical Institute, estimated that there were 1.5 million Canadian telecommuters in 1992.

Telecommuting can save on office space, reduce turnover, and save employees valuable commuting time. With the rapid advance of information technology, employees can have all the business equipment they need to run self-contained work sites with a minimal investment. Gil Gordon, management consultant and telecommuting expert with Gil Gordon Associates of Monmouth Junction, New Jersey, says that telecommuting workers can be 15 to 20 percent more productive than office workers.

Telecommuting is particularly viable for customer service representatives (CSRs). Most CSRs need only a computer, a phone, and a way to route incoming calls directly to their homes. Most call centers have extended hours; an on-site location can handle base volume, and telecommuters can log on during peak hours. This means that 24-hour customer service lines won't need to be kept open for only a handful of employees, which will save money.

> Working from home allows CSRs to schedule their work at preferred times and with fewer interruptions. It also allows for an extended workday and permits access to the computer at off-peak times.

Telecommuting is receiving wide attention as a method of not only greatly reducing car exhaust pollution, but fostering healthier and more family-oriented life-styles for millions of "freeway slaves."

> Letting workers telecommute, linked to the office by a computer, fax and phone, is one of the ways creative companies are responding to their employees' wants and needs.

A 1985 study conducted in the United States by the National Academy of Science found that telecommuting raised productivity by 15 to 25 percent among managers and clerical workers. Linda Russell, a senior partner with Telecommunications Consultants International Inc., a Canadian firm, found that her clients show productivity gains ranging from 10 to 50 percent.

Telecommuters often convert commuting hours into work hours, putting in extra time that would normally be spent sitting in rush-hour traffic. They start each workday less stressed, they reduce nonwork activities (such as gossiping with fellow employees) during the day, and they choose to work during their high-energy times. Absenteeism tends to be low, and telecommuters will often work even when they are sick because they are able to work part days. A California state government telecommuting project reported a 20 percent reduction in sick leave.

Telecommuting has other potential benefits: job commitment and job satisfaction increase; quality of life improves; output increases; auto insurance premiums, parking, gas, and, in some cases, clothing expenses decrease. And, crucial to providing support to a more diverse and stressed work force, telecommuting relieves pressures of child care and elder care and facilitates employment for staff who are physically challenged. Time formerly spent commuting can be converted into recreational or family time—a boon to single-parent families and working mothers.

Telecommuting also offers cost savings when work is reorganized into new organizational structures. Jocelyne Côté-O'Hara, President and CEO of Stentor Telecom Policy Inc., reports:

> Four years ago, when IBM Canada decided to get serious about cutting costs, it zeroed in pretty quickly on real estate. Owning, renting, leasing and maintaining office, plant and laboratory space had become the number-two cost item on the computer company's books.

To help reduce these costs, a task force came up with Flexiplace, a long-term program to move employees out of expensive corporate offices and into suburban satellite centers and home offices. The program began in early 1992 with 150 employees. By October 1992, 700 employees had become part of the program, and 450 of them were working out of their homes. In some regions, IBM estimates that up to 30 percent of its sales and marketing staff will be at home. It also projects $5.7 million in real estate savings.

Telecommuting means that employees are often remote from their supervisors, but this shouldn't be the case all the time. Experts tend to agree that home telecommuters should come into the office at least once a week. IBM's Flexiplace employees usually come in once or twice a week for group meetings or to retrieve mail and faxes.

> The benefits of telecommuting are simply too many and too great to ignore, especially in an increasingly competitive marketplace.

Pitfalls and Remedies

In a survey of over 22,000 corporate employees, conducted by Professor Chris Higgins of the University of Western Ontario School of Business, 70 percent of all employees said they would like the option of working at home at least some of the time. But it's not all wine and roses with telecommuting. Some very serious problems can arise:

- Managers may resist the idea, fearing a loss of control over employees and a perceived reduction in their own value to the company.

- Social isolation, a tendency toward workaholism, and the stresses of trying to keep work and home life separate can combine to reduce telecommuter productivity and even lead to burnout.

- On-site employees may come to resent their telecommuting peers, creating morale problems.

- If experienced employees are working away from the office, new recruits will lose the benefit of ad-hoc, on-the-job cross-training.

- Confusion over contractual obligations on both sides can create distracting worker–employer conflicts.

- Unions are often suspicious, believing that telecommuting will reduce unity and solidarity and lead to exploitation of workers—as may happen in some cases.

- Technical problems with phone lines, computers, and modems, outside the immediate control of corporate MIS and telecom groups, can wipe out productivity gains.

Here are some practical telecommuting "do's and don'ts" that will help your enterprise avoid the problems associated with poorly planned moves toward telecommuting.

Do:

- Look for real business problems that telecommuting can solve;

- Secure senior management support for telecommuting and find a champion to carry the ball;

- Pick the right managers and telecommuters (they must be volunteers);

- Expend sufficient time and effort on training both supervisors and telecommuters;

- Find ways to measure present employee productivity so you can track productivity gains (or losses) later; plan your project in detail and in advance.

Don't:

- Pick jobs that require a lot of face-to-face interaction with colleagues (unless you buy videoconferencing);

- Assume telecommuters know how to work on their own;
- Assume telecommuting means employees must be at home all five days of the workweek;
- Let telecommuters begin with the assumption that telecommuting is an answer to their child care problem.

HOW TO ADOPT NEW INFORMATION TECHNOLOGY

Just when enterprises reach internal consensus about upgrading their technology to increase their competitive advantage, newer technologies emerge, often making relatively new systems archaic within months. Unfortunately, enterprise decision making tends to be slower than the present pace of technology development.

> The global development of new technologies is growing at an explosive rate, accompanied by enormous increase in complexity of the technologies themselves. . . . As this explosion of new technologies is happening, however, it is matched by a much slower rate of organizations adopting them.

Organizations are constrained in their capacity to rapidly adopt new technologies because:

- Often, a vast number of very complex choices must be made; technical people may understand the physical technologies well, but many users in the adopting organizations have much lower levels of comprehension, particularly given the huge number of choices.
- Human capacity is inadequate; because of delayering and recession pressures, fewer managers are able to deal with technology-related decisions or to cope with the complexity of integrating adopted technologies.
- Financial capacity is insufficient; many potential adopting organizations have increasingly limited cash flow to finance rapid adoption of new technologies, regardless of their appeal or utility.

Important business factors influence decisions on technology "architecture." The two most important factors are (1) business stability and (2) the relationship with suppliers and customers. Fast company growth calls for the use of smaller modular systems; slow growth argues for the use of larger systems. Growth resulting from frequent buying and selling of portfolio companies requires modular systems, and growth from within requires larger systems that will allow smaller units to take advantage of existing applications.

Meanwhile, a close relationship with suppliers and customers necessitates a tight interconnection of systems. A loose association with suppliers and customers, on the other hand, requires only good on-line query capabilities. Close relationships call for the use of somewhat isolated systems interacting via electronic data interchange (EDI) networks, which customers and/or suppliers are permitted to access. On-line query can be handled by normal systems, such as mainframes that contain the entire set of customer files.

Improperly conceived and implemented "techno-fixes" fuel enterprise leaders' fear of expensive infotech failers. For example, Hewlett-Packard's (H-P) Sales Productivity Program (SSP) was launched in 1987 and lies in ashes today.

SSP comprised giving 2,000 H-P field operations sales representatives the technology necessary to conduct their business in the filed—Portable PLUS laptop computers and ThinkJet printers. Initially, time spent with customers went up from 26 to 33 percent, with future estimates running as high as 67 percent. Today, H-P is out of the laptop market altogether, and all of the SSP champions have either left or been relocated. One former insider says:

> We were naive. We thought we knew what the sales process involved and how to automate it. We didn't. Because we didn't understand the process, the tools we pushed on the reps didn't help.

Today, H-P is still interested in boosting sales force productivity, but it's using fewer computer-oriented programs to achieve that goal.

Your decision to adopt new infotech as an enabler for a high-performance enterprise should be based on choosing technology that meets these tests of profit improvement:

1. *Market share.* Will your market share in a targeted product-market segment increase?

2. *Market size.* Will your company be enabled to enter product markets that are significantly larger in unit size?

3. *Unit sales.* Will unit sales for a product, process, or system be helped?

4. *Price.* Will the price for your products increase or decrease disproportionately to changes in variable costs?

5. *Variable cost.* Will the unit variable cost for your products decrease or, at least, increase less than the price increase the technology allows?

6. *Unit margin.* Will the unit margin increase?

7. *Fixed cost.* Will the fixed cost base be reduced relative to the total margin produced?

8. *Investment.* Will the investment base for the product or market be reduced relative to the total margin produced?

Is "Do It Yourself" the Best Option?

There's no question that up-to-date information technology is an imperative for the high-performing enterprise. But should the infotech function be handled in-house or outsourced? The Gartner Group estimates that, by 1995, at least 50 percent of all information services functions will be outsourced by the Fortune 500 companies. The group provides a list of questions to ask before making this crucial decision:

- Does the infotech function focus on the core business or is it viewed as nonstrategic and as a diversion of top management's attention? In other words, will incorporating infotech in-house benefit your enterprise from an overall strategy perspective?

- Is there company pressure to reduce costs? Will in-house infotech cost you more money or save you money?

- Does the company need to raise funds by selling off its in-house infotech equipment?

- Does the operation of the business require a more robust level of infotech delivery than can be managed by existing infotech infrastructures?

- If the infotech infrastructure is weak because of chronic underfunding, is the situation likely to improve?

- Does the company have the resources to migrate to the next level of technical competence?

- Does the company have the ability to attract and retain the best infotech staff?

Choosing the Right System

Choosing a system that fits into your organizational processes, vision, culture, and budget and offers the crucial elements your system needs isn't easy. Here are six principles that will help to guide you:

1. *Complete connectivity.* All workstations must easily communicate with all computers and other workstations.

2. *Information consistency and integrity.* All applications must use a common set of data definitions; information must pass validity checks before it is used to update databases.

3. *Resource sharing.* Wherever possible, scarce resources, such as trained communications and data processing personnel, communications networks, and specialized computer resources, will be shared by all users.

4. *Computer input/output (I/O) bandwidth sharing.* Computers intended to support an application or a specific set of applications must be chosen more on the basis of the amount of I/O activity they can accommodate rather than on their computing capacity alone.

5. *Disaster resiliency.* Mission-critical systems must rapidly recover from all levels of disaster, ranging from the loss of a data file to the loss of a major computing center.

6. *Appropriate security.* Systems must be reasonably protected from threats ranging from malicious employees to hackers and industrial spies.

Infotech has tremendous potential as a key enabling competency of high-performing enterprises. Infotech can help to cut costs, improve quality, enhance service, and speed customer response—all the important elements of value. But, as powerful as infotech is, it is only a means to the end of increased competitiveness. Without a robust business strategy that is well deployed throughout your enterprise, infotech is just so much high-tech glitz. Strategy development, which may well be the pivotal organizational competency, is discussed in the next chapter.

TOUCHSTONE
7

Strategy Alignment

In the long run, men hit only what they aim at.
Henry David Thoreau

Your successful delivery of value to your customers depends on your ability to develop a coherent value strategy and to deploy this policy effectively throughout your organization. Aligning your organization with your value strategy is the seventh and critically important competency of the high-performing enterprise.

A value strategy is anchored in the requirements of the customer groups that you choose to serve. Customer requirements must be defined in terms of the essential elements of the value equation: quality, service, cost, and time. Your strategy should (1) recognize that value is created through the effective management of cross-functional processes, and (2) identify a few essential areas where core processes need to be improved in order to deliver an offering that is superior to the competition.

Finally, there should be a high degree of consensus within your enterprise regarding the value strategy and the critical factors that will lead to success.

LOSING SIGHT OF THE FOREST FOR THE TREES

In your zeal to adopt the new paradigm of the high-performing enterprise, it's easy to become lost in the maze of exciting tools and techniques, forgetting what you were trying to accomplish in the first place. No matter what a company's strategic priorities are, senior management's first and most vital task is to focus the enterprise on the things that really matter. This is particularly true of organizations that embark on "quality" or "service excellence" initiatives. The desire to "better serve the customer" can get in the way of a thoughtful understanding of how to best allocate enterprise resources to achieve the desired outcome. You must guard against failing to link your high-performing enterprise transition to the critical elements of your business strategy. The high-performance enterprise is continually strengthening those few critical abilities that result in superior value for customers.

A good example of a company that almost lost its way, but got back on track, is Aetna Insurance (Canada). Mike Stephen, CEO of Aetna, launched a corporate "service excellence" initiative in 1987. He began with the design of a corporate mission statement encapsulating the company's goals and values. This stage took some ten months, as senior executives wrestled to arrive at a statement that would be "the engine driving the company's renewed commitment to service."

Two years later, more than 60 programs had been implemented in an effort to carry out the "new mission": service guarantees, rewards and recognition, breakfast meetings, and employee committees focused on service improvement. During this time, each employee received a mounted copy of the mission statement. Staff awareness of corporate direction was estimated to be very high, but an overall "game plan" and a set of clear priorities were still missing. People were working very hard at delivering what they thought service was; but without a coherent and cohesive strategy, their efforts were scattered.

Senior Vice President Dobri Stojsic, then newly arrived, made devising a service strategy his highest priority:

> We needed to clearly identify what Aetna stands for in the operational terms of service, what it means to people in their jobs. We needed a few measures and standards of performance to answer the question: tell me what you want me to do. And we needed to provide a consistent approach to service, to bring harmony to all the many unrelated activities.

Stojsic and Stephen, working closely with other members of the executive team, took another look at the business and commissioned more research into customer expectations. They eventually defined five "critical success factors" (CSFs) that affected customers' perceptions of service quality: (1) reliability, (2) responsiveness, (3) assurance, (4) empathy, and (5) tangibles. Each CSF was then linked to one of the following keynote strategies: speed, accuracy, promptness, accessibility, caring, and quality staff. For each keynote strategy, Aetna devised a strategic goal and a statement of intent that clearly laid out the actions necessary to achieve that goal.

For example, the first keynote strategy was "speed":

Aetna will use processes that are fast, competitive and dependable to exceed our service commitments by: streamlining processes (reliability); turnaround standards and performance better than key competitors (responsiveness); treat requests for speedy service with understanding and concern (empathy); understand and respect turnaround commitments (assurance); use service blueprinting, high tech systems and simplified customer documentation to meet time commitments (tangibles).

Broken down into well-defined areas, the statements were easy to understand and measure. This allowed linking the visionary mission statement to a clear set of working principles that could be adapted and applied by all of Aetna's employees. The strategy development process was further "humanized" by the use of Quality Action Teams made up of a cross-section of employees from different levels and departments. Their task was to identify areas that needed to be improved in light of the newly articulated strategic goals. By involving the employees in the effort, Aetna reaped valuable ideas and a greater level of employee commitment. "I believe that employee involvement leads to employee commitment," says Stojsic. "Their ideas and input were very worthwhile."

THE THREE VALUE STRATEGIES

A value strategy may be reduced to a concept as simple as striving to become ever more "useful" to customers. But good intentions must be transformed into practical reality. The enterprises that will succeed in the decades ahead are not those with advantages defined in terms of internal functions, but those that can become truly market-focused—able to profitably deliver sustainable superior value for their customers. This means doing the following:

- Choosing the right target customer and the combination of benefits and price that, to the customer, would constitute superior value.

- Managing all functions to reflect benefits and prices, so the business actually provides and communicates this chosen value, and does so at a profit.

Your fundamental responsibility as an enterprise leader is to know what is valued by the user and continually improving the organizational systems that—when used by the people in the business—result in increased user value.

From Mass Production to Mass Customization

The method you choose to create superior value hinges on understanding the trends in customer purchasing behavior in your industry, and knowing what type of company you are now. Harry S. Dent, Jr., in his book, *The Great Boom Ahead*, argues (as have others) that our economy is in a state of transition. We are moving from a "standardized economy" to a "customized economy."

The standardized economy:

> . . . consists of countless varieties of products, but they result from a common economic formula. That formula is one of mass-produced, standardized goods and services made cheaper by assembly-line production.

This approach has obviously been very successful in the past; it has raised our standard of living tremendously. Value was created by longer and faster production runs that produced standard quality goods at cheaper prices and made them affordable to the masses. Economies of scale required the development of massive organizations, structured as functional command-and-control centers that effectively managed this particular value paradigm.

However, since the early 1970s, a new value-creating pattern has been emerging, based not on mass markets but on "mass customization." The foundation of this new approach is infotech, discussed in Touchstone Six.

> We've been creating an entirely new economy on top of the old. The micro-computer industry and the broad range of new niche products and services will increasingly dominate our economy in the coming decades. Micro technologies increasingly allow us to custom design, market and produce products and services at lower cost.

Dent proposes that there are three basic segments in every industry: (1) premium, (2) discount, and (3) standard. Depending on what segment you're in, there are different ways to achieve high-value performance.

- *Premium value.* In every industry, this segment is characterized by companies that have found a way to serve customers in a superior way: high quality, superior personalized service, an offer that can be highly customized to buyers' needs, and very fast response to customers' orders and requests for information and support. Dent predicts that infotech will revolutionize production and service delivery in the future, and that the great majority of all future markets will be comprised of the premium "customized" segment, as costs and prices continue to fall.

Examples of premium value companies are: Nordstrom, Lexus, BMW, President's Choice (makers of the "Decadent Chocolate Chip Cookie"),

The Body Shop, Westin hotels, Federal Express, and Midwest Express. A good small business example is Canadian designer Linda Lundstrom. She is currently offering a unique service to customers: she will precisely readjust her clothing to fit breast cancer patients' breast prostheses.

- *Discount value.* This segment is populated by companies that have found radically different ways to deliver familiar products or services to customers at dramatically lower prices, thus providing better value. Some of these companies have found ways to actually improve quality and service while lowering costs. This segment is rapidly growing.

These are the Wal-Marts of the world; the Toyotas and Nissans; Domino's Pizza and Taco Bell; Red Roof Inn and Journey's End hotels; United Parcel Service; and "generic" products instead of brand-name goods. Factory outlet stores and "price clubs" are other examples of successful, new retailing concepts that focus on delivering discount value.

- *Standard value.* This is the segment of the past, one in which your enterprise may now be stuck. Here, you offer the standardized product or service with little ability for it to be customized. You aim for the "mass market" and produce standard quality outputs through inflexible assembly-line processes. This segment will continue to decline in the value decade. Standard value is no longer good enough to compete.

To name a few standard value companies: Sears; GM, Ford, and Chrysler; Fruit Of The Loom and Arrow; Merrill Lynch; Pizza Hut; Holiday Inn, Ramada, and Best Western; and the U.S. Postal Service! These types of companies face major difficulties in the value decade.

Strategies for Standard Value Companies

How can you change your company's value strategy to bring it in line with today's marketplace realities? Let's start first with standard value companies. If your company is one of these, you're in trouble! Because your enterprise is not aligned with current or future buyer trends, you'll need to take some urgent action.

- *Restructure to become a discount value enterprise.* Forget about offering premium value. If you can't compete in your own markets against discount companies, you won't have a chance of becoming a premium value company. That leaves you little choice but to become more competitive with the discount segment.

In recent years, it has become apparent that fast-food champ McDonald's has taken this approach. The company made the mistake of many previously successful mass-market players: prices got too high, and low-cost competitors were scoffed at. For example, Taco Bell has been innovative in reengineering food preparation techniques, lowering prices, and, as a result, offering consumers substantially better value. McDonald's customer counts and profits began to sag in the United States. "We got spoiled by our success," admits Jack Greenburg, Vice Chairman and Chief Financial Officer.

The company has responded with a "value pricing" strategy that has sliced prices by as much as 30 percent, and with the introduction of "extra value meals"—combination menu offerings that act as incentives for customers to spend a little more during each visit.

To support this approach, McDonald's also cracked down on costs. In five years, the chain had let the cost of developing a new restaurant balloon by 60 percent. Competitors, particularly Taco Bell, were shrinking their kitchens and building new units ever more cheaply and quickly.

The strategy is working. By offering customers a better value and working to become more efficient, McDonald's earnings are growing again and are expected to top 12 percent annually. However, lower-cost competition won't go away. McDonald's is learning that flexibility is the key to success in a cutthroat, low-cost, discount-driven market.

- *Sell out while you can.* If you cannot make the change to become a discount value player, think about getting out while some of your assets (for example, locations or certain skilled employees) still have some appeal to another company. You simply cannot remain "stuck in the middle" with an offering that is neither truly price-competitive nor highly customized. This might be the best option for Sears. It may be impossible for this classic mass-market retailer to ever get its costs down to meet the discounters' prices. By contrast, all efforts to move the store's image "upscale" to compete with specialty shops have also failed.

Strategies for Discount Value Companies

If you're currently enjoying success as a discount value provider, look to the future and recognize that your approach might not be the best as the decade unfolds. In particular, you need to find out how to participate in the growing premium value segment of "mass customization." Your choices include:

- *Moving overseas.* Don't be myopic. Think globally. Look first to other developed countries, like Western Europe, Korea, and Japan;

then consider Mexico, Eastern Europe, and the Third World countries around the Pacific Rim. You may instantly become a premium product the minute you move to less developed geographic markets.

Sometimes just crossing the border helps. The Gap went from being a discount retailer to a premium value company when it finally opened up in Canada. All through the 1980s, Canadians were crossing the U.S. border to purchase The Gap casual wear (jeans, T-shirts, and so on). When The Gap finally opened its doors in Canada, it was considered a premium company by Canadians, who previously had not been able to buy the chain's goods. Canadians felt they had been missing out on The Gap fashions.

- *Entering premium value segments.* By the year 2000, the premium value companies will rule. Discount companies will find they have to adopt some of the traits of the premium value players.

The Canadian "Ice Beer" wars serve as a classic example. The major Canadian breweries were suffering erosion of market share from specialized premium brewers. Labbatts Breweries, along with Molson's Breweries, invented a new "ice brewing" process that bolstered their beer into a premium segment to compete with imported labels. Now, many beer companies are copying that move.

- *Buying into premium value segments.* This idea involves partnering with a premium value company, using some of the principles discussed in Touchstone Five. Usually, this means making available high-end products by taking advantage of the efficient distribution systems of the discount competitor.

Strategies for Premium Value Companies

If you are a premium value player, the future is yours as long as you can find ways to move your value delivery into mainstream markets. The choices facing the premium value enterprise are:

- *Jump to a higher niche.* When discount companies suddenly begin offering premium products, you'll need to jump to an even higher premium segment. The idea is to go into a higher, narrower niche to try to improve margins. This is what Porsche and BMW did when Lexus introduced comparably featured cars at significantly lower prices.

- *Move into the mainstream.* Instead of fighting with the discount segment to hang on to your market, become more appealing to the mainstream customer and dominate the product or service category.

Federal Express originally started as an entrepreneurial company that dominated a particular niche. It then decided to move into the mainstream to compete with United Parcel Service, instead of losing mainstream customers to UPS.

- *Partner with a value discounter.* Imagine what would have happened to BMW if it had partnered with Toyota before Lexus arrived, or even had helped create Lexus? BMW would be in a significantly better position that it is currently in. This is a case of: "With our looks and your brains [discounters' marketing ingenuity], we'll go far."

- *Build alliances with other premium players.* Several premium players serving different niches may be able to "buddy up" to become a larger entity, sharing sales forces, production and R&D facilities, management, and support staff. For example, a small specialty publisher may be able to cut down on the distribution costs involved in getting its books into the bookstores by forming an alliance with other specialty publishers facing the same dilemma.

- *Build other niches one at a time.* Add more niche items to capitalize on the core specialty positions you now enjoy. Windham Hill, a small music label, appeals to a sophisticated but devoted group of acoustical music fans. Known for its quality, the label branched off into jazz and is now appealing both to former customers, who are "growing" with Windham Hill ("I love their acoustical music; I think I'll try this jazz CD!"), and to jazz listeners who bought other labels ("Oh look— Windham Hill is getting into jazz now too. I'll give this label a try for a change.")

In summary, your strategic plan for success must incorporate a clear view of how your enterprise will deliver superior value for customers. Your best value strategy will, of course, depend on your current market position and the enterprise capabilities that you feel can best distinguish you from your competition.

COMPETING ON CAPABILITIES

Touchstone Two discussed how an organization's ability to deliver value is embedded in the core processes of the enterprise. Some management theorists believe the ability to develop "core capabilities," which are manifested in effective business processes, is the basis of true competitive advantage.

. . . the goal is to develop the hard-to-imitate organizational capabilities that distinguish the company from its competitors in the eyes of the customers.

For example, the success of Honda, the automobile and motorcycle manufacturer, is often attributed to its innovative design and manufacturing quality. Originally, however, Honda was successful to a large degree because of the company's distinctive capability in "dealer management." Honda managed its motorcycle dealers by making them successful business people. It provided operating procedures and policies for selling, merchandising, floor planning, and service management. Honda trained entire dealer staffs and provided a computerized dealer–management information system.

When Honda moved into other areas—lawn mowers, outboard motors, and cars—it recreated the same dealer–management arrangements in these new businesses. Honda regularly receives the highest ratings for customer satisfaction among American auto dealerships.

The four basic principles of capability-based value strategy are:

1. The building blocks of corporate strategy are business processes, not products and markets.

2. Competitive success depends on transforming a company's key processes into strategic capabilities that consistently provide superior value to the customer.

3. Companies create these capabilities by making strategic investments in a support infrastructure that links together and transcends traditional business units and functions.

4. Because capabilities necessarily cross functions, the champion of a capabilities-based strategy must be the chief executive officer (CEO).

George Stalk, Philip Evans, and Lawrence E. Shulman, in a recent *Harvard Business Review* article, observe:

> The starting point is for senior managers to undergo the fundamental shift in perception that allows them to see their business in terms of strategic capabilities.

They recommend the adoption of the following approaches for transforming an enterprise into a capabilities-based competitor:

- *Shift the strategic framework to achieve aggressive goals.* Abandon traditional function, cost, and profit-center orientation, and move toward identifying the competencies that deliver a response to changing customer needs.

- *Organize around the chosen competency.* Make sure employees have the necessary skills and resources to achieve it. This requires making an initial investment into the management of the competency in question, then relinquishing power to the key front-line players who will turn it into a source of competitive advantage.

- *Make progress visible, bringing measurements and reward into alignment.* With a competency-based approach, new types of measures of process performance (not department activities) will have to be developed. Because capabilities are embedded in cross-functional enterprise processes, reward systems will have to emphasize teamwork rather than individual excellence.

- *Retain the leadership of the transformation in the hands of the CEO.* Because competencies are cross-functional, the change process can't be handled by middle management. It requires the hands-on guidance of the CEO and the active involvement of top-line managers.

Reversal of Fortune

The "reversal of fortune" experienced by retail giants K mart and Wal-Mart is a prime example of how the new "competing on capabilities" strategy will play out in the business environment of the future. In 1979, K mart was the top discount retailer, with 1,891 stores and average revenues per store of $7.25 million. Its enormous size allowed economies of scale in purchasing, distribution, and marketing that were considered crucial to competitive success in a mature and low-growth industry.

At the same time, Wal-Mart was a niche retailer in the southern states, with 229 stores and average revenues per store that were half those of K mart. By 1989, Wal-Mart had transformed itself—and the industry—by growing nearly 25 percent per year. It achieved the highest sales per square foot, inventory turns, and operating profit of any discount retailer. In 1989, Wal-Mart's pretax return on sales was 8 percent—double that of K mart. Today, Wal-Mart is the largest and highest-profit retailer in the world, with 32 percent return on equity, and market valuation more than ten times book value.

In trying to identify how Wal-Mart was able to rise to the top so quickly—and at the expense of chief competitor K mart—experts have come up with a number of explanations. One key innovation was the culture of "service excellence" that Wal-Mart's founder, Sam Walton, worked hard to create. The company is famous for creating the job of a "greeter" who welcomes customers at the front door of each store location. Other important elements of Wal-Mart's success include: employees own part of the business; its "everyday low prices" strategy gives value to customers and saves on merchandising and advertising costs; and its large stores offer economies of scale and a wider choice of merchandise. However:

> The real secret of Wal-mart's success lies deeper, in a set of strategic business decisions that transformed the company into a capabilities-based

competitor. The starting point was a relentless focus on satisfying customer needs.

Wal-Mart's goal was to provide customers with quality goods on demand, on the spot, and at a competitive price. The key was to make the process of replenishing inventory the centerpiece of this competitive strategy. Wal-Mart's "cross-docking" system—goods are continuously delivered to warehouses where they are selected, repacked, and dispatched to stores, often without ever sitting in inventory—is considered the fullest expression of the strategic vision. Goods cross from one loading dock to another in less than 48 hours, thereby saving the cost and time associated with warehousing. Wal-Mart runs 85 percent of its goods through its warehouse system, reducing costs of sales by 2 to 3 percent. These savings are then passed along to the customer. By comparison, K mart runs only 50 percent of its goods through its warehouse system.

Cross-docking, then, translates into "everyday low prices" which, in turn, translate into high traffic, reduced advertising costs, more predictable sales, and, ultimately, reduced stock-outs and no excess inventory.

With all these tremendous advantages, it's understandable that cross-docking isn't the easiest inventory system to implement.

> To make cross-docking work, Wal-Mart has had to make strategic investments in a variety of interlocking support systems far beyond what could be justified by conventional ROI criteria.

To make the system work effectively, constant contact with distribution centers, suppliers, and every point of sale in every store is needed. Orders flow in, are consolidated, and are executed within hours. A private satellite communications system sends out point-of-sale data directly to 4,000 vendors daily. To ensure fast and responsive transportation of goods, the company's 19 distribution centers are serviced by nearly 2,000 company trucks. Shelves can be replenished in less than 48 hours; the industry average for shelf replenishment is once every two weeks.

To make the most out of the cross-docking system, Wal-Mart also had to make fundamental changes in its approach to managerial control. In the retail industry, decisions on merchandising, pricing, and promotions are made at the highest levels of the corporation. With the cross-docking system, the retailers don't push products into the system; the customers "pull" products into the system when and where they need them.

This approach requires frequent, informal cooperation among stores, distribution centers, and suppliers. Senior management's task at Wal-Mart is not to dictate how individual stores should be run, but to allow individual store managers to learn, from the market and from each other, how to run their outlets.

A fleet of company airplanes regularly flies store managers to the Bentonville, Arkansas, headquarters for meetings on market trends and merchandising. Wal-Mart has also installed a video link in all its outlets, allowing managers to keep in contact with each other and with Bentonville. Store managers are able to hold videoconferences to discuss such topics as which in-store promotions work and which products are selling.

Another important aspect of Wal-Mart's competency strategy is its front-line employees. Wal-Mart realized early that employees in direct contact with customers play a huge role in the success of a retail organization. Stock ownership and profit-sharing programs have helped to impress on the employees that "what's good for the customer is what's good for Wal-Mart is what's good for them."

While Wal-Mart was rewriting the book on how to operate a large-scale retail chain, K mart was rereading how to implement the traditional way. K mart continued to manage its business by focusing on a few product-centered strategic business units (SBUs). Each SBU was a separate profit center run under strong centralized line management, and each defined its own strategy, deciding which products to promote and at what prices.

K mart evaluated its competitive standing at each stage along the value chain; activities that managers determined others could do better were subcontracted out. K mart moved out of trucking when it found that an outside company could perform the function at a lower cost. Similarly, K mart kept switching suppliers to find the lowest costs possible on every conceivable product. K mart also leased out many of its departments to other companies in an attempt to maximize the amount of rent money it could make per square foot. It's apparent that most of K mart's efforts were clearly focused on the short term, using traditional retail strategies.

> . . . Wal-Mart emphasizes behaviour—the organizational practices and business processes in which capabilities are rooted—as the primary object of strategy and therefore focuses its managerial attention on the infrastructure that supports capabilities. This subtle distinction has made all the difference between exceptional and average performance. . . . The story of K mart and Wal-Mart illustrates the new paradigm of competition in the 1990s. In industry after industry, established competitors are being outmaneuvred and overtaken by more dynamic rivals.

• • •

As more and more companies make the transition to capabilities-based competition, the simple fact of competing on capabilities will become less important than the specific capabilities a company has chosen to build. Given the necessary long-term investments, the strategic choices managers make will end up determining a company's fate. . . . The capabilities are often mutually exclusive. Choosing the right ones is the essence of strategy.

STRATEGIC PLANNING: STILL RELEVANT?

All this talk about "competing on capabilities" is well and good. But how do you build the strengths needed to compete? Do you need a strategic plan? Are there better ways to get to the high-performing model?

The answer is "yes." You do need a strategy for building critical capabilities, but the way in which plans are formulated needs to change. High-performing organizations place a great deal of emphasis on trying to achieve employee alignment with crucial elements of the strategy. "Technical elegance" in planning is less important than the enthusiastic support of those who must carry out the actions.

A Brief History of "Corporate Strategy"

Experts have a hard time agreeing on what corporate strategy is, let alone which strategy works best for a given company. Lack of understanding hasn't led to a lack of discussion, though. In fact, "no single subject has so dominated the attention of managers, consultants and management theorists as corporate strategy."

The concept of business strategy has been undermined by the sheer multitude of theories. Industry originally borrowed the word "strategy" from the military in the aftermath of the Second World War. The goal was to win "territory" (markets) through a series of goal-oriented business maneuvers. By the 1960s, "strategy" meant a complex plan based on detailed forecasts of economies and specific markets; many observers feel this resulted in over-diversification and poorly performing conglomerates. Markets and competitors change too quickly to be anticipated by static models.

In 1980, Michael Porter, of the Harvard Business School, argued that the characteristics of the industry, and the firm's position therein, should determine its strategy. The firm's primary task was to find a niche that would defend it from competitors. It might become a low-cost producer, or differentiate its products and create a high profit margin. And, it might erect barriers to prevent new rivals from entering the market. Porter's book, *Competitive Strategy*, was a big hit.

Every firm would like to have a niche to defend, but few are given the luxury of that choice. So, in the 1980s, strategy started to mean strengthening your firm's skills (or capabilities, as discussed earlier)—rapid product development, high-quality manufacturing, technological innovation, customer service—and finding markets in which to exploit these skills.

By contrast, Gary Hamel and C. K. Prahalad, professors at the London Business School and University of Michigan, respectively, argued that the function of a company's strategy is not to match its resources to opportunities, but rather to "stretch" the company beyond what most would believe its capabilities to be. They cited Toyota, CNN, British Airways, and Sony as "small" companies that have become extremely successful in recent years by stealing market share from their rivals because they had expansive ambitions. Thus, strategy can be viewed as a rallying cry—or, as some call it, a "strategic intent."

> How a company views strategy does depend largely on its circumstances. Small firms determined to challenge behemoths may find it helpful to call their aspirations a "strategy." Big companies defending a dominant position may find Mr. Porter's industry analysis illuminating. All firms should try to exploit and hone their skills.

More Participative Approaches

There is little argument that enterprise strategy essentially boils down to decisions about allocating scarce resources in ways that will allow your business to deliver differential value to a chosen group of customers. Perhaps the most fundamental change in strategy development during the value decade has been the manner in which it is formulated and deployed. The influence of total quality management, and similar concepts that place great emphasis on employee participation and work process improvement, is changing the way in which enterprise value strategies are being formulated.

The traditional approach to enterprise strategic planning attempts to improve an organization's competitiveness by channeling the ideas of senior management downward, to be applied by the work force in a cost-effective and efficient manner.

> Traditional models are characterized by top management deciding on a set of goals and objectives for the overall organization, with each succeeding level of the organization developing supporting goals and objectives.

By contrast, newer ways of planning call for an interchange of ideas within the organization. The premise is: everyone within the enterprise can generate new ideas and solve problems. Under this approach, senior leadership sets the overall strategic direction for the organization, establishes an organizational infrastructure to support change, and initiates the process of cultural transformation. But employees are actively involved in applying the overall direction to their daily work activities, particularly in improving work processes. This philosophy of policy planning also emphasizes a more flexible and innovative approach to establishing goals and objectives. Senior leadership must provide strong and clear direction, but they must also promote employee ownership, where each staff member takes personal responsibility for improving his or her own process area and, in turn, the organization as a whole.

Linking "Quality" to Strategy

It is particularly important to mesh your "quality" and "service" improvement efforts with the core commercial strategies of the enterprise. Quality/service investments must be clearly linked to demonstrable customer needs and benefits in productivity and asset utilization.

Conrail (Consolidated Rail Corporation) is a good example of a company that embarked on its "quality journey" with the goal of both improving its competitiveness and gaining employee acceptance. Conrail began its Continuous Quality Improvement (CQI) initiative in the summer of 1990. Company representatives began by visiting companies such as Xerox, IBM, Kodak, Motorola, and Milliken, to learn how they had deployed their quality process. Conrail also had leaders from 3M, Corning, and Polaroid present lectures to the company's top 50 managers.

Using all this information, Conrail's deployment strategy focused on the need for top-down expression of Conrail's "vision." The company leaders set out to "paint a picture" of the company in the future. They set goals to define how the corporation and employees could make the vision a reality. Next, a set of guiding principles, or values, were put in place to guide the corporation along the path.

The process of developing the future direction for the company was highly participatory. *Step one* of Conrail's Quality Deployment Process began with company officers taking part in a one-day visioning session to write the vision, goals, and guiding principles. One day was long enough for this step because Conrail had been working on strategic planning efforts since 1988. Each senior executive came up with a personal version of the vision. A format everyone could agree on was constructed, then the group was divided into four teams to decide on the final wording of the corporation's vision, goals, and guiding principles, based on the 19 versions developed individually.

Step two was the ownership-sharing process. The company officers used their draft versions of the vision to stimulate discussion with 50 labor/management employees and 30 middle managers. These groups were asked to critique the draft versions and to indicate whether they could take ownership of the statements. Using these critiques as guidelines, revised versions were drafted and awareness sessions were arranged to introduce the vision, goals, and guiding principles to the company's 4,000 employees.

Step three involved moving the deployment of the quality process to the departmental level. Twenty people in each department drafted their departmental visions and defined their roles in making the corporate vision come true.

> The entire process enabled the corporation to align itself in a way that meshed the quality improvement process with the corporation's business objectives so that Conrail can now say, "Quality is our business." Not only has this alignment helped to increase the probability of doing the right things right the first time and every time, but it has also created a climate that fosters ownership and empowerment at all levels.

Once there was broad acceptance of Conrail's direction and priorities, employee teams were formed around the key processes that were identified during the top-down visioning process. Thus, all quality improvement teams are aligned directly with achieving the vision, not working on irrelevant issues.

MAKING THE DREAM REAL

There is no doubt that the high-performing enterprise needs to create a vision; it serves as a beacon the organization can focus on. But the vision must be broken down into more concrete elements to act as an effective framework for change. You need to define the specifics of your enterprise vision if you expect anyone in it to make the dream come true.

John N. Younker, Senior Vice President of The Institute, Inc., suggests a comprehensive set of terms (Figure 7.1) for defining the principal elements involved in enterprise direction setting (enterprise planning). These components comprise the enterprise *direction statement,* "the reason for which an organizational unit was created and the major guidelines under which it can be expected to operate." The direction statement describes what the organization is and what its customers can expect from it.

An organization exists to accomplish some purpose. Therefore, the choices and actions of individuals within the enterprise must be directed within some reasonable boundaries. Younker observes:

> [Employees] will invest more creative effort and have more personal commitment if they understand the objectives of their organization and if they are allowed some individual choice on how to contribute to them.

The direction statement is a "bridge" spanning the distance between the enterprise's current state and its desired future.

The direction statement has seven elements.

1. *The vision:* "A statement that describes the 'ideal state' of an organization. It energizes and mobilizes its members to realize this ideal. It empowers

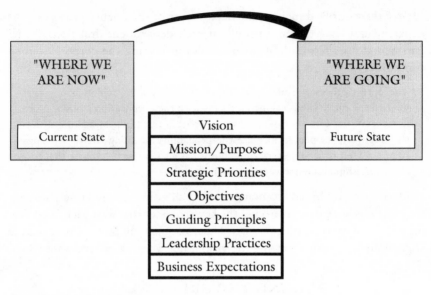

Adapted from: John N. Younker
　　　　　　 The Institute Inc.
　　　　　　 Tapping the Network Journal
　　　　　　 Fall/Winter 1991

Figure 7.1　The direction statement.

people and creates enthusiasm describing the unique and distinctive contributions that the organization will make in its chosen field of endeavor." The vision states what makes the enterprise special and what the future will look like. It's the result of the effective integration of the individual needs of the people with those of the overall organization. "It is a rather personal statement which must be sensitive to changing business trends, challenges, opportunities and marketplace conditions."

Generally speaking, the vision can be boiled down into a series of short descriptive phrases, images, slogans, and other devices that make the vision accessible and understandable to everyone. It's a statement that captures people's attention with its zest or provocativeness. A good vision statement describes "the kind of company we want to become." In companies without an existing mission statement, the vision serves as the precursor; in companies with an existing mission statement, the vision serves as a statement of what the organization will "look and feel" like while the mission is accomplished.

2. *The mission or purpose:* "A statement describing the nature and scope of the work to be performed; the organization's reason for existence." The mission describes the business the organization is engaged in; it's a concise

description of what the enterprise was formed to do. The mission establishes the foundation on which other components of design and direction are built.

3. *Strategic priorities:* "Statements identifying the major outcomes around which the organization allocates its resources and prioritizes its efforts. If accomplished, these outcomes significantly move the organization toward accomplishing its mission." Priorities serve to identify the areas of particular focus and attention that are beyond the business-as-usual requirements of the organization. They are not so much measurable objectives as they are important targets to keep shooting for. Strategic priorities, usually covering a three- to five-year period, describe the strategic positions to be attained, new areas of business, or improvement and innovation efforts. They force an organization to identify the few activities that will move it toward the vision.

4. *Objectives:* "Statements of short-term (usually one year or less, sometimes longer), measurable and specific results to be achieved that fall logically within a given Strategic Priority and that are essential to achieving that priority." Objectives state clearly what is to be accomplished, by whom, and when. To achieve the objectives, numerous intermediate results must be first achieved. Each result is defined by action plans, and each plan has its own set of action steps, resources, and time frames.

Tracking objectives informs everyone of progress and ensures that day-to-day work is moving in the right direction. Clearly stated objectives provide all employees with a statement of what an organization intends to do in response to a particular strategic priority. Objectives may also be tracked for areas of business that fall outside the realm of strategic priorities but are nonetheless important—safety objectives, for example.

5. *Guiding principles:* "A series of statements that serves as a code of ethics for operating the business. A criteria against which people can test future decisions and choices." Guiding principles are derived from a consensus of the organization leadership on what behaviors and attitudes are important to build into the fabric of the day-to-day operation of the organization. In organizations heavily involved with customer value creation, this series of statements usually encompasses four areas: (1) customer-focus, (2) quality, (3) continuous improvement, and (4) employee involvement/empowerment.

The key is to make the principles a meaningful part of the organization's life; this is accomplished by identifying key behaviors and associating them with the principles. Guiding principles are only useful and effective when people see them in action, applied to everyone, day in and day out. Employees readily detect discrepancies between espoused enterprise principles and management behavior.

6. *Leadership practices:* "Statements that describe the leadership's approach or intention in regard to dealing with major groups or elements of the organization and its environment." These statements communicate what the leaders of the enterprise promise can be expected from them. For example: "To provide the type of work environment that permits and encourages each individual member to apply his/her talents, knowledge and efforts to the fullest in the accomplishment of our Strategic Priorities." Some leaders find that statements of leadership philosophy are an effective step toward developing operating principles that can be embraced by the organization as a whole. Public statements of this type foster improved communication and an increased level of commitment from the organization's employees.

7. *Business expectations:* "The hard numbers and specific expectations which must be met if the organization is to continue as a successful entity." Business expectations usually take the form of specific profit numbers, expected accomplishments, or minimum acceptable conditions. The more explicit the expectation statement is, the better; as employees are working, they know what they are being measured against.

> A well thought-out and effectively communicated Direction Statement is an extremely powerful mechanism to inspire and empower people, and to align their individual efforts.

The front-end investment of the time and energy necessary to create the elements of the direction statement pays off later. There is less need to detect, manage, and correct second-guessing; as a result, conflicting norms and work done at cross-purposes decrease.

THE PROCESS OF STRATEGY DEPLOYMENT

In companies where a value strategy is making a lasting impact, there is simplicity and clarity in "where we're heading." There is also relentless communication from the top.

> You can ask any employee in the lunchroom what is important in the company, where the company is going strategically, how that strategy is tied to their daily tasks, and they'll give you the same answer as top management.

Most importantly, there is a deployment process to link the value strategy to day-to-day work, and a process to review and measure the value improvement goals of the enterprise. Successful enterprises create a system of organization improvement whereby their resources are aligned against customer priorities. In other words, customers' concerns drive the improvement plans of the enterprise and of the separate groups within the organization.

Hoshin Kanri

Often, business strategies don't succeed because management fails to balance "planning" with "doing." Don Weintraub, a Senior Vice President with Organizational Dynamics Inc. (ODI) says:

> These companies craft a vision statement and then sort of stop—they say it's time to go back to real work. We used to help client companies develop their quality strategy, and then hope that at some point in the future, that strategy would get linked magically to a business strategy. We don't do that anymore.

Your enterprise value strategy can be strengthened through a method of policy deployment known as *hoshin kanri*. The literal translation is: "ho-" —direction; "-shin"—needle; and "kanri"—management, administration, or deployment. The Japanese translate hoshin kanri as "policy management"—"a process for developing achievable long- and medium-term range business plans, deploying them down to the implementation level."

Hoshin provides a planning structure to bring selected critical business processes from their current level of performance up to a higher level that will contribute to competitive advantage. Hoshin planning helps the enterprise continuously "self-diagnose" and improve performance in critical areas. In the hoshin planning process, planning (setting targets), doing (taking action), checking (evaluating), and acting (making corrections) are integrated in one continuous cycle of both "thinking" and "doing."

This Japanese methodology for planning strategic direction is:

> . . . a step-by-step planning, implementation, and review process for managed change. Specifically, it is a systems approach to management of change in critical business processes.

Hoshin operates on two levels: the first is what Dr. Joseph Juran calls the "breakthrough" management, or strategic planning; the second is at the daily management level. Hoshin kanri has also been referred to as Dr. Edwards Deming's "plan–do–check–act" procedure applied to the management process.

A particular characteristic of hoshin planning gives it special power. Each year, during the planning cycle, only a few (two or three) important objectives are established as the focus of the improvement effort for the entire enterprise. These targets are judged to be the most critical to moving the organization toward its long-term vision. Once defined, the key targets are "deployed" systematically throughout the business. This is done in such a way that each department, and every employee, can set subobjectives that are in full alignment with the overall enterprise priorities. The entire organization then embarks on a systematic effort to achieve those few critical goals, measure progress, and, if unsuccessful, understand the root causes of failure and put countermeasures in place.

Hoshin planning is widely practiced in Japan but is relatively unknown in North America. Companies that have used the hoshin approach report the following benefits:

- Creates an established process to achieve breakthroughs, year after year.
- Creates a commitment to both the overall strategic direction for the enterprise and the tactics chosen.
- Draws on and reinforces the process of continual improvement—plan–do–check–act (PDCA).
- Creates a planning and implementation system that is responsive and flexible, yet disciplined.
- Gives leadership of the enterprise a mechanism to understand the key problem area(s) of the company.
- Creates a quicker and more accurate feedback loop to spur enterprise learning.
- Provides a common focus around which to rally the efforts of the organization.

Principles of Hoshin Planning

The hoshin approach rests on seven basic principles. The hoshin philosophy blends broad participation with individual accountability. Particular attention is paid to thoughtful analysis of what works (or does not work), and why.

Principle 1: Participation by all managers. Together, senior managers define a five-year vision. This entails the top group (president and staff) putting together a vision and sending it "down the line" for comment; feedback from middle managers is then incorporated into the next draft version; eventually, everyone in a management position is expected to contribute.

Principle 2: Individual initiative and responsibility. Each manager sets monthly and yearly targets for himself or herself that are in line with the overall priorities set out in the enterprise vision; subordinates, in turn, decide what they think their targets ought to be, then meet with other individuals to align those targets.

Principle 3: Focus on root causes. Each manager sets monthly targets and, each month, evaluates progress toward meeting them. This is done by focusing not on the "symptoms" but on the root causes. The essence of hoshin kanri is to encourage each individual to think in a systematic way about what is (or is not) working to reach the targets.

Principle 4: No tie to performance appraisals. In Japan, companies want employees to "buy in" to hoshin planning so that it will be a team effort; there is no tie to individual performance evaluations.

Principle 5: Quality first. There is a focus on quality first, not profits; a focus on the planning process system, not the target. If you do this, good results will become a regular by-product.

Principle 6: Catch ball. There is extensive communication—vertically and horizontally, back and forth, in order to ensure that everyone in the organization understands the enterprise vision and key priorities.

Principle 7: Focus on process. Each manager sets a numerical goal for what he or she is going to accomplish for the year. Then, each month, the manager evaluates progress toward the goal. Again, the focus of hoshin kanri is the thoughtful pattern of assessment followed by action. The power of "continual improvement" is captured by this simple cycle.

Steps in the Hoshin Process

In 1989, GOAL/QPC, a management research organization, formed a consortium of interested companies to study the process of hoshin planning (policy deployment) among practicing organizations in Japan and North America. The group found that there are various ways to carry out hoshin planning, but concluded that the basic elements are those shown in Figure 7.2. The steps involved for each element are:

1. *Establish the enterprise vision:*
   - Review data on internal and external performance.
   - Stay customer-focused.
   - Include all environmental factors (social, regulatory, economic, etc.).
   - Circulate the draft vision statement within the organization for a "reality check."
   - Communicate the finalized vision clearly to everyone at all levels.
2. *Develop three-year objectives:*
   - Focus on the "gap" between present organizational capability and required performance to reach the vision.

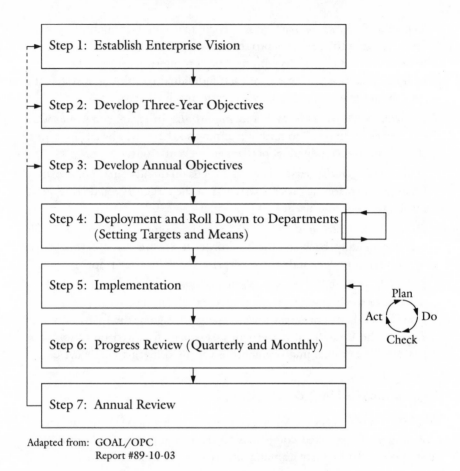

Adapted from: GOAL/OPC
                Report #89-10-03

Figure 7.2   The hoshin planning process.

- Gather accurate data about past performances to determine the present capability of the enterprise and the means that should be pursued over the next three years.
- Communicate three-year objectives clearly to everyone, at all levels.

3. *Develop annual objectives:*

- Integrate the one-year objectives with the three-year objectives and the vision.
- Select a small number of focus points; "fewer more important efforts vs. a scatter shot approach."
- Select the one-year objectives based on accurate data, minimally filtered.

- Make the "reason for improvement" compelling; a convincing case must be made to justify working on the selected objective rather than on something else.

- Use data to identify broad problem areas; identify the truly "broken systems."

4. *Deployment/roll down to departments to develop plans (including targets and means):*

- Compose clear, disciplined action plans that state the direction of improvement, what is to be measured, and the process that is to be improved.

- Expect continuous give-and-take (catchball) between levels around the chosen targets and the organization's capabilities.

- Emphasize the plans of the departments/units, not just the individuals.

- Have a team coordinate plans across departments.

- Designate responsibilities clearly.

- Ensure that the sum of the plans really reaches the overall target.

5. *Implementation:*

- Use disciplined data collection and a measurement system implemented "in process," not after the fact.

- Select a visible process (targets and means) to allow for recognition and reinforcement in "real time."

- Reduce manager-to-manager variability in outcomes by standardizing the process.

- Keep problems visible, so that management can put its support where needed.

6. *Progress review (quarterly and monthly):*

- Keep a strong emphasis on self-diagnosis of targets and process.

- Standardize the review format and language.

- Emphasize simple analysis.

- Continuously build plan–do–check–act into the process.

- See problems as opportunities, not skeletons to be buried.

- Emphasize recognition, support, and corrective action, not punishment.

- Give system problems that are not directly related to the plan a place to surface.

7. *Annual review:*

- Continue data collection and review all year, to provide accurate and relevant diagnosis of missed targets and poor processes.

- Examine plans even when the target is hit, in order to learn how the plan helped. Emphasize understanding which plans led to the achievement of which targets so that the resulting process can be standardized.

- Review the hoshin process itself; aim to improve it for the next year.

Hoshin Planning Tools

From the discussion above, it's obvious that hoshin planning places a great deal of emphasis on establishing a consistent process for surfacing opportunities for improvement. Associated with hoshin method is the use of a set of problem-solving tools to enable people to work together more effectively to diagnose issues and resolve them. The purpose of the tools is to find out the root cause of the obstacles to high performance. You must work on improving the work processes in your enterprise, but you need to know what is right or wrong with the system before you start to make changes.

The tools used in hoshin planning are sometimes called "the seven new management tools" or the "seven planning tools." They contrast to the "seven basic tools" commonly used by problem-solving teams when they attack quality/service improvement issues.

The seven basic tools (Figure 7.3) are simple ways for teams to use statistical data. If you are involved in quality and/or service improvement, you probably already know about the seven basic tools:

- Check sheets
- Pareto chart
- Histogram
- Scatter chart
- Control chart
- Flow diagram
- Cause–effect diagram

In hoshin planning, the seven basic tools are used for problem diagnosis, but seven "new" management tools are added, to help deal with non-numerical and conceptual data. These additional tools are ideal for structuring complex

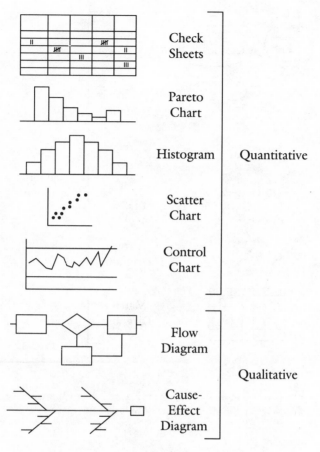

Figure 7.3 The seven basic tools.

issues with uncertain outcomes, for example, business planning, new product development, or planning a brand new activity.

The American Supplier Institute describes the functions of the seven new management tools (Figure 7.4) as follows:

- *Affinity diagram:* for grouping unorganized ideas into a structure of related concepts;
- *Relationship diagram:* for identifying cause–effect relationships between related concepts;
- *Tree diagram:* for evolving objectives into specific supporting actions;
- *Process decision program chart (PDPC):* for identifying potential problems and establishing appropriate countermeasures;

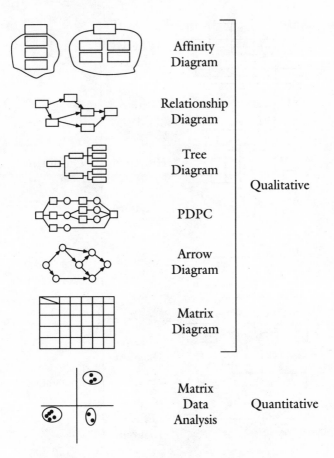

Figure 7.4   The seven new management tools.

- *Arrow diagram:* for identifying the time sequence of steps needed to complete an objective;
- *Matrix diagram:* for displaying relationships between lists of items to clarify complex interrelationships;
- *Matrix data analysis:* for surfacing hidden relationships in otherwise chaotic numerical information.

POLICY DEPLOYMENT IN ACTION

McDonnell Douglas Space Systems Company (MDSSC) is a good example of policy deployment in action. MDSSC provides products and services for space transportation, space utilization, and strategic defense; rocket launch vehicles for putting satellites into orbit; earth-orbiting labs; surveillance and tracking systems; and aircraft nose assemblies. More than 80 percent of its business is with NASA and the U.S. Department of Defense. MDSSC currently has 13 divisions, which employ 11,500 workers.

In the early 1980s, MDSSC started to make a concerted effort to change its cultural philosophy. This effort resulted in an early attempt to develop a vision of the type of organization it wanted to become, and the most important capabilities that needed to be developed within the enterprise. The vision became known as the Five Keys to Self-Renewal: (1) strategic management, (2) participative management, (3) ethical decision making, (4) quality and productivity, and (5) human resources management.

In 1985, MDSSC discovered that sales were lagging because its structure impeded its ability to satisfy customers; this led the company to adopt a strategy that had the goal of becoming more customer-driven.

"We moved to four product divisions and organized around our products with the goal of increasing customer satisfaction," says Bonnie Soodik, Vice President and General Manager of the Quality Systems Division.

Later, however, the company noticed that it was developing, between divisions, inconsistencies in how customers were served. So, in 1989, MDSSC identified six major disciplines in the company that were common to each product division: (1) business, (2) quality, (3) human resources, (4) subcontract management/purchasing, (5) product engineering and definition, and (6) production.

A key executive from each discipline, in each division, was placed in one of six horizontal teams. For example, the key business executives from each of the product groups came together to form the Product Engineering Horizontal Team.

Soodik reports:

We told them, "Your job is twofold. You have to run the function in your program area and represent the enterprise on a Horizontal Team."

• • •

Each Horizontal Team identified all the processes they own. The teams then empowered subteams to develop continuous improvement plans for each of their processes.

• • •

The Horizontal Teams run the processes and are empowered to make decisions. They keep the systems common and audit themselves to make sure the discipline is there and that we don't fail a [government] audit.

The horizontal teams govern their own disciplines, but they are reviewed by an executive council of senior executives every quarter. Through the formation of the horizontal teams, MDSSC was looking for a way to align groups of employees to address enterprisewide issues in a coordinated way.

In addition to the horizontal teams, MDSSC devised another way to deploy business policy and involve employees in the improvement effort. Thirteen productivity centers have been established to act like quality improvement teams; all of the people related to a specific product line are on the team, ensuring that if there is a problem, the team can fix it and prevent it from happening again. Teams such as these were further empowered by MDSSC's employee suggestion programs.

Eventually, MDSSC evolved its thinking to more formally "deploy" the organization's business objectives throughout the enterprise. "Another way we're making sure our people are empowered and that we've touched everyone is through our Strategic Business Objectives, a flow-down process," says Soodik.

In 1989, a few vice presidents and 200 employees worked on creating a vision and mission. Then the group asked, "Of the 'zillions' of things we could do to reach our vision, what is most important?" It defined the three most critical strategic business objectives (SBOs):

1. *Customer*—to become the preferred supplier in our key market segments;

2. *Culture*—to become a company that is the embodiment of TQM;

3. *Financial*—to achieve sales growth greater than 6 percent per year; to increase after-tax return on investment from 16.4 percent to 20 percent over the next 10 years.

Says Soodik:

Next, each division chose three SBOs to support the top level SBOs. Then their direct reports developed three SBOs to support the division, and their employees each individually developed SBOs. So, in this flow-down fashion, each employee has objectives that they document and that are part of their performance appraisals. Each year, we set new SBOs, which are part of our rewards and recognition program.

MDSSC's successful policy deployment process strategy has paid off. In a three-year period, MDSSC saw a 25 percent reduction in hardware nonconformance costs as a percentage of manufacturing costs; a 70 percent reduction in machine shop scrap and a 50 percent reduction in rework; a reduction in cycle time for a purchase order from 54 days to 28 days; and an inventory turnover rate that's gone up by 40 percent.

Soodik makes a final observation:

Leadership at the top, companywide quality improvement, and the empowerment of our managers and employees are all vital elements of our success. Ours is an evolutionary, not revolutionary, journey—in style and intent.

• • •

Overall, I'd say we're about "10 years into our five-year journey" and we think we're halfway there. It's not a lot of giant steps at all times. It's taken a lot longer than we thought it would, but it's been worth it.

Strategy alignment is not about doing "things right" but about doing the "right things right." You need a clearly defined value strategy to guide you through the hazards of a turbulent marketplace. Your planning process must be designed to ensure that everyone in the enterprise is working on the same few critical issues that will move you toward your enterprise vision. Hoshin kanri, or policy deployment, provides your organization with a systematic way to continuously improve the areas of the business that will really make a difference in performance.

The essence of the hoshin kanri philosophy is to enable the enterprise to learn from the results of the actions it takes in the marketplace. Are there other ways to foster "enterprise learning"? Yes! In fact, this ability is essential to success. The way for your organization to learn faster than your business rivals is the critical competency described next.

TOUCHSTONE
8

Fostering the Learning Organization

Genius is one percent inspiration and ninety-nine percent perspiration.

Thomas Edison

The discipline of policy deployment helps to get your enterprise "on target" and reach its high-performance goals. But more than sheer "willpower" is necessary for success in the value decade. With rapid changes in customers, competitors, and technologies, only the nimble and determined will win the race. The capacity to reinvent your enterprise, so that it can cope with the unexpected and capitalize on new opportunities faster than the competition, will become a crucial skill as we enter the 21st century. The capability to sense change, glean lessons from past successes and failures, and turn these lessons into creative new responses is the eighth critical competency of the high-performing organization: enterprise learning.

To foster the "learning organization," you must understand how to support innovation within the enterprise and how to extract "learnings" from day-to-day experience. You will also need openness to the wisdom of outside organizations, and a climate that encourages creativity from everyone in the business. Tom Peters writes:

> The manager's job is like that of the teacher. He or she has but one objective: pursuing improved performance by fostering long-term personal (and team) engagement, learning and continuous development.

182

HAS AMERICA LOST ITS ABILITY
TO INNOVATE?

Enterprise learning is the ability to sense and respond to changing market conditions, draw insights from previous experiences, and apply these lessons in the form of winning innovations. Some observers of North American business fear we are falling behind in our ability to innovate.

A disturbing report, published in the *Total Quality Newsletter* in 1992, revealed that the United States seems to have lost its domination in the area of new and profitable ideas. Grant Thornton, a Chicago-based accounting and consulting firm, found that 50 percent of the 250 manufacturing executives it polled felt the United States has lost its role as world leader in product innovation. Of those who said the United States had lost its advantage, 75 percent picked Japan as the new leader and 13 percent picked Germany.

The executives surveyed were from industrial companies with annual sales ranging between $10 million and $500 million. Eight percent of the executives polled felt that the United States had always been a leader in terms of innovation and would continue to lead; 38 percent said they felt that, although the United States was on top, it was in danger of slipping.

According to the survey, the following companies are the most innovative companies in the world: Sony, Toyota, IBM, 3M, Mitsubishi, Merck, General Electric, Hewlett-Packard, Honda, and Nissan. Half of the companies on the list are indeed American, but the others are all Japanese.

Where has all the innovation gone? American entrepreneurs seem to be still leading in creating new ideas. CNN/Turner Broadcasting and Microsoft are two prime examples of old-fashioned entrepreneur-style big business. American scientists have won 51 of the 85 Nobel prizes for science awarded from 1976 to 1988—an indication that risk taking, creativity, and drive are still present in America. But patents granted to Americans accounted for only 52 percent of the world total in 1988, compared to 62 percent in 1978.

During the 1980s, 40 percent of the Fortune 500 companies dropped from the list because of acquisition, bankruptcy, or attrition. The troubles faced by large American corporations were severe indeed. But the rate of sales growth for the *Inc. 500* small-growth companies accelerated from 59 percent between 1977 and 1981 to 95 percent between 1985 and 1989. These numbers indicate that the bulk of creativity and innovation in America is occurring within small enterprise rather than big business.

The result is that most new jobs in America are being created by small companies, manufacturing as well as service jobs. Unless large U.S. corporations can learn to be more innovative and grow their revenues faster, there will be further waves of severance packages and early retirements among the bluechips as in many industries they lose share to foreigners and small American companies.

• • •

The failure is an institutional failure, not an individual failure. The failure is a failure of management. Unless large U.S. corporations can emulate the vision and flexibility of American entrepreneurs and small companies, our industrial base will continue to erode against global competitors.

Innovation and creativity seem to be casualties of a rigid enterprise structure. To correct this, enterprise leaders need to ask: What are the characteristics of innovative companies? What steps does my company need to take to build innovativeness?

Andrew J. Parsons, a director with McKinsey & Company, identifies three "institutional skills" that lead to innovative enterprises:

1. *Invention:* the ability to generate new ideas for providing value to customers.

2. *Innovation:* the capacity to develop and commercialize the new product, service, or business system that derives from the idea. This includes developing distinctive new methods of production or distribution as well as new products or services.

3. *Innovativeness:* the power to capture ideas and commercialize value to the customer time and again, continually for years. Innovativeness is a broad concept that encompasses the whole organization of a firm, its mode of operations, and its relationships with customers. Innovativeness demands that an institution develop self-renewing characteristics.

Innovative companies share a number of important traits. The first is *a focus on customer value.* Commercial success requires that an innovation provide better value than existing alternatives. Fred Smith of Federal Express pioneered the express letter and package delivery business in the early 1970s by arriving at the concept of serving the entire country from a central hub. Prior to the arrival of FedEx, the fastest service had been two- to three-day ground transport. Smith perceived a customer demand for faster service and created a new way! The door to new opportunities was opened.

The second important characteristic is *the ability to promote cross-functional innovation*—throughout the enterprise and between suppliers and distributors. Ted Turner focused on creating an entirely new business to deliver unprecedented customer service—news around the clock, as it happens, on CNN. Utilizing the merging satellite and cable technologies and high-quality portable video equipment, CNN arrived at a whole new way of delivering the news: on demand. With the "news on demand" system, a lightly edited "video river" is flowing responsive to world events and crises.

The third characteristic of innovative companies is *the ability to improve products and services quickly and continuously*. Canon perceived a gap in the photocopier market for small, convenient, slow, but high-quality photocopiers for use by small businesses and other low-volume users. Its response was a light, reliable, cheap, easy-to-maintain machine that delivered good quality copies: the PC-10. Canon revolutionized production and distribution with the PC-10: it used standard parts and mass production techniques (Xerox was using special parts and low-volume techniques); it distributed the machine through trade dealers and department stores instead of direct sales; the PC-10 was sold, not just leased, to customers; and after-sales service was vastly improved through the dealer rather than the manufacturer.

Stretching the Enterprise Imagination

You can unleash creativity and innovation within your organization by "setting it free." This involves "quickening" the enterprise imagination.

> Conventional wisdom says it is almost impossible for big companies to be truly innovative. New businesses that wriggle out from under the deadweight of bureaucracy and short-term thinking exist despite the system not because of it. Yet no one believes that big companies' employees are any less imaginative than their peers in smaller companies. So to protect imaginative individuals from corporate orthodoxies, senior managers in many companies tend to isolate them in new venture divisions, skunkworks, incubators, and the like. . . . Individual imagination must become corporate imagination.

Here are some ideas for opening up your enterprise vision to include new possibilities:

- *Escape the tyranny of the served market.* The search for unconventional market opportunities is smothered by overly narrow business charters. Instead, the company should be viewed as a portfolio of core competencies, not as a portfolio of products. Because Motorola sees itself as a leader in wireless communications, not just in pagers and cellular phones, it explores diverse markets such as wireless local area computer networks and global positioning satellite receivers.

Kodak convinced its managers to explore the "white space" in between business units. It explicitly looked for markets that fell across its traditional areas of competence in chemicals (film) and electronic imaging (copiers), and came up with something called the "electronic shoebox." In many homes, old photographs sit in shoeboxes. Kodak's chemical and electronic engineers devised a process that would let customers store their photographs easily and safely, watch them on television, and rearrange them at the touch of a button. The process, available through photo developers, turns chemical images on film into electronic images to be viewed and edited on a videodisk player hooked up to a television.

- *Search for innovative product concepts.* "New competitive space is created when a dramatic innovation in a product concept reshapes market and industry boundaries." Innovations can add an important new function to a well-known product. Examples are Yamaha's digital recording piano and Toto's "intelligent" toilet, which uses biosensors and microprocessors to provide medical diagnostic data. Innovative companies also develop novel forms in which to deliver a well-known functionality, such as automated teller machines, or Sharp's "Electronic Organizer" pocket calendar. Finally, innovative companies deliver a new functionality through an entirely new product concept, such as fax machines and camcorders.

- *Overturn traditional price/performance assumptions.* "Managers and product designers typically think about price and performance in linear terms, which limits the potential for radical innovation. Overturning this assumption often reveals undiscovered competitive space." Sony and JVC used this approach in the late 1950s, when they looked at Ampex's $50,000 video tape recorder and predicted the same machine costing $500 in the future! Recently, Sony introduced a video sketch pad children can use to draw colored pictures on a television screen, mimicking much more expensive computerized workstations. Parents are reportedly in awe of the product; they are literally unable to figure out how anyone could think up such a thing.

Yamaha was making traditional pianos, but later transformed the industry by first distinguishing the piano's functionality (the keyboard) from its traditional form (uprights and baby grands). Yamaha then applied new technology (digital sound recording) to give customers new and unexpected products. Its new "high-tech" piano stayed in tune could be kept in a small space, used with headphones, and provided musical accompaniment at the touch of finger. The competition was left dumbfounded, "In contrast, few of Yamaha's competitors understood the threat the new technology posed to their business, nor were they able to separate the piano's function from its traditional product form and construction process."

- *Get out in front of customers.* This is the ability to differentiate need from want—to predict what people will line up to buy! Hollywood provides an effective analogy for this differentiation: the "sequel." Movie studios rack their brains to predict what films audiences will pay eight dollars to see. But once they hit on a successful movie—one that grosses in the neighborhood of $100 million—the preparation for a sequel to that movie is already under way.

Building the Capacity to Innovate

Parsons prescribes these guidelines to help you foster innovativeness:

1. *Assess whether there is an innovation problem.* "If your company has the strategic need for innovation and is not successful, there are three possible causes for failure: a strategic failure, a procedural failure, or an organizational failure." Strategic failure may be due to lack of fit with the competitive environment or to inadequate investment. Procedural failure may be the result of a poor transition from prototype to market or of inadequate overall project management. Organizational failure may be caused by a lack of necessary skills, by poor systems, or by company values that do not support innovation.

2. *Determine how innovation should fit into the overall competitive strategy.* Do you want to be an industry leader or a fast follower? "It is critical . . . that a company identify clearly what its predominant approach is going to be. The implications for the whole organization differ greatly according to the approach." The so-called "big bang leader" may want to invest in leading-edge research. A "fast follower" may want to master the ability to respond quickly to new industry developments. Different approaches require a different set of priorities.

3. *Create a cross-functional approach.* "Often traditional functional organizations are not comfortable with innovation, since it inevitably demands the obsoleting of existing knowledge as well as radical changes in organizational linkages and procedures. Successful innovators help overcome this problem by establishing cross-functional project teams." Teams consisting of five to 500 people, handpicked by upper management and led by champions willing to break the rules, work together to accomplish a task.

4. *Manage the innovation process.* "Successful innovation doesn't just happen. It has to be managed. Successful companies don't reinvent the process each time they want to commercialize their ideas." The initial stage—the idea generation stage—will be somewhat unstructured, whereas the latter stages of commercialization should be tightly disciplined. A timetable, clear benchmarks and goals, development, testing and launching, and continuous risk assessment and management will all play a part in the latter stages of successful innovation.

Moving from Innovation to Acceptance

The problem often facing innovative, high-performing enterprises is not generating exciting new ways to create value for customers, but gaining acceptance for unconventional approaches. Customers may be leery of new concepts because they seem to upset the status quo—that is, the former equilibrium in relationships among the market players. The introduction of new solutions in the marketplace must be done with care. To illustrate how to gain acceptance of new ideas, author Joel Barker recounts how Thomas Edison overcame resistance to use of the light bulb.

- *Innovation must deliver perceived advantages.* When Edison introduced the light bulb to gaslight users, he emphasized the advantages of safety, low heat, and steadier light.

- *Innovation must be compatible.* Edison installed his bulbs in the same locations as gas lamps.

- *The user must perceive the innovation to be simple.* Edison always simplified his explanation of electricity for customers: bulb, switch, and fuse box.

- *Innovations must be divisible.* Edison was happy to install one light bulb at a time rather than wiring an entire building.

- *Innovation must be easily communicable.* People resist newfangled language. Edison called light sockets "electrical burners."

- *Innovation must be reversible.* Says Barker: "You have to be able to get out of it if people don't like it. That reduces people's fear of taking risks."

- *Innovation's relative costliness must be understood—and reduced.* People confronted with change see time, anxiety, fear, and frustration as potential costs.

- *Innovation must connect to credibility.* If you're driving innovation but the user doesn't perceive you as a credible innovator, partner with someone who is.

- *Innovations must be reliable.* People don't like to be guinea pigs. Make sure your innovation will work—that it will do what you say it will.

- *Understand the failure consequences if the innovation does not work.* The fewer the failure consequences, the more likely the innovation will be accepted.

CAN AN ENTERPRISE REALLY LEARN?

If increased innovation is necessary for survival in the value decade, then your organization must "learn how to learn." The term "learning organization" has become a popular term for describing an enterprise's ability to adapt and innovate to changing circumstances. Jocelyne Traub, of Xerox Canada, proposes this definition:

> A learning organization is one that continually enhances its capacity to create its future. It is characterized by its speed and innovation in responding to the needs of its customers. It does this by consciously managing its collective learning to continually optimize organization structure, strategies, processes and opportunities.

Witness some of the effective learning processes going on at Amil-Assistencia, the $250 million Brazilian health insurer that averages 40 percent in annual growth. President Edson de Godoy Bueno spends 90 percent of his time teaching other employees because, he says, "The best way to learn is to teach."

Each of the company's 12 directors teaches an average of 100 hours of classes per semester in the company's own MBA program, Amil Business Administration (ABA). (ABA is rated so highly, outsiders apply to take courses.) It offers 16 courses, including economics, strategic planning, personal leadership, and time management. Classes are held one day per week and feature heavy homework assignments. Each year, 150 employees apply for 60 spots in ABA.

Another program, Amil Selling Administration (ASA), is designed "to develop the most modern and well-prepared salespeople in the world." Amil spends 3 percent of revenues on training and personnel development. Workers can earn bonuses up to 40 percent of their base pay by participaton in skills development, and they're rewarded for cross-training and studying hard. More than 200 high-level employees write for the president a 5- to 10-year personal development plan, then write strategic action plans for reaching their goals. Every three months, all employees read a leading management book and discuss ways to implement the ideas contained therein.

Amil's customer service department also sponsors its own three-stage training program. In Stage 1, leaders from all ten Rio branches train eight hours a week on company products, procedures, and service attitudes. Managers also discuss specific front-line problems and solutions. For example, branch agents review the reasons for Amil's high premiums so they can explain pricing to customers.

In Stage 2, at the end of each month, all 150 front-line agents meet with Customer Service Director Carlos Eduardo Santiago for four hours. They discuss their successes and failures in applying what they learned from Stage 1. Finally, in Stage 3, on one Sunday morning every other month, a team from each branch discusses a specific topic, such as cutting client waiting times.

Amil's 300-seat auditorium is decorated with balloons, whistles, and confetti for the event, which is more a spiritual ceremony than an informational meeting. When he can, Bueno participates by explaining his aspirations for the company and for the employees, bringing a positive attitude and real warmth. The best team presentation wins prizes ranging from chocolates to Sony Walkmans.

Amil also sends employees abroad to teach others about the company's productivity program. Bueno's investment in education and training efforts are intended to extend beyond Amil's boundaries; he wants to inspire the people of Brazil to focus on education for their children and to remain open to new technology. "Getting rich is very easy," Bueno says. "But there is only one way to increase the wealth of a nation, and that is to train and develop people all the time."

The "Knowledge-Creating" Company

Training individuals is one thing, but how can we conceptualize "enterprise knowing?" Professor Ikujiro Nonaka, of Hitotsubashi University, feels we should think of businesses as "knowledge-creating companies."

> The essence of innovation is to recreate the world according to a particular vision or ideal. To create new knowledge means quite literally to recreate the company and everyone in it in a nonstop process of personal and organizational self-renewal. In the knowledge-creating company, inventing new knowledge is not a specialized activity—the province of the R&D department or marketing or strategic planning. It is a way of behaving, indeed a way of being, in which everyone is a knowledge worker—that is to say, an entrepreneur.

• • •

> The centerpiece of the Japanese approach is the recognition that creating new knowledge is not simply a matter of "processing" objective information. Rather, it depends on tapping the tacit and often highly subjective insights, intuitions, and hunches of individual employees and making those insights available for testing and use by the company as a whole. The key to this process is personal commitment, the employees' sense of identity with the enterprise and its mission.

Nonaka believes the four basic patterns for creating knowledge in any organization are:

1. *From tacit to tacit:* when one individual shares tacit knowledge with another. Matsushita software developer Ikuko Tanaka studied the head baker at Osaka International Hotel to try to learn how to bake the best bread. In this way, the apprentice learns the master's skills, but neither gains much systematic insight into the craft knowledge. Because the knowledge never becomes explicit, it can't be easily leveraged by the organization as a whole.

2. *From explicit to explicit:* when, for example, a controller gathers information from the entire organization and uses it to create a financial report. The report is new knowledge because it synthesizes information from many different sources, but it doesn't really expand the company's existing knowledge base.

3. *From tacit to explicit:* when, for example, a software developer explains a baker's knowledge to a project-development team, converting it from tacit to explicit knowledge; or, when a controller uses the financial report to suggest an innovative new approach to budgetary control.

4. *From explicit to tacit:* when new, explicit knowledge is shared throughout the organization and is internalized by employees so that it broadens, extends, and reframes their own tacit knowledge. When the controller's proposal is used by employees who eventually take it for granted as part of the background of tools and resources necessary to do their jobs, it has moved from explicit to tacit.

Five Critical Learning Skills

New ideas are essential if learning is to take place, but, by themselves, ideas cannot trigger organizational improvement unless an enterprise can change the way that work gets done. Many organizations have been successful at acquiring new knowledge, but less successful in applying that knowledge to their own work activities. Peter Senge, author of *The Fifth Discipline,* says: "We should think of learning as the expansion of one's capacity—to create, to produce results, ... not as simply taking in information."

David Garvin, of the Harvard Business School, believes that effective learning enterprises are skilled at five main activities: (1) problem solving, (2) experimenting with new ideas, (3) learning from mistakes, (4) learning from the success of others, and (5) transferring knowledge quickly and efficiently throughout the organization. Many companies practice these activities in isolation; the learning organization creates systems and processes that support the activities and integrate them into daily operations.

1. *Problem solving* can be made more effective by using the philosophy and methods espoused by the total quality management (TQM) movement, a "scientific method" for diagnosing problems, such as Edwards Deming's plan–do–check–act cycle, and simple statistical tools to organize data and draw inferences. Problem solving emphasizes the use of data, not assumptions, as background for decision making, often called "fact-based management."

2. *Experimenting with new ideas* involves searching for and testing new knowledge. Unlike problem solving, it's motivated by opportunity and expanding horizons. Enterprises need to be concerned with two forms of experimentation: (1) ongoing programs and (2) one-of-a-kind demonstrations.

Ongoing programs involve a continuous series of small experiments designed to create incremental gains. Corning experiments with diverse raw materials and new formulations to continuously create better grades of glass. Successful ongoing programs create a steady flow of new ideas, even if they come from external sources. Chaparral Steel sends first-line supervisors on sabbaticals around the world to visit academic and industry leaders, study new practices and technologies, and then incorporate viable findings into the company's daily operations. (Chaparral is one of the five lowest-cost steel plants in the world.) GE's Impact Program used to send manufacturing managers to Japan to study factory innovations; today it sends them to Europe to study productivity improvement practices.

Ongoing experiment programs have incentives that promote risk taking, so that employees perceive the benefits of experimentation as exceeding the risks. Managers, however, must attempt to maintain accountability and control without stifling creativity. For example, Allegheny Ludlum keeps expensive, high-impact experiments off the "scorecard" used to evaluate managers but requires prior approvals from four senior vice presidents before a new experiment can begin. Allegheny's productivity improvements average 7 to 8 percent annually.

Ongoing learning programs also require managers and employees to be skilled in performing and evaluating experiments. They must learn:

> . . . statistical methods, like design of experiments, that efficiently compare a large number of alternatives; graphical techniques, like process analysis, that are essential for redesigning work flows; and creativity techniques, like storyboarding and role playing, that keep novel ideas flowing.

Demonstration projects are often larger and more complex than ongoing programs, and they include holistic, systemwide changes used to effect new organizational capabilities. Projects are usually started from scratch, representing a sharp break from past procedures. For example, General Foods' Topeka plant, one of the first "high-commitment work systems" in the United States, was set up as a pioneering demonstration project to introduce the concepts of self-managing work teams and worker autonomy.

Demonstration projects tend to share the following characteristics:

- They are usually the first projects to embody principles and approaches that the organization hopes to adopt later on a larger scale. For this reason, they are more transitional efforts than end points, and they involve considerable "learning by doing." Midcourse corrections are common.

- They implicitly establish policy guidelines and decision rules for later projects. Managers must therefore be sensitive to the precedents they are setting.

- They often encounter severe tests of commitment from employees who wish to see whether the rules have, in fact, changed.

- They are normally developed by strong multifunctional teams reporting directly to senior management. (For projects targeting employee involvement or quality of work life, teams should be multilevel as well.)

- They tend to have only limited impact on the rest of the organization if they are not accompanied by explicit strategies for transferring learning to other parts of the enterprise.

The Copeland Corporation, a highly successful compressor manufacturer, launched a project in the mid-1970s designed to transform the company's manufacturing approach. Previously, all manufacturing was done in a single facility at high cost and with questionable quality. CEO Matt Diggs felt the problem was too much production complexity. A small, multifunctional team was assigned to design a "focused factory" dedicated to a newly developed product line. With an initial project budget of $10 million to $12 million and a time period of three years, the team learned that drastic improvements were indeed possible.

The final project, which cost $30 million, yielded unanticipated breakthroughs in reliability testing, automatic tool adjustment, and programmable control. During the setup and early operations, the quality manager was placed as second-in-command, a significant move upward. Production was gradually raised to full scale, and all efforts to proliferate products were resisted. Once the first focused factory was running, it captured 25 percent of the market in two years and held the advantage in reliability for over a decade. Copeland quickly built four more similar factories, with members of the original team involved in the design and then rotated among the factories once they were operating.

Whether they are demonstration projects like Copeland's or ongoing programs like Allegheny Ludlum's, all forms of experimentation seek the same end: moving from superficial knowledge to deep understanding. At its simplest, the distinction is between knowing how things are done and knowing why they occur. Knowing how is partial knowledge: it is rooted in norms of behavior, standards of practice, and settings of equipment. Knowing why is more fundamental: it captures underlying cause-and-effect relationships and accommodates exceptions, adaptations, and unforeseen events.

3. *Learning from mistakes* means the enterprise reviews failures as well as successes, assesses them logically, and records the "moral of the story" in a form that is accessible to other employees. Managers who are indifferent or hostile to the past lose the opportunity to gain valuable knowledge. IBM's 360 computer series, one of the most popular and profitable ever, was based on the technology of its failed predecessor, the Stretch computer.

Boeing studied the difficulties with its 737 and 747 planes to ensure the problems were not repeated. "Project Homework" compared the development processes of the 737 and 747 with those of the 707 and 727, two of Boeing's most profitable planes. After spending three years on the comparison the study group came up with a set of "lessons learned" and a one-inch-thick guide filled with hundreds of recommendations. Several members of the group were then assigned to the start-up teams working on the 757 and 767 planes; they produced the most error-free planes in Boeing's history.

British Petroleum has established a postproject appraisal unit to review major investment projects, write case studies, and derive lessons for planners. The lessons were incorporated into the company's revised planning guidelines. The five-person unit reports to the board of directors and reviews six projects per year.

These kind of reviews can be relatively inexpensive. You can enlist the help of faculty and students of colleges or universities who consider internships and case studies as valuable experience; they can bring fresh perspective from outside.

4. *Learning from the success of others* is often the basis for the most powerful insights. The outsider looking in can bring the benefit of a unique perspective that isn't clouded by "enterprise myopia." "Benchmarking is one way of gaining an outside perspective; another, equally fertile source of ideas is customers. Conversations with customers invariably stimulate learning; they are, after all, experts in what they do. Customers can provide up-to-date product information, competitive comparisons, insights into changing preferences, and immediate feedback about service and patterns of use." For example, Worthington Steel's machine operators pay unscheduled visits to customers' factories to discuss their needs.

5. *Transferring knowledge* involves the ability to communicate new knowledge quickly and efficiently throughout the organization. "Ideas carry maximum impact when they are shared broadly rather than held in a few hands." Written, oral, and visual reports; site visits and tours; personnel rotation programs; education and training programs; and standardization programs are among the mechanisms available to promote enterprisewide learning.

Reports and tours are the most popular methods for knowledge transfer. Reports summarize findings, provide checklists of do's and don'ts, and describe important processes and events; tours are tailored to different audiences and needs. The NUMMI automotive plant is introduced to visiting managers through a series of specialized tours describing the policies, practices, and systems most relevant to the level of management in attendance.

Because tours and reports are cumbersome, with knowledge absorbed secondhand through reading or seeing, personnel rotation is a more powerful method of transferring knowledge. In many organizations, expertise is held locally, by specialists with little influence; through a hands-on transfer of expertise, the organization as a whole becomes more knowledgeable. For example, the CEO of Time Life shifted the president of the music division to the book division in an attempt to resurrect flat profits and invigorate marketing approaches by bringing the successful ideas from the music business to the book business.

In 1986, PPG launched a new float-glass plant that used a radical new technology and human resources innovations. Workers were put into small, self-managing work teams with responsibility for assignments, scheduling, problem solving, improvement, and peer review. After several years, the plant's manager was promoted to Director of Human Resources for the entire glass group. Based on his experiences at the plant, he developed a training program for first-level supervisors that taught them how to manage employees in a participative, self-managing environment. By moving him to a new position in the company (Human Resources), the benefit of his experience could be transferred to other areas of the business.

LEARNING FROM OTHERS THROUGH BENCHMARKING

When it comes to learning, why reinvent the wheel? Take somebody else's wheel (ethically, of course), and speed ahead of the competition! The high-performing enterprise recognizes that it doesn't have a corner on the best ideas in the world and actively seeks to learn from other organizations: customers, suppliers, competitors, and even companies in completely different businesses. You would have to have been living on a desert island during recent years, not to have heard of one of the newest ways to spur enterprise learning, one that has gained enormous popularity: benchmarking.

Benchmarking is a process through which an organization compares its internal performance to external standards of excellence, and then acts to close whatever gap(s) exists. The objective of benchmarking is to achieve and sustain best-in-class performance through continual improvement activities.

In 1979, the modern benchmarking boom began when Xerox Corporation discovered that rival Canon had a new midsize copier that *sold* for what it cost Xerox to manufacture a comparable model. The American company rushed to study and adopt Japanese manufacturing techniques, to reduce its own unit production costs. Xerox was successful in its efforts, regaining market share.

In 1980, Ford dismantled 50 midsize cars built by competitors to define 400 "best-in-class" features; 80 of those features were designed into the Taurus and Sable models introduced in 1985.

In 1988, the Malcolm Baldrige National Quality Award featured benchmarking in the judging criteria.

The International Benchmarking Clearinghouse, founded in February 1992 by the American Productivity and Quality Center in Houston, had 128 members in the late months of that year; today, it boasts 10 new members or more per month. It provides benchmarkers with networking services, information services, training, and publications. Early on, it received 300 calls weekly for information; more than 100,000 requests for information have been received. An International Benchmarking Clearinghouse ad in *Fortune* generated 900 inquiries, the greatest response to advertising the magazine had ever received.

Studies conducted by Towers Perrin, the Massachusetts Institute of Technology, and the American Productivity and Quality Center indicate that, by 1995, most American companies will engage in benchmarking.

Benchmarking can be applied to all kinds of activities and outputs of your enterprise: external customer products and services; broad business functions; and narrow business practices and procedures. The goal of benchmarking is to learn how other organizations perform critical business processes so you can duplicate these outstanding results now beyond your present ability.

Which Flavor of Benchmarking?

You should consider using the following types of benchmarking to foster learning and innovations in your business:

- Strategic benchmarking;
- Cost and performance benchmarking;
- Customer benchmarking.

Strategic benchmarking focuses on identifying the premier level of shareholder value creation, comparing your company to that standard, and figuring out why there is a gap between your performance and the best performer. By definition, the premier company has the greatest positive spread between its return on capital and its cost of capital, the best market-to-book-value ratio, and the highest shareholder return averaged over a long period. If, after comparing your company to the industry leader, there is a large performance gap, your managers must redefine strategic goals to enhance revenue, reduce costs, improve asset management, and reconstitute the business portfolio. Once the gap is measured, managers must backtrack to determine which specific areas require performance improvements.

Cost and performance benchmarking is concerned with measuring operational components: the relationship between productivity and direct costs. Productivity and cost buildup are compared at distinct points in the value chain. In developing operational benchmarks, the greater the level of detail, the more meaningful the comparisons. This information is usually obtained through direct exchange among peers or through industry associations. Studying a competitor's (or "best practice" company's) facilities and operations; researching supplier, distributor, and customer data; reviewing public records; and interviewing former employees are methods used to gather information.

As part of your cost and performance benchmarking, you may want to focus on organizational components. This means clarifying the sources of organizational capability and staffing efficiency, and comparing indirect costs—both attributable and allocated—for each employee. This method is used primarily to compare indirect cost structures and staffing efficiency among peer companies. Indirect cost structures include those associated with management, professional, technical, and administrative employees—costs such as salaries, wages, benefits, rent, training, and computer expenses.

Analysis of process components defines best practices for certain processes, both within and across the industry, and even compares completely different industries that perform the process well. The focus here is on transaction processes, such as invoice processing and/or the administration of benefit programs. Policy and decision-making processes, such as strategic planning, business planning, budgeting, and capital allocation, can all be benchmarked. Process performance evaluation can highlight reasons for significant gaps between your company's accomplishments and that of "best of class."

The third type, *customer benchmarking,* is also important: it determines the position of your products or services relative to alternatives in the eyes of buyers and users. This is a four-step process that involves:

1. Identifying the attributes that influence customer value perceptions;

2. Assessing your performance against these customer's value criteria;

3. Analyzing competitors' performance and standing;
4. Devising a plan for closing gaps between your current performance and customer expectations.

Guidelines

Here are some guidelines that will help you undertake an effective benchmarking study.

1. *Research your own company first.* Understand what's really important to your company's success; these key success factors should be the focus of benchmark comparisons.

2. *Establish the scope of, and the basis for, benchmark comparisons.* Select the benchmarking forms (strategic, cost, customer) that best meet your company's needs.

3. *Select the group of comparators.* Identify and screen companies to be compared paying attention to differences (often structural) that could make comparisons invalid. Data collection, if difficult, should be done through a shared arrangement with a peer or premier company.

4. *Develop a detailed plan for data collection and processing.* Identify all useful sources of data: employees, customers, trade associations, joint venture partners, cooperative data exchanges, interviews, and surveys.

5. *Develop conclusions and establish performance targets.* Once the benchmark data are in place, identify the source of the comparators' primary advantages.

Consider this example of how one organization prepared to carry out a benchmarking project. Florida Power & Light Company (FP&L) needed to improve its service to one of its most important customer groups—commercial and industrial—which included shopping centers, factories, and government office buildings. Despite the fact that these customers received more individual attention from sales reps than any other market sector, surveys by FP&L indicated that they were less than satisfied. A 1989 internal review showed that the division responsible for these customers, who represented 40 percent of FP&L's revenues, lacked direction, had conflicting agendas and priorities, and was very bureaucratic.

FP&L's Management Services Division recruited volunteers for pilot benchmarking projects in May 1990. The benchmarking team consisted of two commercial–industrial sales reps, a sales analyst, and one person from corporate marketing. First, the team met for two intensive days to figure out what was to be accomplished by the benchmarking effort. The team concluded that it needed to focus on six areas: (1) the commercial–industrial division's organizational structure; (2) the recruitment of topnotch sales reps; (3) motivation of sales reps; (4) communication with customers and employees; (5) performance measurement methods; and (6) training.

To come up with a list of benchmarking partners, the team put together a list of 100 electric-light-and-power companies. The selection criteria included the following: Did any team member have an "in" at a particular company? Did the company have a reputation for stellar customer service? Had the company been cited in any industry journals for its forward-thinking management? In the end, although FP&L originally intended to benchmark only against other utility companies, it added an office products manufacturer, a computer company, and a medical clinic to the list. The medical clinic, for example, offered FP&L insight into a "single point of contact," which the clinic provided in the form of a primary care physician. FP&L wanted to adopt a single point of contact in its billing and customer service departments.

The team's next step was to devise a questionnaire that would explore how other companies managed their commercial and industrial sales organizations. Among the questions asked were: Did the companies have mission statements? Did they segment their markets? How did they view the position of sales manager in the enterprise—as a stepping stone, or a dead end?

Before FP&L sprung the questionnaire on its potential benchmarking partners, the utility company answered the questions as they applied to itself. This helped to eliminate some questions but raised others. For example, the team decided not to ask what percentage of revenues was devoted to sales efforts when it realized it couldn't answer the question itself.

In the end, because of the intensive preparation phase it went through, the team took only two weeks to contact and secure a benchmarking partner. The team succeeded because it knew clearly what it needed to find out, was able then to select the best partner, and approached the partner in an intelligent way to secure cooperation.

What happens if your potential benchmarking partners are reluctant to work with you? There are other ways to gain cooperation. When Jeanette Frick, the head of the benchmarking program for GTE Directories, the Dallas-based subsidiary of GTE Corporation and the world's largest publisher of Yellow Pages, attempted to launch benchmarking efforts concentrating on the telephone industry, she found that these companies were far more secretive than companies in other industries. In late 1990, GTE Directories approached the Yellow Pages Publishers Association (YPPA) with the idea of starting a benchmarking consortium.

After forming a task force to investigate the idea, YPPA decided to act as a coordinator but placed Ernst & Young, the management consulting and accounting firm, in charge of overseeing and compiling the benchmarking database. The secretive telephone companies' fear of losing proprietary information necessitated the neutral third party; all information collected was to be disguised so no one would know which company provided which data. All members would contribute information and would receive reports that summarized everyone's input. The 12-company study looked at such areas as production cycle time and the time needed to resolve customer complaints.

Benchmarking Etiquette

The "heart" of any benchmarking effort is usually a series of "site visits" to a benchmarking partner, to learn firsthand how it achieves the results you admire and wish to emulate. In turn, the partner may wish to visit your enterprise to learn from you. These visits require some finesse. Otherwise, instead of reaping the benefits of a smooth and insightful benchmarking collaboration, your enterprise could end up embarrassing itself. Michael J. Spendolini and Neil H. Thompson, of The Benchmarking Partners, Inc., warn:

> Proper benchmarking can lead to extraordinary improvements in products, services, processes, and profits—if done properly. Sadly, it seems that more well-intentioned benchmarking efforts will fail than will succeed. Poor planning, poorly prepared people and just plain bad manners are prime causes of most failures.
>
> • • •
>
> Many organizations are beginning to realize that the professional etiquette of benchmarking—the "protocol" involved in approaching a prospective partner— is a critical determinant of the success of the benchmarking effort. In fact, if the suitor is not effective in their initial approach, they may never get the opportunity to benchmark at all.

Here are some rules you can use that will help ensure proper benchmarking protocol:

- *Understand your own organization before you begin to investigate others'.* Without a significant level of internal diagnosis and understanding, the benchmarking investigation will lack focus, purpose, and depth, and will be a random information-gathering exercise (a "fishing expedition"). Your target organizations may also want to gather information about you; if your organization isn't forthcoming, or is unorganized or secretive, your reception will be poor.

- *Prepare a briefing package.* Assemble the following information: a statement of purpose; a project description indicating how the target was identified; a description of the benchmarking topic outline; a list of other target organizations to be contacted; a statement of what the target organizations might receive in exchange for participating in the benchmarking process; the identification of key contacts in your organization; and an estimated timetable for project completion, including reasonable and conscientious estimates of the time required to complete the project. A typical briefing package is two to three pages long; it should be faxed prior to contacting the target, then followed up with a phone call.

- *Do not overburden your benchmark partners.* Don't use lengthy questionnaires, telephone conversations, or surveys, and avoid excessive information-gathering. Don't spring unplanned and unnecessary site visits on the target.

- *Be conservative with site visit requests.* Generally, site visits are overused. Valuable information can be collected in other ways, such as over the phone. When visits are necessary to physically inspect some process or object, don't bring a large entourage to the site; one or two people are usually enough to handle the assignment, and small numbers can encourage valuable one-on-one talks.

- *Follow through on commitments.* Returning phone calls promptly, being on time for site visits, and providing information when requested should all be automatic.

- *Select your benchmarking team wisely and then train them well.* The team should be comprised of well-trained, highly informed employees who have effective interviewing skills and information-gathering abilities. Good communication skills are crucial. The team should not appear defensive, arrogant, or overly demanding. Discussions should be conducted with a high degree of professionalism, respect, courtesy, and deference. First impressions are critical.

- *Be sensitive to ethical issues.* Do not press for information that may be sensitive or proprietary; conduct the benchmarking investigation through the "normal" target organization hierarchy, then work downward through the hierarchy until the desired contacts are made. Always inform prospective benchmark partners of your intentions and purposes for benchmarking; make sure that any third agents (consultants, observers) under your aegis represent themselves as your representatives or agents; never divulge information collected to any outside sources, unless prior explicit, written permission has been granted.

AT&T Universal Card Services (UCS), a 1992 Baldrige National Quality Award winner, uses benchmarking to achieve its award-winning performance. As its first step, the company hired managers from the credit card industry who already possessed considerable expertise. Rob Davis, Vice President and Chief Quality Officer, reports:

> They brought with them quite a bit of knowledge, and we put our business together [by drawing upon that expertise.] We decided that kind of benchmarking, if you will, was enough to take us through two years.

The company then did more formal benchmarking, ". . . entering into a few carefully chosen partnerships to study particular issues, such as [how to] heighten awareness of corporate values." For example, it studied Walt Disney Company to learn how the "world-class performer instilled its corporate culture in its employees." UCS learned that Disney begins building in corporate culture "from the time prospective workers interview." UCS took the lesson to heart. As a result, says Davis:

> When somebody comes to work, before we tell them about insurance and other benefits, we tell them about what's important to the business [in terms of] our philosophy and our values.

Where to Go for Help

Three principal resources are available to enterprises seeking assistance with benchmarking:

1. *Consultancies.* Because consultants aren't really needed every time a benchmarking effort is launched, they've turned to offering benchmarking training programs and seminars to teach companies how to "do it yourself." Consultants can also help in researching best-in-class companies. One of the greatest strengths of a consultant is the ability to put benchmarking in its proper perspective and to provide objective assessment of the data collected and the application of results.

2. *Consortiums.* As a cheaper alternative to consultancy, there is always "sharing." Orval Brown, Director of Business Process Architecture and Benchmarking for Ameritech, says, "Sharing the cost of a study lets a company benchmark many more processes than it could afford by contracting with a consultant individually. Having to spend only a 17th the amount to get a comprehensive benchmarking study is a real plus."

Ameritech and Brown became the guiding force behind the Telecommunications Industry Benchmarking Consortium. They sent letters out to telecommunications companies to drum up interest, and they contracted with the consulting firm, A. T. Kearney, to avoid potential antitrust and regulatory conflicts and to ease the data recording and analysis load. The project's progressing but a delay has arisen because of the need to work out legal agreements between A. T. Kearney's counsel and the 17 participant companies' lawyers. Once the consortium is firing on all cylinders, the members want to benchmark three or four processes per year.

Another consortium, Best Practices Benchmarking, of Lexington, Massachusetts, founded in 1991, will offer a subscription to companies interested in gaining access to their human resources management, customer satisfaction, and strategic planning databases.

> It's clear that the consortium is an efficient way to share information within an industry. For smaller companies with limited staff and tight budgets, a consortium may also be the only way to afford comprehensive benchmarking. Another asset: A consortium can help define industry benchmarking standards.

3. *Clearinghouses.* American Productivity and Quality Center (APQC), a nonprofit organization in Houston, has set up an ambitious information clearinghouse project. Following eight months of planning and data collection, the APQC International Benchmarking Clearinghouse has benchmarking data covering many industries and many topics, from customer service to flexible manufacturing, with the process information to explain the numbers. APQC also offers training and assistance in benchmarking.

Another clearinghouse, created by Ernst & Young in conjunction with the American Quality Foundation, has a benchmarking database of management practices aimed at improving quality. This clearinghouse was developed from the International Quality Study, an examination of more than 1,000 quality-focused management practices within the automotive, retail banking, computer, and health care industries in the United States, Canada, Germany, and Japan.

FOSTERING CREATIVITY IN INDIVIDUALS

When you think about it, it's obvious that the innovative, learning enterprise must be comprised of innovative individuals. Any effort to foster a learning organization has to address the issue of prompting purposeful creativity on the part of every member of the business. Creativity has become a subject of intense interest among leading enterprises in recent years—and a big business in its own right.

A *Training* magazine annual survey of 2,600 corporations and other organizations having more than 100 employees found that, in 1990, 32 percent offered creativity training, up from 22 percent in 1989. Attendance at the Center for Creative Leadership, in Greensboro, North Carolina, jumped 65 percent between 1988 and 1990, says Stanley S. Gryskiewicz, a director of the Center. Three years ago, 5 percent of attendees were executives; in 1991, 24 percent were executives. Frito-Lay, a division of Pepsico, trained all 25,000 of its employees in creative thinking methos during the 1980s. Corning trained 26,000 employees in several countries. Exxon has trained 7,000 employees in the sales, exploration, and chemical divisions since 1988. Texas Utilities trained its top 400 executives in an array of creative thinking techniques, and is now offering similar training to other employees.

Some critics argue that creativity training is a fad, and that it doesn't address concrete problems facing businesses. Creativity advocates maintain that coming up with a new idea is only the first step. The real goal is innovation—turning an idea into something of value to the business.

Does creativity training, then, lead to innovation? The answer is "yes." New products, new ways to attract customers, new solutions to shop-floor problems, and new insight into how to budget, plan, and strategize, are all the results of creative thinking.

> Creativity training has been regarded by business as "off-the-wall" and frivolous. Indeed, some of the methods used to teach creativity—writing down dreams, donning different-coloured hats—seem plain silly. That is, until one weighs the results.

At Kodak, workers used creativity techniques to reinvent the way they ran a huge film processing machine that deposits the emulsion coating on photographic film. The machine had to be shut down periodically (often during large production runs) for preventive maintenance and capital improvements.

To solve this problem, a dozen maintenance employees, working with a Kodak creativity trainer, imagined themselves at a party, celebrating their ability to do the job in four days instead of seven, without interrupting the production schedule. They imagined who was at the party and what was said, and began to extract real solutions from the daydreamed party banter. They refined these ideas, using modular equipment and making creative use of production schedules, and successfully made the necessary changes.

Through a problem-solving method called "metaphoric thinking," a Du Pont scientist came up with a way of adding dyes to Nomex fibers' tight structure. In metaphoric thinking, the problem is likened to processes that are completely unrelated, with the mind leaping to make connections, occasionally discovering something worthwhile. The scientist, who grew up in West Virginia coal country, thought of how mine shafts are prevented from collapsing by structures that keep them propped open. Using this idea, he came up with a technique for propping open a hole in the Nomex structure as it's being manufactured, to allow it to be filled with dye later.

Creativity on Demand

There are many different methods to "extract" creativity from your enterprise staff, and the methods are not exactly conventional. Du Pont employees, as mentioned, use dreams and metaphors to solve manufacturing problems; Eastman Kodak, Hoechst Celanese, and Amoco employees use a technique called "imagination-enhancing." Texas Utilities, a Dallas-based power company, had its managers solve a capital planning problem by imagining themselves as a kilowatt traveling through the company's systems.

> Fantasy, games, and dream analysis are the kind of inspiration-kindling strategies that poets might practice in their search for novel expressions. But these are just a few of the creativity techniques used by employers at a growing number of companies. Managers promoting use of these activities hope to spark creative thinking throughout the corporate ranks, from maintenance workers to CEOs. Ultimately, they see creativity as a means to enhance quality, performance, and innovation within the company.

Creativity techniques you'll find useful fall into one of four categories: (1) fluency techniques, (2) excursion sessions, (3) pattern breakers, and (4) shake-up exercises.

1. *Fluency techniques* help stimulate the generation of ideas. The techniques include brainstorming, brainwriting, mind mapping, storyboarding, and using words or pictures to stimulate ideas.

One of the greatest barriers to creativity is criticism, the picking apart of a suggestion or new product idea—along with the employee's confidence—until it's no longer valuable. It's crucial for enterprise leaders to listen to even half-baked suggestions. John Seeley Brown, director of the Xerox Palo Alto Research Center (PARC), reminds us:

> Creativity demands openness, integration, and collaboration, a willingness to try to bridge differences in disciplines and methodologies, and a willingness to listen for glimmerings of useful ideas, however raw.

The destructiveness of criticism has been long recognized in traditional brainstorming sessions. Brainstorming, the oldest fluency technique, was developed by Alex Osborn, the famous advertising executive, in 1938.

> . . . brainstorming has become primarily a group activity in which participants fire off as many ideas as possible. The premise is that a group will

produce a far greater number of ideas, from different perspectives, than an individual can. In an ideal brainstorming session, all thoughts are treated as welcome guests; judgment is deferred. Criticism is forbidden until afterward, when ideas are evaluated and prioritized.

Today, some organizations are abandoning brainstorming because it rarely achieves this nonjudgmental ideal, and participants tend to remain silent in the presence of superiors. Instead, an offshoot to this traditional corporate pastime is emerging: *brainwriting*.

During a group brainwriting session, employees write down their ideas on slips of paper, usually in a manner that protects anonymity. Then they exchange papers and try to build upon each others' insights. That way, the loudest voices don't necessarily prevail, and employees feel less pressure to perform for the boss.

Through electronic communication networking, information technology can facilitate anonymous brainwriting. Electronic Data Systems, the computer management systems arm of General Motors, maintains automated brainwriting facilities over a bank of networked Macintosh computers.

Similar techniques involve "mind mapping," where individuals or groups "draw a primary idea in the center of the paper, then depict new or related ideas as vines growing in all directions." Boeing engineers used mind maps to better understand how their technical manuals are developed, and to pinpoint ways to improve work flow by eliminating redundancies.

Another technique is *storyboarding:*

. . . participants in a group jot ideas down on index cards, which are then displayed on large bulletin boards or conference room walls. This technique is especially handy for thinking about processes. Each step in a process is a frame in a narrative. Employees readily reshuffle, rewrite, or even eliminate cards, with an eye toward improving the efficiency of the flow.

At Xerox PARC, researchers sketch ideas onto a large white wall in a common area, inviting researchers from other disciplines to make suggestions on the wall. At Bell Atlantic, large sheets of brown wrapping paper are hung in a hallway or in the conference room so employees can draw and change and comment on process diagrams, slowly redesigning them.

Another way to cue new ideas is to use *unusual stimuli* to get people thinking in new ways. Suzanne Marritt, a creativity specialist, asked a group of managers to look at some paintings, describe what they saw, then force-fit the impressions from the paintings to the original task of figuring out how to improve departmental harmony. One painting showed crows in a tree beside a pool of fish, which some interpreted as meaning the fish were vainly trying to communicate with the unhearing crows. As the discussion evolved, people from marketing and R&D realized that they saw themselves as the fish; researchers, preoccupied with scientific matters, spoke a technical language, and marketing was thought of as being deaf to new technical insights. As a result, teams of marketing and research employees will meet quarterly to "learn how to talk to each other."

Unleashing the "child" in the employee is another important concept Ann McGee-Cooper, a Dallas creativity consultant, relies on 10-year-olds to help with her clients.

> In a creativity session, McGee-Cooper brings together a dozen senior executives and six 10-year-olds, who have been recruited from the Dallas school system for their high scores on creativity tests. After a get-acquainted period with the executives, the youngsters join in the brainstorming, often attacking real-life corporate problems. They contribute children's uncanny ability to rattle off new ideas in a nonstop, uninhibited fashion, as well as the perspective that comes from being outside the problem.

2. *Excursion sessions* push the mind to grope for illuminations. These techniques teach workers to dream day and night: "By imagining themselves inside products or processes . . . , employees use mental images summoned from the unconscious. A Du Pont researcher, trying to find ways to control colors in one product, visualized himself inside the material. He imagined light penetrating it and reflecting off individual particles—and saw a solution (which, for proprietary reasons, Du Pont won't yet disclose.)"

Another example is a group of workers at Texas Utilities. The utility uses power-generating machinery such as turbines, generators, and boilers, which have an average life expectancy of 35 years but carry a high maintenance expense. A team of managers spent three months in a study designed to shave costs.

Part of the study included having them visualize themselves as a kilowatt traveling through the various fossil fuel and nuclear power systems. They saw that instead of trying to replace whole systems, they could replace key constituent parts as a form of maintenance. The new plan will bring down the company's equipment costs tenfold or more during the next decade.

3. *Pattern breakers* force thinkers to restate problems in novel ways.

Synectics, an innovation consulting firm, asks clients to walk around taking pictures with an instant camera, then use the photos as prompts. One client, a large management consulting firm trying to develop services for corporate R&D units, came back with pictures of a glass jar, a household wash product, a Federal Express package, and other sundry items.

The jar, surrounded by colorful trinkets, raised the notion of how to sell a service that seemed practical to the consultants who developed it but was lost in crowd of business services. The Fed Ex package prompted discussion about how that company had created a successful business system to help other companies to perform better: this led to the consulting company's designing a new service to help clients accelerate their R&D.

Xerox PARC pushes researchers to wrestle with risky and adventurous problems and to pursue cross-disciplinary work. They are encouraged to visit universities, other parts of the company, and research institutes.

Medtronics, a medical devices company, invites elite researchers who have been awarded a lot of patents to help top managers set the technical direction of the company. Hewlett-Packard, 3M, and Texas Instruments invite select groups of employees to spend on-the-job time thinking about new products and ways to improve business.

4. *Shake-up exercises* (such as games) help loosen up groups and make them more receptive to unusual ideas.

These exercises, intended as relaxation techniques, are designed to ease employees' anxieties so they'll feel freer to "create." Deborah Nicklaus, a creativity specialist from Kodak's management services department, uses a collection of 30 different hats in relaxation games. She might ask one person to don a Santa Claus hat and describe a camera or film product from Santa's perspective. How could Kodak target a customer like Santa, who would only need the camera once a year? Can a Kodak camera capture an image using only the light from Rudolph's nose? Would the camera work in freezing temperatures? And so on. The idea is not to devise a product or marketing strategy specifically, but to use the exercises to shake up the group's imagination in preparation for attacking business problems.

Kodak also has a "humor room" stocked with games, objects (toy robots, juggling balls), creativity books, and Monty Python videotapes. A financial planning group uses the humor room as a conference room; others go in there to loosen up and relax.

Dallas-area companies have toured children's playgrounds to watch how kids play, how they discover things, make rules, and change rules. Says Ann McGee-Cooper:

> Kids discover, and when they tire of their own rules, they change them. . . .
> The executives then try to look at their own problems as games where the
> rules can be changed, where nothing is set and all alternatives are possible.

With all these ways to foster creativity, innovation, and wisdom in your enterprise, what are the critical steps to building the learning organization?

- Foster an environment that is conducive to learning; set time aside for reflection and analysis—for thinking about strategic plans, dissecting customer needs, assessing current work systems, and inventing new products.

- Free up employees' time for learning purposes, and have top management teach employees techniques such as brainstorming, problem solving, evaluation of experiments, and other core learning skills.

- Break down enterprise boundaries to stimulate the exchange of ideas; boundaries inhibit the flow of information and keep individuals and groups isolated, reinforcing preconceptions.

- Convene conferences, meetings, and project teams that cross organizational levels; or, link the company with suppliers and customers.

- Design learning forums—programs or events that have explicit learning goals. Strategic reviews, systems audits, internal benchmarking reports, study missions, and jamborees or symposia are all good ideas.

If an enterprise is learning, that enterprise is changing. Indeed, without an organizational culture that embraces change, it is very difficult to nurture innovation. The high-performing organization knows how to effectively manage change, using the techniques explained in the next chapter.

TOUCHSTONE
9

Mastering Change Management

> *There cannot be any crisis next week. My schedule is already full.*
>
> Henry Kissinger

In the value decade, there are only two choices: (1) be a leader of change or (2) be a victim of change. Mastering change is the ninth competency of the high-performing enterprise. Are you facing any of the following challenges? If so, you need to become a "change master":

- Initiating major *reorganization* plans;
- Improving competitiveness through the implementation of *total quality management* processes;
- Incorporating *computer systems* as an integral part of business and/or production strategies;
- Integrating *customer focus* mentality and behaviors throughout the organization;
- Accommodating the turmoil associated with *mergers, acquisitions, and leveraged buy-outs;*
- Responding to new or increased *worldwide competition;*
- Redefining the *organization's culture* to be more supportive of the corporate business objectives;
- Initiating *cost containment* mechanisms;
- *Right-sizing* the work force;

- Establishing *employee involvement* mechanisms to generate a sense of empowerment and commitment among the work force;
- Launching *new products and markets;*
- Incorporating *new production/manufacturing procedures* or machinery;
- Adjusting to the *changing profile and needs of today's employees;*
- Complying with new *government regulations.*

The above list is unnerving. Few organizations would not be facing at least one of these issues. Most are coping with several at the same time. Even if your enterprise enjoys relative tranquillity now, beware!

> Few markets remain stable for long. When they are stable, it usually means that some discontinuity is either just around the corner, or is already starting to happen. This is not accidental. Stable technologies and markets are symptomatic of approaches which have neared the end of their useful lives. There is limited scope for future improvement. When that situation arises businesses start to look for fundamentally different ways of tackling the problem. The discontinuity soon follows.

Enterprises that have failed to cope with change successfully share a common pattern:

- They misunderstand the inevitable resistance to change that arises within the organization.
- They fail to put in place specific tactics to reduce the resistance.
- They lack knowledge of the proper sequence for the appropriate steps in the change process.
- They lack a clear understanding of the various roles that need to be played by individuals in the enterprise to facilitate effective change.

The burst of technical evolution makes it essential for consultants and client managers to have sharp change-management skill[s]. It is no longer enough simply to plop change into place and expect employees to take it from there. The technical solutions are more complicated, and like the tools they work with, employees are more sophisticated.

ASSESSING YOUR CORPORATE CULTURE

The essence of change management is aligning the organization's people and culture with changes in the business strategy, organizational structure, systems, and processes. Business strategy and processes are relatively "tangible" and therefore easy to grasp; insight into enterprise culture is not. You would no doubt agree that you have an enterprise culture ("the way we do things around here"), but it is difficult to describe in a meaningful way. You need to decode your current enterprise culture as the first step toward recasting it to support your enterprise strategy for creating value.

> Organizational change can be defined as a process of letting go of existing behaviors, attitudes and ways of working and establishing new behaviors, attitudes and work methods that achieve desired business outcomes. It is a process of moving from the old to the new, from the "as is" or present state to the "to be" or desired future state.

York University's Gareth Morgan observes that employees see their organizational cultures as taking the following forms:

- *A mechanism* in which activities are programmed, repetitive: powerful, reliable, efficient, and precise.

- *An organism* in which growth and development are stressed; employees are cared for and nurtured, and interdependence among them is created.

- *A brain* in which learning from experience and processing complex information are accomplished.

- *An aesthetic culture* that creates beauty, comfort, and satisfaction for customers.

- *A political system* in which the corporation is seen as a power and a bargaining structure between contending groups.

Attempting to change corporate culture can be a dangerous mission. You will need to open up numerous "cans of worms" that many people in the enterprise will resent. You must find out how individuals within the enterprise perceive the existing culture and whether you have the same perceptions.

Some change "experts" believe using an outside consultant will help discover and clarify the dimensions of enterprise culture. Although an outsider may have an objective view, he or she may be blind to certain subtleties observed by someone inside. The best approach is to have the outsider assist in making discoveries and in mapping the culture, then have influential insiders assist in validating and adding additional insights to the findings.

Uncovering the Hidden Secrets

Gaining insight into your enterprise's customs is difficult; they're so pervasive, you may not even know they are there. Dan Richards, president of a Toronto-based marketing consulting firm, calls this phenomenon the "Takla Syndrome." Richards writes in *The Wall Street Journal:*

Early in my career, business took me to a pulp and paper mill in Takla, a small community in the interior of British Columbia. As I approached, I was hit by a distinct and overwhelming odor, which I subsequently discovered was sulphur. As discreetly as I could, I asked my client, a longtime resident, how people could put up with the smell. His response? "Smell? What smell?"

He was quite serious. After a while, people who lived in Takla simply became inured to the smell—they didn't notice it anymore. And that, I believe, is what's happening when we encounter non-responsive customer contact employees. Often, they've lived with the smell of poor customer service for so long they don't notice it anymore.

You can follow these five steps to uncover the characteristics of your present enterprise culture and develop insight into the way to bring about the changes in attitudes needed to support your value strategy.

1. *Find the ones that "don't fit in."* Just as most families have "black sheep," so do most organizations. When you locate the "corporate black sheep," you need to ask: "Why don't they fit in?" Discovering why some people don't fit will tell you a lot about the current culture in place and will expose its built-in biases, or "rigidity."

Automotive executive John Z. DeLorean was an example of a "black sheep" working within a conservative corporate culture at General Motors. He challenged GM's rigid culture, and his rebellion exposed GM as being run according to these unstated tenets:

- A company the size of GM can largely have its own way with its environment.

- Power relationships with subordinates, suppliers, dealers, and subcontractors are legitimate ways of transacting business. Those with clout should use it.

- Human nature responds well to large monetary rewards or punishments tied to short-term profits.

- GM as an organization is more important than the individuals who serve it, who should efface themselves accordingly.

- Years of dutiful subordination give to those promoted the right to inflict on their subordinates similar humiliations.

- What cannot be easily counted and monitored by the finance department is not important—that is, safety, quality, and customer satisfaction.

DeLorean attacked this culture. He publicly stated that mediocrity was promoted at GM; he talked back to superiors; he campaigned for better quality and safety; he denounced short-termism and "group think." He had valid criticisms, but he was forced to resign because ". . . shouting your opposition to your corporation's culture is the quickest road to martyrdom rather than success."

2. *Bring conflicts into the open.* This step involves interviewing and observing managers and rank-and-file employees to elicit feedback about the conflicts and dilemmas within the culture. Interviewing is at the heart of a culture investigation, the skills of the interviewer are crucial. These interviews should focus on finding out what the individual truly believes. During interviews, care must be taken to manage the stress those interviewed feel from the conflict between their loyalty to the corporation and the need to point out valid problems within the business.

> The interviewees may be trying to use the interviewer as a messenger for what they are culturally constrained from saying. If this message is passed on it may cause offense, and its originators may deny authorship. Yet if it is not passed on, those who gave it may feel betrayed. Indeed, this situation can be a serious trap for consultants.

British Airways used interviews and group discussions with staff to discover a key problem in the airline's management practices: cabin and ground staff's contact with customers could make or break the airline, but these employees had little power to control events or bring about improvements. The airline concluded that staff couldn't be expected to care for customers if management wasn't taking care of them.

> Much work in the service industries and especially the work in cabins and on counters is not personally fulfilling. People do not get to know customers enough for their efforts to win due gratitude and friendship. If employees are to be convinced that their efforts are worthwhile, then that confirmation must come from colleagues and supervisors and must be attributable to the culture.

3. *Play out corporate dramas based on the findings.* This step is a little like a "creativity training session" (see Touchstone Eight). The findings of the interview process are shared with a representative group of employees through role playing. The purpose of this activity is to make the observed cultural norms more explicit and open for discussion. It also helps to answer the question: "Will private complaints be denied in public?"

British Airways used "Putting People First" (PPF) seminars as a discussion forum. Feedback from employees from these sessions revealed that the company was "cold, aloof, uncaring and bureaucratic" to its employees. "Customer First" quality circles and other means now empower employees to make on-the-spot decisions to help change this perception.

4. *Unearth your enterprise "mythology."* Like any other society, companies have their own distorted versions of history, archetypes, and symbols (in the form of logos, awards, or corporate colors). In this sense, every company is rooted in its own "mythology." To fully understand your enterprise you need to unearth its mythology; investigate the company's history, symbols, and heroes—as employees like to tell it.

For example, when John Sculley joined Apple Computer Inc. in 1984, he heard an often repeated "myth" that spoke powerfully about the beliefs of the people in the company. The tale went something like this:

> Once upon a time there were only corporate computers, which gave vast powers to U.S. institutions but which left individuals feeling powerless. But two youths in their early twenties, Steve Jobs and Steve Wozniak, struck a telling blow for the counterculture. In a garage, they created the first computer designed to give power to the person and liberate the individual.

> Just as Prometheus stole fire from the gods, Steve Jobs "stole computing from the corporation" and brought it back for the use of ordinary persons. So fast is technology developing that the corporate super computer of three to four years ago can today empower each individual.

> Steve Jobs taught his employees that "the journey is the reward." By this he meant that the accumulation of skills and knowledge in a continuous process of accelerated learning was the key to personal satisfaction and corporate success. Even great products would soon be obsolescent; every great discovery would soon be bypassed. All these were "ports of call" in an endless journey of discovery to expand the human mind.

> The logo, or symbol, chosen by Apple depicted a multicolored apple from which a bite had been taken. We are in an "electronic Eden" rediscovering fateful knowledge.

> Knowledge is inherently different from selling objects in exchange for money: those who give knowledge can never lose it. It stays with them in a paradigm beyond scarcity, which is why Steve Jobs gave Apple computers to every high school in California. Computer literacy is in the mutual interest of all. The computer is coextensive with mind itself. The computer network is a global village. Apple is in the business of learning and discovery by a world community of scholars. And they all lived happily ever after.

However, at the time Sculley took over the reins at Apple, the organization was badly in need of change. It needed to move from being a hugely successful start-up venture to adopting the practices of more mature enterprises. Sculley faced a major alteration in how the employees at Apple viewed themselves and the company's role in society. Gaining insight into enterprise mythology helps you to understand the vision and symbolic purpose that employees and executives see in their work.

It is possible to change the enterprise mythology to support a high-performance culture. Goran Carstedt, who was President and CEO of Volvo Svenska Bil AB from 1986 to 1990, turned around Volvo sales in France through this method. As general manager of Volvo France, he helped increase sales from 10,800 to 21,000 cars per year between 1982 and 1986. From 1983 to 1985, it posted average annual profit of Fr19 million versus average annual loss of Fr13 million from 1980 to 1982.

> The change in fortunes was almost entirely due to the way one man, Goran Carstedt, succeeded in infusing a cooperative Swedish corporate culture into the French dealers' network and marketing the values behind Volvo to a French audience.

Carstedt was faced with the following "myth" when he joined Volvo France: Swedish people don't understand the fiery, romantic, dashing French; and, Volvos are too sober, too safe, too practical, and too pedestrian to be successful in the French marketplace.

To change this "mythology," Carstedt arranged for French Volvo dealers and their wives to go on a grand tour of Sweden, and forever altered the notion that Volvos are dull cars made by moody people. Instead, the French visitors learned that Volvos are made by dedicated craftsmen. The cars symbolize individualism married to social concern, and promote the virtues of safety and reliability. Furthermore, the dealers became convinced that there were enough discerning French people who value the safety of their families enough to desire an automobile manufacturer that values the same thing.

5. *Look at the symbols, images, and rituals.* This step explores the metaphors, images, symbols, and rituals that characterize your company. What does the design of your logo say about your company? What are your traditional "corporate colors"? Grey symbolizes something different from rose or mauve. Easy-to-observe rituals include those used to celebrate achievement, such as corporate-sponsored awards for top performers, or the way business meetings are conducted, or how people of different rank dress.

Changing symbols can alter how the enterprise sees itself. For example, Carstedt replaced the Volvo logo (four hands, each "pointing the finger" in a loop) because it conveyed the idea that blame was being assigned and reassigned. The new image has a "clenched wrists" motif, signifying people working together to accomplish a common purpose.

6. *Create new ways of working.* This step involves introducing "new paradigms" to replace outmoded patterns.

British Airways (BA) took this approach in 1983 when Colin Marshall became CEO. The demands of privatization forced the airline to cut

20,000 employees and many international routes. The organization also badly needed to improve how it served customers and motivated its employees.

Marshall created a plan to install a new way of working within BA. He first wanted his employees to become more involved in decisions. Next, he wanted them to look outside of the organization, focusing more on the customer. Furthermore, he decided that no one should be able to hide behind titles or job descriptions. Tradition at BA dictated that the chief executive officer be called "CX"; he demanded to be referred to as Colin Marshall. He disbanded large committees and formed small ad hoc groups with responsibilities that cut across many functions. He also reduced the number of levels in the hierarchy.

Marshall decided to try to change the BA culture through training programs; BA enlisted the help of Time Manager International, an organization that had helped Scandinavian Airline Systems (SAS) with its turnaround. The first training program, carried out from 1983 to 1987, was called "Putting People First" (PPF).

> Staff were encouraged to utilize delays, bad weather, running out of preferred food, lost baggage, and so on to show their own ingenuity and concern in the shape of personal initiatives designed to compensate for such difficulties.

Colin Marshall attended 97 percent of the PPF gatherings and set up "Customer First" teams of cabin staff, encouraging them to contribute their ideas, experience, and reflections. Over 100 quality circles were launched; 75 of them were still running by 1990. Together, these groups generated some 700 improvements.

PPF was then extended to include non-customer-contact staff; "Managing People First" was designed for BA's 1,400 managers who received the training through a five-day residential program. Managers were schooled in how to create a vision for their organization, and were advised on how to build a support network for helping one another, and how to show subordinates the way their job contributed to the whole. To gauge managers' performance on supporting the principles of BA's new culture, an evaluation system in which managers checked each other's progress was designed and implemented.

Culture Change Is Difficult

Another lesson in "change management" can be learned from the case of the Dutch giant, Philips Electronics. When Jan Timmer joined the company as president in 1990, he sliced 45,000 jobs and streamlined its business activities by selling off appliances, computers, and other products. He then launched a program to create innovative consumer electronics products, but discovered his company's culture wasn't up to the demands of the change.

Philips is the only large European competitor left to battle the Japanese dominance in the electronics field. The market is demanding, but Timmer found his company's bureaucracy to be a much bigger challenge than the Japanese, "You just can't change a deep-rooted corporate culture in one or two years. It takes at least five years or longer."

The first new product to come out of Timmer's program was the Imagination Machine—also called CD-1—which hooks up to a television set and uses compact disks to reproduce sound and pictures. The next product to be realized will be the digital compact cassette (DCC), which records and plays music with the fidelity of compact disk sound. For the future, Philips is preparing high-definition television (HDTV).

The plan is a solid one, but Philips fell behind in the projected introduction of DCC by setting an overly ambitious schedule. Initial reviews of the Imagination Machine were mixed; Tandy Corporation dropped it from its Radio Shack chain. HDTV appears to be in trouble as well; most Europeans receive television signals from earthbound transmitters, so they would prefer to use the digital high-definition system being developed in America instead of Philips's satellite-based standard.

In the first half of 1992, Philips lost $250 million. Timmer forecasts that corporate profits may not show up until 1994. As a result, investors are deserting the company. Stock value dropped 35 percent from June to October 1992. Philips, successful creator of the video cassette recorder and the audio compact disk, has witnessed less inventive companies passing it by:

> The problem is that technological superiority is no longer the key to success in consumer electronics. Marketing agility, and price, areas where the Japanese hold a distinct advantage, have become crucial competitive factors. In his war to save Europe's electronics standard-bearer, General Timmer simply may not have a nimble enough army to overcome his Japanese foes.

UNDERSTANDING RESISTANCE

Changing an enterprise comes down to changing the behavior of individuals within the enterprise. Even the most advanced technical solution to improve business performance won't work if the solution doesn't have the support of the employees who have to implement the new ideas. A William Schiemann & Associates, Inc. survey of executives found that employees' resistance accounted for 74 percent of the biggest obstacles to organizational change. Inappropriate culture to support change was responsible for 65 percent; poor communication of purpose/plan for change accounted for 45 percent; incomplete follow-through to change initiative accounted for 42 percent; lack of management agreement on business strategy accounted for 39 percent; and insufficient skills to support change accounted for 39 percent.

The resistance of employees (both management and front-line personnel) to change should not only be anticipated, it should be expected. People naturally seek the comfort of ritual and habit in the workplace. People in an organization resist change for the following reasons: loss of control; feelings of uncertainty; loss of face; and concerns about future competence in coping with new job demands.

To offset these resistances, top managers should become more actively involved in the change process. They need to provide complete information and disclosure to employees; make change "manageable"; put past actions in a positive light; and supply adequate training to employees to help them cope with change.

How we perceive change is perhaps more important than the change itself:

> Change is not perceived as negative because of its unwanted effects as much as because of our inability to predict and control it. Bad events in our lives would not be so unpleasant if we could stop them as they occur or at least anticipate them and then prepare for the consequences. We view change as negative when we are unable to foresee it, when we dislike its implications and feel unprepared for its effects. Thus, a critical factor affecting our perception of change as positive or negative is the degree of control we exercise over our environment.

People's strong need for control can be met when they can dictate (or at least anticipate) their future. When specific expectations are established, based on what can be dictated or anticipated, and perceived reality matches expectations, people achieve a sense of control and equilibrium. When perceived reality does not match expectations, people lose the feeling of control and must adjust to changes they were unprepared to face.

On a personal level, change events can be characterized as one of the following types, each with a different effect on the individual:

1. *Micro changes.* These affect you, your spouse, your family, or your close friends and associates.

2. *Organizational changes.* These occur not just at work but with any institution that affects your life—your church or synagogue, a professional association, a union, and so on.

3. *Macro changes.* These affect you as part of a large constituency. For example, the global implications of Third-World debt and progress in

reducing racial tension in South Africa are events that have macro implications.

Daryl R. Connor of ODR Inc., a change management specialist, says: "Micro change is when 'I' must change; organizational change is when 'we' must change; macro change is when 'everyone' must change."

He believes that, in order to strengthen the enterprise's ability to "assimilate" change, it's important to understand the nature of "human resilience." "Resilience," in this context, is the ability to absorb high levels of disruptive change while displaying minimal dysfunctional behavior; resiliency is being able to bounce back repeatedly after being subjected to the stresses of change.

> In fact, when resilient people face the ambiguity, anxiety and loss of control that accompany major change, they tend to grow stronger from their experiences rather than feel depleted by them. Resilient people experience the same fear and apprehension as everyone else when they engage change. However, they are usually able to maintain their productivity and quality standards as well as their physical and emotional stability while achieving most of their objectives.

Connor, in his book, *Managing at the Speed of Change,* proposes the idea that people can be divided into two "change personality types":

1. *Type-D or danger-oriented people* ". . . view the crisis of change as threatening and generally feel victimized by it. Such people usually lack an overarching sense of purpose or vision for their lives, and therefore, they often find it difficult to reorient themselves when the unanticipated disrupts their expectations." Type-D people typically feel insecure during periods of change, are unaware of the dynamics of human change, fail to recognize the need for change, and often feel the need to defend themselves against the random emotional reactions they have during disruptive times. Their common defense mechanisms include: denial, distortion, and delusion. When faced with change, they respond in a reactive fashion. When they do acknowledge the need for change, it is often late; therefore, they are unprepared when change becomes absolutely necessary.

2. *Type-O or opportunity-oriented people* recognize the dangers inherent in change, but also see change ". . . as a potential advantage to be exploited, rather than a problem to be avoided." They usually have a strong life vision that serves as a source of meaning and steers them through turmoil. Type-O people have often achieved a sense of purpose through religious beliefs, political convictions, philosophy toward life, or a compelling task they are trying to accomplish in their lifetime. They view life as ever-shifting, and they assume that tomorrow will produce even more demanding situations. Type-O people consider disruption and

discomfort as necessary to the adjustment process and they constantly challenge their own assumptions and frames of reference. In times of duress, they rely on nurturing relationships to bounce back from the strain of change. "They view change, even major, unanticipated change, as a natural part of human experience. It is seen as a challenge replete with problems to solve and opportunities to exploit, rather than something terrifying to avoid."

OVERCOMING RESISTANCE

Every successful change program is fraught with its own set of problems, resistances, and complaints. To overcome the natural resistance to new ways, change leaders need to have a clear understanding of the effect of change on the organization. Crucial questions to consider are: What specifically are we changing? Why do these things need changing? Where is the starting point? Have we charted a reasonable direction? What particular part of the organization are we changing or could we change, as a result of this effort?

To establish a focus for action, change leaders must confront these critical issues:

- *Is there a motivation for change?* When people resist change, it's because they associate it with previous negative "change" experiences. In addition, some people have a hard time letting go of the comfort that comes with status quo. Other people lack the motivation to change because the reasons for change haven't been communicated properly. It's crucial to explore different ideas, solicit input from employees, and communicate the rewards associated with change.

- *Can the right resources be obtained?* Don't announce plans for change until you're sure they are feasible. Secure adequate financial backing as needed, and form teams of talented people to help you implement the change. It's also crucial to do your homework: gather feedback on your plans from key personnel, customers, and suppliers. This information will help you focus on truly feasible goals and opportunities.

- *Can the change effort be made workable?* Planning and the coordination of each phase during the change process are required to reach your goals. Help your change management team to visualize specific plan steps. Suggest ways to improve and achieve personal goals. Make sure you work from a visible, written plan instead of a verbal plan, which can be misconstrued.

Preparing for radical change is a particularly daunting undertaking:

> In dealing with radical change, it's important to extend one's view: to see the future, one has to stretch one's mind beyond day-to-day operating and strategic thinking toward a world that has yet to occur. Instead of extrapolating trends in a logical fashion, one has to sense how a discontinuity might develop and where it will lead.

The case of Niagara Mohawk Power, a gas and utility company based in Syracuse, New York, proves that radical change can be achieved, provided this person leading change has the conviction and the power to see the change through. In 1988, maintenance problems forced the shutdown of a Niagara nuclear power plant, which compelled the utility to spend $225,000 per day on replacement electricity. Cost overruns in the construction of a second nuclear plant necessitated a write-off of nearly $1 billion.

Following these disasters, Niagara appointed William Donlon as the new CEO. Donlon had started out with Niagara in 1948 as a meter reader! In his new role, he began to act like a revolutionary because, he said, "The whole system just wasn't working any longer. It was apparent to me that we had to change." Donlon began a systematic program to change the way the utility operated.

He enlisted the help of McKinsey & Company, management consultants, to reassess the functions of all 11,000 Niagara employees. This uncovered millions of dollars in productivity savings.

> The process convinced Donlon to break his vertically integrated company into four strategic units, each responsible for its own profit and more focused on developing its business: nuclear, gas customer service, electric customer service, and electric supply and delivery.

Perhaps the greatest challenge for any "change catalyst" is dealing with the inevitable "proponents for the status quo."

> No matter how well motivated and activated, radical change exposes status quo agents who cannot be converted. Their interests are directly threatened. For them, yielding to the change pressure is much less attractive than resisting. The wave of motivation and excitement created by successful change during the initial phases of the change process can be dashed on the rocks of this submerged resistance.

Donlon confronted this issue head-on. By 1991, he had hired 20 new senior officers; only one senior manager remains in the same post he had before the new CEO's appointment. To reinforce new priorities within the new executive team, Donlon introduced a new compensation scheme whereby bonuses from 15 percent to 35 percent of salary are given after specific performance goals are met.

Perhaps Donlon's most productive move was to establish a new relationship between Niagara and its customers and regulators. Rather than litigating for new rate increases, Niagara negotiated.

> In two years of talks with the New York State Public Service Commission, he reestablished mutual trust and hammered out an innovative deal: If Niagara meets stringent targets on issues ranging from environmental responsibility to cost reductions and customer service, the government will lift the ceiling it normally sets on utility profits by up to $190 million over five years.

The results? Donlon's company qualified to receive $30 million in extra profit over the first half of 1991, and customer complaints to the Public Service Commission have dropped by 27 percent.

A Salomon Brothers analyst reported on the progress Niagara was making, shortly after the better results started to become evident:

> Niagara's management recognized that they could not continue as an uncaring monopolist providing merely adequate service in a cost-plus rate environment. So instead of a surface change, they made a deep, lasting change.

PARADIGM PIONEERS

Change protagonists are "paradigm shifters." They challenge the contemporary enterprise practices and habit patterns. In his book, *Future Edge: Discovering the New Paradigms of Success,* Joel Arthur Barker categorizes paradigm shifters as typically belonging to the following groups:

1. *A young person fresh out of training*—someone who has studied the existing paradigm but has never practiced it. This person may be an entrepreneurial type along the lines of Federal Express's Fred Smith, or Apple's Steve Jobs and Steve Wozniak.

2. *An older person shifting fields*—someone who brings operational naïveté about the new field and doesn't know what "can't be done." This person often asks "dumb" questions, combined with creativity. Dr. Alex Mueller was the 1987 Nobel Prize cowinner for superconductivity, but his specialty was in physics.

3. *The maverick*—usually an insider who understands that the present paradigm will not work, and who leads the charge for change. This person is knowledgeable about the paradigm but not captured by it. Paul Galvin, founder of Motorola, first developed car radios. But his son, Robert, took the company out of consumer electronics and into integrated chips.

4. *The tinkerer*—someone who runs into a special problem with the current paradigm and devises an innovative solution. Almond B. Strowger, a Kansas City undertaker, lost business because the local telephone operator's husband was a competitor; she routed all the calls for an undertaker to her spouse. Out of frustration with this circumstance, he developed and patented the automatic switching system that took the operator out of the loop in directing calls.

Resistance to new paradigms comes from those who have the most to lose. Barker observes:

New paradigms put everyone practicing the old paradigm at great risk. The higher one's position, the greater the risk. The better you are at your paradigm, the more you have invested in it, the more you have to lose by changing paradigms.

Paradigm pioneers also face these additional dilemmas:

- *New paradigms can both solve problems and create new ones.* Sometimes, new paradigms open up new complications while offering solutions to others.

- *Paradigm shifters are usually outsiders.* A paradigm shifter is often a "black sheep" who doesn't play by the old rules. The enterprise at large finds it easy to isolate and ignore the change being suggested by the "outsider."

- *Paradigm pioneers will never have enough proof to make a "rational judgment" in the eyes of their resisters.* Pioneers will choose to change the paradigm because they trust their intuition. However, no matter what kind of proof the paradigm shifter can offer the "hard core" resister, it will not convince him or her that the change is logical.

Unitel Communications Inc. (Canada) is an interesting example of the complex interrelationships that must be managed to successfully introduce new management patterns into a traditionally run enterprise.

In June 1992, the end of Bell Canada's monopoly of the long-distance telephone market launched companies such as Unitel into a completely new area of business. Prior to that date, Unitel was restricted to providing only specialized business communication services, such as private lines and data links. Changes in telecommunications regulations provided the opportunity for Unitel to establish a network to serve the "mass market" of homes and businesses across Canada.

These changes were indeed challenging, "but none of the upheaval is more daunting than Unitel's internal shakeup," insists George Harvey, president and chief executive. "Changing our culture is more challenging than taking on Bell Canada." Before 1990, Unitel was known as CNCP Telecommunications, owned by the century-old Canadian National Railways and Canadian Pacific Railway Company. The parent company, perhaps understandably, was old-fashioned, with a "highly centralized and bureaucratic" organizational structure. The corporate culture was engineering-oriented and male-dominated, and decisions often took a long time to be made.

Harvey took over the reins of the company in 1987, just as its Telex business was beginning to take a nose dive. Demands for the then-new fax technology were sounding a death knell. When the telephone rang at CNCP Telecommunications offices, more often than not, it was to cancel existing service contracts.

> Mr. Harvey set to work on four goals for the company: to revitalize products and services; to build a modern communications network; to reduce the cost structure; and to establish a new culture focusing on market needs.

In late 1988, the company launched a discount fax service, some two years ahead of the phone companies. Then, Harvey reorganized the sales and marketing departments into three regional groups whose purpose was to better solve customer problems.

New managers joining the company, however, found it to still be an "old boys' network." Paradigm Consulting Inc., Unitel's consultants, described the company as a classic example of "functional chimneys" separating departments from each other and from their external customers. Following two years of study, Paradigm unveiled the new organizational model for Unitel.

Customer support groups were assigned a key role, with cross-functional teams organized around categories of clients, such as finance and banking, or around geographic territories. Support staff were moved out of Toronto to regional offices, thereby cutting down on the time needed to process orders. Three layers of middle management at the head office were eliminated. Client service employees embraced quality improvement programs to root out the causes of problems they were previously working overtime to correct.

Through all these measures, Unitel's service performance has improved. The monthly failure rate of its lines fell almost seven percentage points, from 11 percent in 1989 to 4.1 percent in 1992. And when a line does go dead, the average time to repair the problem has been slashed from 9 hours to 3.2 hours. Revenue rose to nearly $400 million in 1992, up from $283 million in 1988. Unitel has reduced staffing costs by offering retirement incentives. Personnel count was reduced by more than 400 people to 3,200 in 1988, then reduced again to 2,600 by late 1990. Revenue per employee was $90,000 in 1988; in 1992, it was up to $150,000. Unitel's costs per employee are among the lowest in the North American telephone industry; five years ago, they were among the worst.

To create a more customer-oriented culture, Unitel:

- Reassessed its strategy, establishing the primacy of customer service as the central enterprise value to guide employees;

- Revamped the organizational structure and analyzed all job functions to determine which tasks could be restructured or eliminated;

- Downsized through voluntary buy-outs, often accepted by those employees most resistant to change;

- Recruited new blood from successful market-driven companies, but also promoted enthusiasts of change from within;

- Reduced hierarchy and allowed multidisciplinary teams in sales and product development to be responsible for customer and market needs;

- Placed service and quality at the core of all procedures and policies, and trained staff to understand the use of standardized measurements and software.

Innovation . . . Again!

Being open to change is the secret to successful innovation, as discussed in Touchstone Eight. In *Winning the Innovation Game,* Denis E. Waitley and Robert B. Tucker explain why innovators prosper: they *welcome* change rather than resist it; they have learned how to make change work for them rather than against them; and they have developed a unique set of skills that enables them to create opportunities.

> There's nothing mysterious about why innovators benefit from change. They are creating some of it themselves. Like surfers, they ride the Wave, using its power to take them where they want to go. Rather than trying to resist change, they seek to harmonize with it.

Here's a list of the "ten secret skills" of paradigm pioneers:

1. *Innovators are opportunity-oriented.* They search for unsolved problems, market inefficiencies, unmet wants and needs, and new customer groups.

2. *Innovators are strategists.* They attempt to anticipate the future in order to maximize their ability to thrive and prosper in that future; they continually define and redefine their goals, and have well-developed but flexible plans to reach them.

3. *Innovators "unhook" their prejudices.* To better solve problems and create opportunities, they constantly rid their thinking of preconceived beliefs, biases, thinking ruts, and unchallenged assumptions.

4. *Innovators are trend-spotters.* They monitor change—social, attitudinal, and technological—to spot new opportunities before everyone else; they look at where things are headed and try to imagine the "big picture."

5. *Innovators are idea-oriented.* They constantly generate ideas, borrow concepts from other fields, and develop and experiment with new ideas.

6. *Innovators rely on intuition.* They assess risks, read people, spot emerging patterns of change, and make complex decisions.

7. *Innovators are extraordinarily persistent.* They are willing to "face the heat" in pursuit of their dreams; their passion for ideas helps them overcome what might otherwise be roadblocks; they are long-term thinkers.

8. *Innovators are resourceful.* Their skill and persistence at gathering strategic information knock down walls to implementing new ideas; they realize that specialized, state-of-the-art knowledge and insight are key in today's "innovation age."

9. *Innovators are feedback-oriented.* They constantly poll their customer group to determine how products and services can be improved; feedback is used as a "checks and balances" mechanism, guiding their decisions and helping them avoid prejudices.

10. *Innovators are superior team builders.* They need teams to help them implement ideas; sometimes rely on the support networks of fellow professionals, mentors, friends, and advisers.

ROLES IN THE CHANGE PROCESS

Four principal roles are involved in the change process. Most people are not aware of these roles, nor of how they must be played out in order to effect successful change. The roles are: (1) the change patron, the individual or group who legitimizes the change; (2) the change catalyst, the individual or group who is responsible for implementing the change; (3) the change target, the individual or group who must actually make the change; and (4) the change booster, the individual or group who wants to achieve change but does not have the appropriate authority to legitimize it.

"The biggest single factor contributing to the failure of change projects is the lack of commitment by people in these primary roles." All of these roles must be played out in concert with each other for the change process to run as smoothly as possible. For example, the patron may be the CEO, the catalyst may be in middle management, and the target may be the front-line supervisor. Individuals within the enterprise may take turns wearing each "hat." Some projects may require you to wear your patron hat; others, your target hat; still others, your catalyst hat.

It is important to understand how the relationships among the roles can help, or hinder, the change process:

1. *The linear relationship:* This is the usual management chain of command. The target reports to the catalyst, and the catalyst reports to the patron. The patron delegates responsibility to the catalyst, who in turn deals directly with the target to ensure that the change occurs. This is easy to implement in a hierarchical structure because everyone is used to these roles in the normal course of doing business. Problems arise, however, if the patron and catalyst misread the effect of change on targets and underestimate the degree of resistance that will be encountered.

2. *The triangular relationship:* These relationships are complicated and usually fail. The catalyst and target both work for a common patron, but the target does not report to the catalyst. This is the classic situation that exists when the patrons are senior executives, the targets are line managers, and the catalysts are in a support function, such as human resources or information systems. Why does this fail? Because when catalysts tell targets who don't report to them what to do, resentment and a lack of cooperation are often the responses. This can work if the patron, target, and catalyst are highly evolved individuals who understand the dynamics that govern triangular relationships, but that doesn't happen very often.

3. *The square relationship:* Dysfunctional change management relationships are created when catalysts report to one patron and the targets to another. The problem this creates is that patron 1 may direct a catalyst to bypass patron 2 and go directly to the targets. But targets rarely respond to major change directives unless these directives come from their specific patron.

A familiar illustration of this pattern occurs when a company vice president of budget and finance asks one of his or her financial officers to go to the firm's marketing manager and insist on new cost-cutting procedures. This just won't work. Instead, the vice president of budget and finance should have his financial officer propose the change to the vice president of sales and marketing. That vice president should then discuss the proposed changes with his or her marketing manager.

The transforming of the Communist world is an example of how understanding change management roles can give clearer insight into why some change efforts succeed when seemingly similar campaigns fail. In 1989, both Communist China and the former Soviet Union had millions of boosters for change, but each country experienced radically different results.

In the former Soviet Union, newly elected representatives openly challenged the old Communist regime, including the man at the helm, Mikhail Gorbachev. Not only was the Soviet leadership allowing dissent, it was encouraging it. In China, students struggled for these same rights of free speech and democracy, but were powerless because there were no patrons for these changes. In both countries, the boosters demanded a loosening of authoritarian control and a promise of freer enterprise. Because the former Soviet Union had patrons supporting the new ways, the boosters for change became both catalysts and targets, and the Soviet government was transformed. In China, there were no patrons, and the powerless boosters were suppressed instead.

The U.S. health reform movement is another example. American citizens, unhappy with their current system, have been previously as powerless to change their health care system as the Chinese students were in Tiananmen Square. They had no patrons for their cause. However, with the election of President Clinton, these once-powerless boosters became influential because the necessary patrons assumed positions of power. Insurance companies and the health care providers have now become change targets, and the government health departments President Clinton seeks to create will become the change catalyst, pushing for change in the health care system.

CHARGING AHEAD WITH CHANGE

To achieve effective and positive change within your enterprise, you need a proven plan. Many methodologies are offered by those who specialize in assisting executives in the change process. However, most change management approaches can be boiled down to the four basic phases shown in Figure 9.1:

1. Evaluate;
2. Design;
3. Activate;
4. Rejuvenate.

Let's take a closer look at each of these phases.

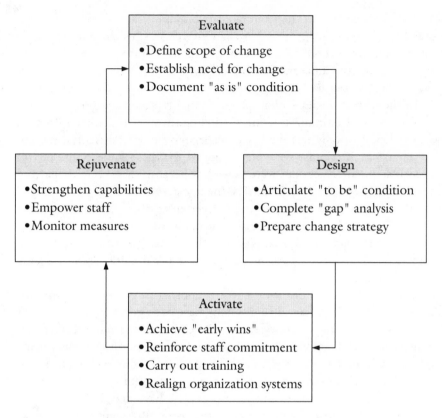

Figure 9.1   Change management plan.

1. *Evaluate:* Define and understand the scope of the desired change; establish the context that creates the need to change; establish the "as is" baseline condition; and outline the change plan.

The initial step in this phase is to obtain the view of major patrons and stakeholders. It is especially important to define and understand the external pressures that are causing the need for change. A workshop involving the key parties should follow, to complete initial preplanning work. The end result of "scoping" the change effort is to better understand the enterprise's "readiness for change" and produce a "change map" that outlines each anticipated phase in the process.

The second step is to define a baseline, the "as is" condition of the enterprise. Establishing the baseline entails: building relationships with patrons and securing commitments; understanding the political coalitions; assembling backers and supporters; and ascertaining financial impacts. You'll also need to assess the mindset of key players, the organizational culture, key organizational systems, and business strategy alignment issues. Most importantly, you will need to understand key areas of actual or potential resistance to change.

The evaluate phase is complete when you've secured the appropriate patron commitment, the "as is" condition is clearly understood, and you've established the measures of success.

2. *Design:* Frame the "to be" condition; conduct gap analysis; articulate the compelling need; and identify and document your strategy.

The design phase comprises the steps necessary to develop a shared vision of what the enterprise will be like after the change is successfully completed. To do this, you'll need to conduct with patrons a visioning process that clarifies the change initiative, articulates why the "as is" condition is untenable, and defines change management roles and responsibilities.

Next, you must bridge the gap between the baseline condition and the future, or between "as is" and "to be." Conduct an analysis to determine patron commitment, the necessary change management skills of catalysts, target resistance, and current cultural alignment with the proposed changes.

Finally, define your strategy for change. Will you start with pilot projects, or create the changes throughout the enterprise? Will you implement changes quickly or gradually? Will you work with existing structures or create new ones? Will the changes you propose be mandatory or voluntary? What will be your process for feedback and communication of the change activities?

3. *Activate:* Create quick successes; support and reinforce commitment; build employee resilience; train; and align organizational systems.

During this phase, it's important to achieve some early successes. Select first some change targets that have a vested interest in the goals of the change program. Seek out allies for support and make sure they understand the rationale for change. Management consultants with Coopers & Lybrand recommend the following guidelines to reinforce commitment during your "rollout" of the change process:

- Plan change in ways that benefit targets:
    —Increase the targets' control over job tasks;
    —Frame change in ways that enhance the targets' self-image;
    —Ensure quick, visible results.
- Involve targets in the change process:
    —Ask for suggestions before implementation (use the targets as consultants to the change program);

—Specify milestones for seeking target feedback;

—Institute methods for gaining feedback (focus groups, surveys, feedback sheets);

—Publicize the way suggestions are being used;

—Build-in incentives for innovation and change.

Try to limit the number of changes attempted so as not to overwhelm departments, and make sure that the reasons why a change is necessary are well communicated.

Implement training that will create the job skills you need to support the new ways of working. Avoid complicated, mass training events; instead, organize training sessions into smaller, more productive groups that emphasize the specific tasks the participants need to learn or improve. Understand the appropriate balance between directive management styles and participatory approaches to secure successful change. Align reward and recognition systems to support the change objectives.

4. *Rejuvenate:* Build capabilities; empower people; and establish change measures.

Rejuvenating is the "people phase" of the change process. You'll need to implement all of the elements discussed in Touchstone Four: empowerment, new types of rewards and recognition systems, continuous training, and so on. The challenge of this part of the change process is to strengthen the core competencies of the organization to cope with future change. This requires providing training opportunities to strengthen team effectiveness, change planning skills, and leadership. Finally, you'll need to adopt a measurement strategy that tells you whether your change initiative is staying on track. Consider measuring the following:

- Internal and external customer satisfaction as affected by the changes made in operating systems and styles;
- The level of patron commitment over time to monitor the level of energy and momentum of the leadership group;
- The level of skills of designated change catalysts;
- Employee capacity to cope with changes;
- Budget and time targets for the change.

Simulating the anticipated change is an excellent way to begin the overall process. It enables those affected to "experience" the change and become more comfortable with new ways of working before the new methods are put in place permanently. One consulting company offers a simulation exercise designed to help participants get a feel for some of the issues that could arise during the change process.

> A high-energy teambuilding exercise which allows participants to experience the effects of non-collaborative team behavior and to then use the insights gained during the simulation to define their vision and the supporting actions for becoming a high-performing team.

BEWARE OF "BLACK HOLES"

In the change management vocabulary, "black holes" are gaps in the enterprise that swallow up the change rhetoric, leaving no trace. In astrophysics, the term black holes refers to areas in space that have a gravitational pull so strong that everything gets sucked down into them—even light! Similar "gravitational pulls" within every enterprise suck into them changes in policy or structure.

ODR's Daryl Connor explains:

> There are spots in the corporate universe that exert the same effect; it is common for management rhetoric to go into bureaucratic structures and then vanish without a trace. . . . Like the black hole in space that captures everything that travels in its vicinity, various levels of management withhold or distort information so that it doesn't get to the rest of the organization. Without proper information dissemination, change will fail.

The cure for black holes is to understand and utilize the role and power of the change patron. The change process will move ahead or bog down as a direct result of how effectively the patron is sanctioning change. When this is not done well, the organization loses confidence in its leadership. The change targets begin to believe management cannot successfully fulfill the promise of change, and learn to ignore change initiatives. The reaction becomes: "Don't worry, this will pass."

> If an initiating sponsor assumes that a major change will sail through the organization without his or her continual guidance, that change is doomed. The initiating sponsor must be able to enlist the support of sustaining sponsors down in the organization, or the change will fail.

To escape the power of black holes, be very clear about following the rules for each player in the change process:

- *Patrons:* Don't take on more changes than you can effectively support. Your physical and political resources are limited. Allocate these carefully, and follow through. If you sustain several change failures, people will start to ignore your leadership.

- *Catalysts:* Don't take on a change if your patron is unwilling to provide the necessary support and resolve. When your patron can't or won't make the effort to legitimize the change, you are headed for failure.

- *Targets:* Don't get involved in a big change if you don't understand your role and how the change will affect you, or if you suspect the patron's commitment is insufficient to see the change through.

- *Boosters:* Don't become blinded by your enthusiasm for the change. Success depends on the committed support of patrons, more than anything else.

In summary, the onus is on leaders to make the change process as smooth and efficient as possible. Here are some guidelines:

1. *Reduce uncertainty:* Conduct informal question-and-answer sessions with employees; actively listen to employees to gauge their early response; use memos and on-the-spot sessions to provide "emergency" response to unexpected resistance; secure and publicize commitment from top management; as much as possible, show what the change entails; train employees about new equipment or methods needed.

2. *Secure a commitment:* Elicit employee involvement; if you are an "outsider," link up with influential employees and managers; demonstrate expertise with new technologies; if the work force is unionized, approach the union leadership before they approach you, and provide full information about the change effort; if the change requires new knowledge or skills, continue the training effort.

3. *Issue a challenge:* Use a company newsletter to issue a challenge; install a formal method, such as an incentive program, to motivate employees; enlist influential employees to monitor improvements; provide telling evidence that change is needed, possibly using comparative data on the company's industry standing; supply employees with objective information that supports the need for change.

4. *Forge a single agenda:* Make sure your management is supportive of the targeted changes, and replace resisting managers if necessary. Identify the functional area or department most directly affected by the change; analyze the link to other functions; determine how other areas will influence and will be influenced by the change; communicate the findings to lead managers in other function areas, making sure they understand the nature and consequences of the change.

5. *Implement fairness:* Change threatens the status quo. It creates a feeling of uncertainty. It calls on people to learn new skills and to assume

new responsibilities. At every stage of the change process, employees will be on guard, evaluating and eventually deciding whether the demands placed on them are excessive. Be conscious of the need not only to be fair to those involved in change, but also to be seen as dealing equitably with all affected parties.

In the end, successful change is the result of effective leadership. However, the leadership skills needed for the value decade are different from traditional patterns. As discussed next, a "new spirit" of leadership is necessary for the high-performing enterprise.

TOUCHSTONE
10

The New Spirit
of Leadership

*There is a great man who makes every man feel small. But
the real great man is the man who makes every man feel
great.*

G.K. Chesterton

How is the high-performing enterprise created? It is the product of determined leaders who are unwilling to accept the status quo. Promoting a new
enterprise vision, new values, and new ways of managing employees; serving
customers; and communicating the need for change—all will require specific
leadership behaviors from the pacesetters in your organization. In fact, one
study of successful transformations of corporate culture concluded: "The
single most visible factor that distinguishes major cultural changes that succeed from those that fail is competent leadership at the top."

This theme is echoed in the remarks of David M. Culver, President of
Alcan, one of the largest resource-based companies in North America.
When first appointed president, he says, the best advice he received was
from a close colleague: "Don't be too full of yourself. Lots of people can
run Alcan, but very few can change it."

The trendsetters in the high-performing enterprise will not always be
those in formal positions of authority. Employees at all levels of the organization will be called on to take on the role of "change agent"; they must
master leading from the "middle," creating the "revolution from within."

The tenth competency of the high-performing enterprise is the ability to
cultivate the leadership attitudes and skills necessary for the value decade.

This competency requires an understanding of the role of leadership in the change process, insight into the talents that must be acquired, and the courage to continually assess your current level of mastery or seek improvement.

Peter Drucker believes that the foundation of leadership is thinking through the organization's mission—defining it and establishing it clearly and visibly. The leader sets the goals, arranges the priorities, and states and maintains the standards. Drucker also feels that a true leader sees leadership as a responsibility, not as a rank or privilege. The effective leader is rarely "permissive"; when things go wrong, yet the effective leader never blames others. The effective leader is not afraid of strength in associates or subordinates; their triumphs and mistakes are the leader's as well.

In the *Total Quality Newsletter,* Hyler Bracey and Warren Smith report that more "meaningful" relationships between the leader and his or her followers are gaining popularity in the business world.

> It's hard to tell if we're creating a "kinder, gentler nation," but there seems to be movement toward a kinder, gentler workplace. The movement is being led by a new breed of leader who understands the power of managing with both compassion and accountability.

The old-paradigm enterprises too often forced employees to hold back their real gifts and creative thinking. The new social contract between employers and employees features the following two tenets:

1. *Meaningful work:* "People are no longer content to be cogs in the wheel. They want to know that what they do makes a difference in the world." The leader, in a vision that goes far beyond next quarter's profits, must articulate: "Why are you in business, and what value does your product or service bring to the world?"

2. *Healthy relationships:* A Fortune 500 company recently researched why its brightest, most creative employees were leaving. Why was the "regretted turnover" rate so high? Poor relationship with the boss was the number-one reason cited. "The best people won't put up with destructive relationships. They want not just bosses, but mentors and leaders; not just coworkers, but colleagues and friends."

Bracey and Smith report that employees have five unspoken requests that, if honored, will allow work relationships to flourish:

1. *"Hear and understand me."* Listening is a powerful way to show employees their input is valuable.

2. *"Even if you disagree with me, please don't make me wrong."* Disagreements should center around the ideas, not the person.

3. *"Acknowledge the greatness within me."* A person's greatness is the sum total of his or her talents, experiences, and abilities. By fully utilizing a person's "greatness," a powerful competitive advantage is created for the organization.

4. *"Remember to look for my loving intentions."* People doing the wrong thing often intend to do something right; looking for the good intentions can encourage further risk-taking and innovation even after initial mistakes occur.

5. *"Tell me the truth with compassion."* Give feedback that is specific and grounded in fact so the individual can learn from their experience.

"The best managers confront people with hard truths, but they do it with great skill and compassion." Honoring these five unspoken requests is "managing from the heart"; it's a style of management based on high levels of compassion and accountability, a "new spirit of leadership" that leads to growth, motivation, and innovation.

WHEN LEADERS ARE AT THEIR BEST

What do successful leaders spend their time on? In the value decade, where knowledge workers are becoming the key members of the work force, helping them reach personal "peak performance" is clearly an important task. In their book, *The Leadership Challenge: How to Get Extraordinary Things Done in Organizations,* James M. Kouzes and Barry Z. Posner report on some interesting research into leadership. They asked leaders to describe when they have been "at their best," and they polled "followers" to identify effective leadership practices from that point of view.

> As we looked deeper into this dynamic process, through the case analyses and survey questionnaires, we uncovered five fundamental practices that enabled these leaders to get extraordinary things done. When they were at their personal best, our leaders:
>
> 1. Challenged the process.
> 2. Inspired a shared vision.
> 3. Enabled others to act.
> 4. Modeled the way.
> 5. Encouraged the heart.

When they *challenged the process,* the leaders searched for opportunities; they experimented and took risks. They played an active role; none of them waited for fate to smile on them. People who lead others to greatness create some kind of challenge: an innovation, a turnaround, or a reorganization.

> Leaders are pioneers—people who are willing to step out into the unknown. They are people who are willing to take risks, to innovate and experiment in order to find new and better ways of doing things.

They may not be the original innovators of a new product, service, or process, but they are responsible for cultivating the attitudes that promote innovative ideas in employees, suppliers, or customers. Effective leaders recognize good ideas, support them, and then challenge the system so that these innovations will get adopted. Leaders are able to learn from both successes and mistakes.

When Stanley Gault, Chairman of Goodyear, arrived on the scene, the tire company was burdened by $3.7 billion in debt and trying to cope with a decline in sales. Gault had come from Rubbermaid, a company he had successfully revitalized. He took on a similar leadership role at Goodyear: he assembled teams to complete work on stalled new products, and he kept his door wide open for complaints or suggestions on how to make the company better. Under his leadership, Goodyear has introduced successful products such as the Aquatread tire, which helps prevent skidding on wet roads (hydroplaning). Says Gault: "The teams at Goodyear are now telling the boss how to run things. And I must say, I'm not doing a half-bad job because of it."

When they *inspired a shared vision,* leaders had to envision the future and get involved with enlisting the support of others.

> Every organization, every social movement begins with a dream. The dream or vision is the force that invents the future. Leaders spend considerable effort gazing across the horizon of time, imagining what it will be like when they have arrived at their final destinations. Some call it vision; others describe it as a purpose, mission, goal, even personal agenda. Regardless of what we call it, there is a desire to make something happen, to change the way things are, to create something that no one else has ever created before.

Leaders breathe life into the hopes and dreams of others and help them see future possibilities. No example of this type of leadership outshines Dr. Martin Luther King. Everyone who was old enough to watch television in 1964 remembers his "I have a dream" speech. This is a classic inspiring-the-vision address. What makes the speech so uniquely universal is that it is inclusive, not divisive, to all who heard it.

> I have a dream that one day men will be no longer judged by the color of their skin but the content of their character.

Leaders must understand the needs of the followers and have their interests at heart; only then can the leaders enlist the followers' support. When they have *enabled others to act,* effective leaders have fostered collaboration and strengthened others. This is crucial to ensuring the success of the entire enterprise.

> Exemplary leaders enlist the support and assistance of all those who must make the project work. They involve, in some way, those who must live with the results, and they make it possible for others to do good work. They encourage collaboration, build teams, and empower others.

This sense of teamwork goes beyond subordinates to include peers, superiors, customers, and suppliers.

> The effect of enabling others to act is to make them feel strong, capable and committed. Those in the organization who must produce the results feel a sense of ownership. They feel empowered, and when people feel empowered, they are more likely to use their energies to produce extraordinary results.

When they *modeled the way,* outstanding leaders set the example, plan small wins, and have detailed plans to implement the vision; they steered projects, measured performance, raised funds, and took corrective action.

> In order to lead by example, leaders must first be clear about their business beliefs. Managers may speak eloquently about vision and values, but if their behavior is not consistent with their stated beliefs, people ultimately will lose respect for them.

Being a role model means showing others that you live your values. Olin Corporation learned this lesson when attempting to implement total quality management practices in 1989. Olin found that, to create a culture that valued quality, senior managers had to lead by example. The company's senior managers discovered they were living in a "fishbowl." To serve as role models, they needed to "walk their talk." Their words and actions were observed closely by employees, who were quick to expose any bogus behavior.

In addition, Olin managers found they had to be prepared to be held accountable for problems within the organization, and to acknowledge their personal responsibility for improving quality. To meet this higher standard of leadership, the Olin executives began to conduct employee surveys to get feedback on their leadership behavior. This method offered employees a forum to express opinions and make suggestions.

Leaders who *encouraged the heart* celebrated successes and offered encouragement; leaders must love their products, their people, their customers, and their work. "People do not start their work each day with a desire to lose. It is part of the leader's job to show them that they can win."

Those who become the best leaders take advantage of the broadest possible range of opportunities. They try, fail, and learn from their mistakes. Leaders develop best when they are enthusiastic participants in change.

When leaders followed the five fundamental principles described above, they were seen by others to: have a higher degree of personal credibility; be more effective in meeting job-related demands; be more successful in representing their units to upper management; have higher performing teams.

LEADERSHIP SKILLS FOR THE VALUE DECADE

Kouzes and Posner's leadership principles are insightful, but perhaps not specific enough in pinpointing the skills your organization's "trail blazers" need. The leader needs to develop a repertoire in the following areas:

1. *Anticipatory skills: leader as prophet:* Effective leaders are expected to "see the future." To do so, they keep themselves open to a wide range of information sources. Richard E. Byrd, in writing on the skills of the leader, observes:

> Foresight is fundamental to leadership. An effective leader intuitively and systematically scans the environment for potential areas of exposure to new historical risks. To develop anticipatory skills, a manager must accept that the world is constantly changing.

Leaders with these skills also focus their attention on the people around them. They excel at networking with constituents throughout the organization, helping them to better sense future trends and build stronger coalitions. Leaders must also be able to anticipate defeat and disappointment, then help their people deal with these issues.

> Anticipatory skills, then, entail projecting consequences, risks, and tradeoffs (having foresight); actively seeking to be informed and to inform (scanning/communicating); and proactively establishing work relationships (building trust and influence).

These abilities allow the leader to keep staff up-to-date on situations in other functions, explain the rationale behind company decisions, and articulate how those decisions affect them, while educating key people about new ideas.

The successful leader in the 1990s will:

- Define success by the rate of improvement. Perpetuating the status quo is unacceptable.

- Ensure that all employees share a consistent purpose that they believe is worthy of their commitment. Slogans, theme programs, and corporate visions that change annually can create more cynicism than commitment.

- Make sure that everyone in the organization plays to win (to create memorable, unique experiences for customers through better listening, constant experimentation, and strategic risk taking) instead of playing not to lose (avoiding responsibility, blame, and mistakes).

- Make excellent performance mandatory. Encourage marginal performers to either perform better or leave.

- Constantly focus on the education and development of all people in the organization, from the chairman to the newest front-line employee. Continuous improvement requires every employee to focus on innovation and improvement. It will demand unprecedented education efforts as we encourage every person to focus on tomorrow's questions instead of learning from yesterday's answers.

- Involve customers and suppliers actively in every aspect of the improvement effort, from design of the customer information system to employee education.

- Develop trust among managers and employees, based on widely shared information. Destroy the "need to know" mentality that ensures that only managers know what's going on.

- Ensure that change is not only accepted but is viewed as a competitive opportunity and as a chance to learn and grow.

2. *Visioning skills: leader as navigator:* It's the job of leaders to establish "creative tension," the result of the perceived "gap" between where the organization wants to be (the vision) and where the organization is at present (the current reality). Creative tension can be resolved by either raising current reality toward the vision, or lowering the vision toward current reality. Author and consultant Peter Senge explains: "The principle of creative tension teaches that an accurate picture of current reality is just as important as a compelling picture of a desired future."

Helping your staff to create a "future vision" for themselves is often a matter of posing the right kind of questions. At Harley Davidson, the "HWIKIIISI" acronym stands for: "How would I know it if I saw it?" Managers use this question to help employees envision a successful outcome. At the Tomahawk, Wisconsin, plant, which makes painted fiberglass parts that eventually get used in producing Harley Davidson motorcycles, managers and supervisors looking for improvements asked questions such as:

If the plant were perfect, how would the customer–supplier relationship work? As a supplier of parts to Harley assembly plants, how should Tomahawk communicate with its internal customers?

After considering these questions, workers decided to focus on improving customer service and the quality of the product. The employees decided that some jobs and production processes needed to be redesigned in order to get closer to their "vision." Impressive improvements were made in less than one year. The plant reduced quality problems dramatically, reduced work-in-progress time (the time it takes for a given product to go through the plant from start to finish) from two and a half days to less than 16 hours, and reduced "float" (the average time a motorcycle in production is pulled off the line waiting for a Tomahawk piece) from 22 days to less than two days.

The long-term vision that provides the enterprise with its sense of direction is a result of thoughtful consideration. The effective leader takes such thinking seriously. Working on the "vision thing," as former President George Bush put it, is one of the leader's primary responsibilities. David R. Gaster, in his essay, "A Framework for Visionary Leadership," observes:

> One of the characteristics that distinguishes outstanding leaders is that they have thought deeply and seriously about the kind of business they want to be running. . . . They have become aware that the leader's task is to create a world to which people want to belong; that all the attention paid to details, to tasks, and to fast decisions while climbing the ranks now needs to be balanced by a much larger and longer view. They have realized that there are many factors that set the tone of the company, and many possible actions to affect it. The key to the company's sense of identity and vision is the person of the leader. . . . Leaders who are able to operate effectively at this level are frequently described as visionary.

3. *Empowerment skills: the keys to the kingdom:* Federal Express is an example of "a company that regularly underlines its culture of empowerment by publicizing heroics its employees perform." Fed Ex knows that people want to do a good job and will do so if they are properly trained and know what is expected of them. The company regularly asks employees for advice on how to improve processes, and it rewards employees with bonuses for both individual and team high performance.

Tennant Company, a Minneapolis-based manufacturer of floor sweepers and scrubbers, began to focus on quality improvement in the early 1980s. The company was quick to jump on the empowerment/enablement bandwagon. "It quickly realized employee involvement was the key to the improvements it needed to make to remain a viable competitor in an increasingly global marketplace." Since that time, it has built processes that encourage and reward employees for taking responsibility; the company suggestion system gives individuals, or teams, 30 percent of the first year's savings that result from their cost-cutting suggestions.

As a result of this encouragement, a group of machinists came up with a way to improve the machining process on an aluminum casting for one of the company's sweepers; the old method took three days and the new method took three hours. The group determined how to reduce setup time, increase capacity, reduce lead time and inventory, and deliver more consistent quality.

> . . . A manager should allow employees to share the satisfaction derived from achievement. It involves developing lower levels of leadership to take the initiative downward and outward throughout the organization.

The experience of Chrysler Corporation teaches us that sometimes leaders can become blinded by their vision and ignore the "nuts and bolts" of the business. In particular, it is important that the "vision" not overwhelm the voices of the people within the enterprise. Chrysler's current chairman, Robert Eaton, is a firm believer in keeping vision "short." He says:

> Internally, we don't use the word vision. I believe in quantifiable short-term results—things we can all relate to—as opposed to some esoteric thing no one can quantify.

Eaton is the polar opposite to Chrysler's former chairman, Lee Iacocca, when it comes to leadership. Observes one writer on Iacocca's style:

> Far from being a good listener, Mr. Iacocca often couldn't stop talking. A candidate for high post at Chrysler tells of being interviewed by Mr. Iacocca. The Chrysler boss, he says, asked and answered his own questions so quickly that the candidate was able to utter a single word—"Well, . . . "—the entire time.

Eaton, a very different kind of guide, is perceived by Chrysler employees as both a "coach" and a good listener. Eaton eschews "power leadership" behavior and instead supports teamwork. Eaton's style is very casual. He often just "drops in" on employees at all levels of the organization, jacketless, just to chat. He has even been known to answer the telephone on his own! Eaton's leadership is "down home." As a result, employees are inspired; they feel they can relate to Eaton. Because Eaton does "walk his talk," he has created a kind of "trickle-down behavior modification," as one Chrysler VP phrased it, encouraging others to follow his empowering style. The result? People at Chrysler have renewed enthusiasm. Says Theodore Cunningham, VP Sales and Marketing, "Eaton lets you run your business."

4. *Value-congruence skills: walking your talk:* The importance of being able to demonstrate values such as trust, respect, teamwork, integrity, and commitment to quality are critical abilities in the value decade.

> Value-congruence skills entail knowing and understanding the organization's guiding beliefs, being willing to act consistently as a person of principle, and having and using the ability to teach others the organization's values.

One of the greatest pitfalls for an enterprise leader is inconsistent demonstration of personal values, resulting in a credibility gap, accusations of hypocrisy, and cynicism on the part of employees. Values must be translated into daily behaviors. Day-to-day decision making should be guided by organizational values and beliefs, and significant time should be spent communicating these values to the employees. Leaders should also challenge colleagues when inconsistencies in values arise.

These skill sets can enable the leader to act as a true change agent. He or she can shift paradigms through personal example. Writer Charles F. Kiefer points out that the most famous leaders in history had the ability to inspire people to follow them, in large part, because of a public commitment to a set of clear values.

> All great leaders stand for something. They have defined some value, issue or purpose to be of overriding importance to them. For Martin Luther King, Jr., it was freedom and civil rights. For John F. Kennedy, it was democracy and America's destiny. For Gandhi, it was freedom in India. Each of these men embodied a strong commitment to his vision. His life spirit was involved in it. Because of their commitment, others were willing to commit themselves under the leadership of these men.

A more recent example of commitment to "purpose" is Dr. Don Francis, formerly of the Centers for Disease Control. Dr. Francis fought for the screening of blood products in the early 1980s, after watching the spread of the HIV virus into the hemophiliac population. Francis took on the blood product industry, which appeared to be more interested in profit than in safety. Eventually, through his persistence and commitment to a single goal, he managed to influence the passing of legislation that required blood products to be screened for the virus.

5. *Self-understanding skills: accepting imperfection:* "For a leader, self-understanding is critical. Without it, leaders may do more harm than good." Leaders should be eager to get feedback on their performance. By knowing their own weaknesses, they can surround themselves with people who can compensate for those limitations.

Self-understanding skills entail being willing to search for personal identity and growth, appreciating that personal ego strength is a requirement for leading, being open to feedback and other performance data, and having a frame of reference by which to understand and arouse motivation.

Here is a checklist to help you pinpoint the personality traits essential for leading in the value decade:

- A passion for seeking new knowledge to improve self and others.
- A strong sense of self; comfort with one's own strengths and weaknesses.
- A firm anchoring in humanistic values; strong personal integrity.
- An ability to see beyond "what is" to "what could be"; a strong sense of purpose.
- A commitment to unite the organization under a shared vision of the future.
- A belief in people and their abilities; a commitment to draw out the best in others.
- An understanding of human behavior and how to influence others; diplomacy.

CREATING A LEADER

Are leaders "born that way" or can leadership skills be taught? This debate has raged for decades. Casual observation supports the view that leadership talents, like musical abilities, are not equally distributed within the enterprise population. However, even the least gifted musical student can learn to create harmonies, if not independent melodies, through diligent training and practice.

The many obstacles facing your organization in becoming a high-performing enterprise make it crucial to assume that leaders can, indeed, be developed. The need for leadership from everyone in the organization is now so acute, to presume otherwise is folly.

William G. Pagonis, in the *Harvard Business Review*, describes his leadership experiences as a Lieutenant General in the U.S. Army. Pagonis's notable accomplishments include leading the 40,000 women and men responsible for theater logistics of Desert Shield, Desert Storm, and Desert Farewell. He writes:

I've concluded that leadership is only possible where the ground has been prepared in advance. . . . If the organization isn't pulling for you, you're likely to be hobbled from the start.

He has been groomed by the Army to become a leader through formal education, informal mentoring, and rotation through a wide variety of postings, all designed to challenge and broaden skills and knowledge base. Training, Pagonis writes, isn't everything, though. Leaders are shaped by their environment, but they must also take an active role in remaking their environment to become more productive.

> . . . a leader is not simply a passive vessel into which the organization pours its best intentions. To lead successfully, a person must demonstrate two active, essential, and interrelated traits: expertise and empathy. In my experience, both of these traits can be deliberately and systematically cultivated; this personal development is the first important building block of leadership.

His philosophy on leadership supports the idea that leadership can indeed be learned. According to Pagonis, hard work develops the skill base and expertise necessary, then luck gives the chance to apply the abilities to achieve mastery.

> I can think of no leader, military or business, who has achieved his or her position without some profound expertise. Most leaders first achieve mastery in a particular functional area, such as logistics, and eventually move into the generalist's realm.

Empathy also plays a big part. "No one is a leader who can't put himself or herself in the other person's shoes." During the Gulf War, American leaders used empathy to smooth relations with their Saudi Arabian hosts. A particularly devout Muslim community objected to U.S. female soldiers with their sleeves rolled up and their hair uncovered; the local religious police were called and female soldiers were jeered. Before the situation turned ugly, U.S. leaders met with Saudi religious and civil officials to learn the cause of the disturbances. They came to an agreement whereby all U.S. military personnel would wear long sleeves, and female soldiers would wear hats; these concessions headed off further problems and pleased the religious police.

However, when Saudi Arabians disapproved of female soldiers driving vehicles and carrying weapons, they were told that soldiers were soldiers and the female soldiers were needed to perform those functions.

Several months after the ground war had ended, Pagonis realized that two inactivated firing ranges were littered with unexploded ammunition and the Bedouins would soon be walking across that land.

> We put ourselves in the shoes of the Bedouins and also in the shoes of the Saudi officials who had to protect the interests of these desert wanderers. We cleaned up the ranges well before the Saudi Arabians had to put

pressure on us to do so. With that we earned their continued respect and cooperation.

During the Gulf War, in a binder known as "the Red Book," Pagonis kept a complete and constantly updated collection of data outlining developments in the conflict. The binder was four inches thick, filled with charts and tables; he kept it at his side at all times.

> By definition, leaders don't operate in isolation. Nor do they command in the literal sense of the word, issuing a one-way stream of unilateral directives. Instead, leadership almost always involves cooperation and collaboration, activities that can occur only in a conducive context.

For Pagonis, the day begins with a "stand-up" meeting at which a representative from each functional area gets the chance to make a quick status report and field questions. At the end of each day, a "sit-down" meeting allows people a more concentrated kind of analysis; attendees identify three areas where operations have been improved and three areas that need improvement, in their respective functional areas.

During the day, Pagonis spends a few hours that are divided into 15-minute segments called "Please See Me" times. He asks people in to elaborate on certain points or he schedules time for people to come in to ask him questions. He also uses 3-inch by 5-inch index cards to further enhance communication; questions or comments are written on the cards, then moved through the chain of command until they reach someone with the authority to respond to them, all within 24 hours. (During the Gulf War, Pagonis received about 100 cards per day.)

> Formal methods of information transfer are very important, but I find that you don't get a complete view of what's happening in an organization unless you also open regular informal communication channels.

Pagonis tries to maintain a regular personal presence in all the different areas under his command; when this isn't possible, he deputizes a group of soldiers, called "Ghostbusters," as his proxies.

> What was the point of all this meeting, mentoring, and moving around? In a sense, it was to touch as many people, and as many kinds of people, as possible. Leaders must be motivators, educators, role models, sounding boards, confessors, and cheerleaders—they must be accessible, and they must aggressively pursue contact with colleagues and subordinates. . . . I'm convinced that if someone works hard at leadership, his or her instincts will tend to be right. His or her hunches will be based on expertise and empathy, and they'll be good ones. Leadership will seem to come easily.

MIDDLE MANAGERS:
FRONT-LINE REVOLUTIONARIES?

Most advice for leaders is directed toward the CEO. In the value decade, however, everyone will be required to be a champion of change—even that seemingly "endangered" species known as "the middle manager"! Like senior executives in high-performing enterprises, middle managers will have to develop new leadership capabilities that differ from traditional models.

Progressive companies are supporting midlevel managers to acquire the skills necessary. For example, Levi Strauss & Company's mission promises "that the company will balance its goal of profitability with fair treatment, teamwork, open communications, personal accountability and opportunities for growth and development for employees." All of the company's 31,000 employees will eventually participate in leadership training. Sue Thompson, director of human resources, says:

> All employees need to take leadership roles in a different way at different times. It may mean not waiting for "them" to take action, or giving open and honest feedback if things aren't going forward.

Brian Dumaine observes, in a *Fortune* magazine, that managers are no longer being called "managers" in some circles.

> Call them sponsors, facilitators—anything but the M word. They're helping their companies and advancing their careers by turning old management practices upside down.

Goodbye, Middle Managers?

Until recently, the trend for the past 35 years has been to add more and more layers of management; now the trend is in the opposite direction. General Motors in the 1990s will probably have five or six levels of management as opposed to the 14 or 15 it had in the past. Proportionately, more management positions in the later 1990s will be "lower," not "middle" or "upper."

The American Management Association surveyed 836 companies and discovered that middle managers accounted for only 5 percent of the work force but *22 percent of the layoffs* in 1992! Middle managers traditionally handle two jobs: (1) supervising people and (2) gathering, processing, and transmitting information. In growing numbers of companies, though, self-managed work teams handle those jobs, including scheduling work, maintaining quality, and administering pay and vacations. In addition, cheaper and faster computers have made information handling an easy and quick job for front-line employees. Towers Perrin management consultant Cynthia

Kellams says, "If you can't say why you actually make your company a better place, you're out."

Tomorrow's top corporate jobs may go to middle managers who are able to master the skills of team building and intrapreneurship and who acquire broad business expertise. The top executives of tomorrow will be team players and brokers of others' efforts, not autocrats.

An example of the "new middle manager" is Cindy Ransom, a "sponsor" at Clorox. She asked 100 workers at Clorox's Fairfield, California, plant to redesign operations three years ago. She supervised a team of hourly workers to establish training programs, set work rules for absenteeism, and reorganize the factory into five customer-focused business units. As her managerial duties were decreased, Ransom was able to spend more time with customers. In 1992, the plant was named the most improved in the household products division. However, instead of moving up the hierarchy, Ransom was transferred overseas to manage another plant.

Another example of new roles for senior managers is found at Drypers, a Houston-based maker of disposable diapers. The company operates with an "office of the chief executive" manned by five managing directors, all with equal power. Each director has a functional responsibility, such as finance, marketing, manufacturing, and so on. No major decisions are made until all five are in agreement, which may take longer but helps put the final decision into effect more quickly.

Working like a middle management team, the group developed disposable training pants called Big Boy and Big Girl in only six months in 1992. This was extraordinarily fast by industry standards. Because of its quick time-to-market achievement, the new line captured 20 percent of the market in six months.

Another story of the new abilities expected from middle managers comes from Dee Zalneraitis, information group manager at a division of R. R. Donnelly & Sons, America's largest printer. She saw her division convert to self-managed work teams in 1992. Her new role is to teach, train, cajole, and comfort her 40 employees as well as to hire, fire, schedule vacations, and so on. Once the teams are able to work alone, she anticipates a move elsewhere; in effect, she is managing herself out of a job.

Zalneraitis found that her hardest task was to let her people figure things out on their own, thereby promoting faster learning. One employee left on vacation without scheduling someone to provide backup; the employee's phone rang until the team acted. Another goal is to bring her people into the decision-making process; at budget meetings, she asks people how *they* think money can be saved.

At S. C. Johnson, the $3 billion-per-year maker of household products, Earl Vander Wielen has been redefining the role of a human resources (HR) manager. An HR manager, who does things such as supervising pay systems and ensuring compliance with government regulations, is usually far removed from the everyday activities of the company.

Eight years ago, when the company moved to implement self-managed teams, Vander Wielen and his staff worked long hours on the factory floor teaching line managers and workers about management techniques such as systems analysis and pay-for-skills. As a result, a team of workers figured out how to reduce the time needed to change a production line from liquid floor wax to stain remover. A three-day changeover time was reduced to thirteen minutes! Johnson's Racine, Washington, plant increased productivity 30 percent in a recent eight-year period, while reducing the number of middle managers from 140 to 37.

Middle managers traditionally have processed and consolidated information as it flowed through the hierarchy. In the value decade, their role will be to ensure that everyone is given the same information that managers receive. Steve Jobs, founder and CEO of Next Computer, believes that, to be competitive, ". . . every employee must contain the company's DNA and therefore must be privy to crucial information like profits, sales, and strategic plans."

At Next, everyone is given information on each other's salaries and stock holdings, if they want to know. Kevin Grundy, Director of Manufacturing and Engineering, devised this concept in part to enforce equal pay for equal effort. Someone complaining about a relatively low salary is told why the salary is relatively low and what the employee can do to rectify the situation. Few people have asked to see the payroll list.

The "Rebirth" of the Middle Manager

There is a profound difference between the "old manager" and the "new manager" in the value decade. Typically, the old manager might be defined as someone who thinks of self as manager or boss; follows the chain of command; works within a set organizational structure; makes most decisions alone; hoards information; tries to master one major discipline, such as marketing or finance; and demands *long hours* from subordinates.

The new manager is someone who thinks of self as a sponsor, team leader, or internal consultant; deals with anyone necessary to get the job done; changes organizational structures in response to market change; invites others to join in decision making; tries to master a broad array of managerial disciplines; and demands *results* from subordinates.

At the Indianapolis headquarters of France's Thomson Consumer Electronics, the head of industrial design in the television division, Louis Lenzi, says:

. . . the trick to working with people to get things done—especially when you have no direct authority over them—is to win their respect. He does this by showing them he has a thorough understanding of their jobs, skills, and needs.

A cross-functional team of managers worked together to develop RCA's ProScan, a successful line of high-end televisions. Lenzi earned his team-mates' respect by demonstrating a broad knowledge of the business, not just the design aspect. His background includes assignments that taught him marketing, manufacturing, and engineering; he spent nine months in-terviewing TV retailers and consumers, met with engineers and manufac-turers to work out technical details for the new set, and helped draft the marketing campaign.

While they were meeting, Thomson managers were still responsible for overseeing their respective departments. In order to handle two jobs at once, says Lenzi:

I had to build trust and confidence. Part of the trick is showing up only when crucially needed. If my people had an issue with the factory on, say, whether to paint the back of a TV—which the designers thought was a great idea and the manufacturers thought insane—I'd go to the meeting and raise hell where I had to raise hell and cajole where I had to cajole.

Because fast innovation is the lifeblood of high-performing enterprises, middle managers in the value decade will have to hone their skills as "intrapreneurs."

Consultants say any new manager worth his or her low-sodium salt substitute must learn to create new businesses swiftly in response to fast and fickle markets.

Anthony Lombardo, General Manager at Sony Medical, has discovered a "formula for rapid-fire innovation": this maker of color printers and other peripheral equipment for medical imaging equipment, such as ultrasound machines, always has to have at least six new seed ventures going at once.

Lombardo and his people spend a lot of time with doctors and HMOs, learning what they need. They scour Sony's other divisions for technology they could use to fulfill those needs. Once a technology is found, a team of ten people work on the idea through constant experimentation. For exam-ple, using Sony's touchscreen and laser–disk-player technology, Lombardo worked with the Foundation for Informed Decision Making to create an interactive system that helps patients learn about their afflictions. Total sales of the system should reach $40 million within four to six years. Lom-bardo says the key is ". . . constantly creating, juggling, shifting, and fi-nally destroying organizations as the market demands."

Okidata's John Ring is another prime example of the new guard. He convinced six stubborn sister divisions on three continents to pool their resources on a project that became Doc-it, a new desktop printer, fax, scanner, and copier. In September 1992, an industry consulting group named Doc-it product of the year.

> When times were flush in corporate America, a manager who wanted to create a new product would simply ask for resources—people, technology, money—and with luck, get them. Today, with budgets tight, the new manager must beg, borrow, and steal anything he can.

The original idea came to Ring in 1988, but he couldn't enlist support from his compatriots at Okidata, the U.S. subsidiary of Oki, a large Japanese maker of semiconductors, telecommunication equipment, and computer printers. Ring pooled the technologies from Japan Oki's fax and printer divisions. When the Japanese doubted a printer would fit in the suggested small size, Ring and a colleague broke up an Oki printer and threw it back together using half the space. It worked; others were then convinced.

Acquiring a broad base of industry experience and leading in innovation are only two of the new abilities necessary for today's middle manager. Attending to the personal needs of employees is also important. Rick Hess is Chief Operating Officer of M/A-Com, a defense company that makes microwave communications equipment, trying to cross over into the private sector. He believes that part of the new manager's job is to make sure that employees don't burn out in the face of competition. Hess takes employees to lunch, plays softball and basketball with them once a week, and tries to find out what's going on in their lives. He constantly prods employees to challenge themselves by putting them in situations where they don't have previous experience.

> Being a new manager is hard. Practically no one has been trained for it, and many companies still aren't sure what to make of the phenomenon. If you want to feel noble about it, reflect that this new generation of smart, aggressive, entrepreneurial managers likely holds the key to America's future prosperity. And if nobility is a little higher than you're aiming, remember that in today's marketplace, with today's workers, the new non-manager has the best chance of producing the results that will advance his or her career.

THE TWELVE TESTS OF LEADERSHIP

In the end, the success of the high-performing enterprise in the value decade depends on you! The critical competencies discussed in this book are little more than alluring concepts unless put into practice by resolute leaders. The 10 enterprise competencies have proved their worth in other organizations: the leading high value-delivering enterprises of today. Do you have the "right stuff" to put these concepts to work in your company?

If you're feeling doubtful, don't despair. Those who have gone before you have felt the same way.

> Most people in our culture have been programmed to fear this thing called failure. Yet, all of us can think of times when we wanted one thing and got another. We've all flunked a test, suffered through a frustrating romance that didn't work out, put together a business plan only to see everything go awry. . . . The super successes of our culture aren't people who do not fail, but simply people who know that if they try something and it doesn't give them what they want, they've had a learning experience.

The skills that are required by today's leaders are neither science nor art. They are, in fact, a combination of attributes and competencies that must be aligned through an understanding of the leadership process. The effective leader requires special knowledge, a burning belief that change is required, and the courage to "stay the course" while balancing the needs of the customer, shareholder, and employees. The leader also needs a "game plan." Leaders who are transforming their companies into high-performing enterprises travel predictable journeys and meet similar obstacles.

You will face the "12 tests of leadership" when embarking on your own voyage. The 12 tests, shown on the rim of the circle in Figure 10.1, comprise the four "challenges" indicated in the inner quadrants. The 12 tests are presented in the order typically faced by pacesetters leading enterprisewide change. By comparing your own obstacles to these benchmarks, you can assess where you are now and anticipate what lies ahead.

Needing Change

At the beginning of your leadership journey, you must understand the need for change in your organization and believe in the possibility of a high-performing future. Unless a leader is willing to face the current reality with an unflinching eye, he or she can't convince the rest of the enterprise to begin the transformation that is necessary. The three tests you will encounter during the needing-change phase are:

1. *Confronting:* facing facts and understanding current reality; gaining insight to the true causes of business performance declines, such as changing customer needs and a changing work force. Accepting the reality of intensified competition; establishing the measures and benchmarks necessary to develop a complete picture of the current performance of the enterprise.

2. *Visioning:* actively seeking a better tomorrow and developing a future vision; knowing what is necessary to create competitive advantage in the marketplace of tomorrow.

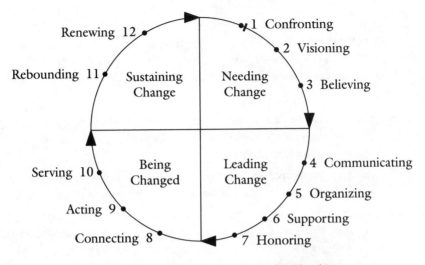

Figure 10.1   The twelve tests of leadership.

3. *Believing:* making a personal commitment to change, and communicating to everyone in the enterprise: "We can do it."

Leading Change

The capable enterprise leader must marshal the needed resources to bring about the change desired. You must be able to pass the following "skill tests" during the leading-change phase:

4. *Communicating:* articulating the need for change and involving others in the change process; defining the key audiences who need to know why the organization must adopt new ways, and developing a communications strategy to get the message out effectively.

5. *Organizing:* planning and structuring the change process; setting priorities and linking them to the enterprise business strategy. Establishing timetables and accountabilities while achieving "early wins" to build momentum for change.

6. *Supporting:* providing the necessary resources to sustain the change effort; enabling others to act. Training staff in new methods while changing outmoded work processes. Investing the time and energy to see the change through, which means becoming personally involved in improvement projects.

7. *Honoring:* "encouraging the heart" while change is unfolding; being proficient in rewarding those around you for adopting new ways; recognizing and publicly celebrating successes.

Being Changed

The capable leader in the value decade understands that, in order to change the enterprise, he or she may have to change his or her own behavior most of all. You will face these tests during the being-changed phase of the leadership process:

8. *Connecting:* building shared values and constituencies; knowing that little can be accomplished alone. Identifying and enlisting allies and disarming opponents.

9. *Acting:* "walking, not talking" the new enterprise values; personally modeling the type of behavior you wish others to embrace.

10. *Serving:* accepting personal responsibility for change; understanding that being a change agent brings with it the responsibility of becoming a "steward" and making a difference in other people's lives. Being conscious of the type of personal "legacy" you are creating in the business.

Sustaining Change

The final two tests are found in the sustaining-change phase. Perhaps the greatest challenge occurs when the leader recognizes the degree of personal commitment necessary to transform an organization into high value-delivering enterprise.

11. *Rebounding:* knowing the power of persistence; moving constantly forward in face of inevitable setbacks. Knowing that each stage of resistance is a sign that the enterprise is getting closer to the "ideal vision."

12. *Renewing:* having the energy and fortitude to start the change process all over again; being aware that even the most effective transformation process will require periodic "jump starting" to keep enthusiasm high.

In the final phase of the leadership process, a fresh look at the challenges facing the enterprise will be necessary. You will have to recalibrate to the prerequisites for continued prosperity. The quest for high performance "ends at the beginning" with an eagerness to discover the new competencies essential to competing in the value decade.

Endnotes

Introduction: Ten New Ideas Revolutionizing Business

3. *If you are prepared . . . "nine-to-five" behavior:* Walter Kiechel III, "How We Will Work in the Year 2000," *Fortune*, May 17, 1993, p. 39.

Touchstone 1: The Four Keys to Creating Extraordinary Value

8. *Edwin L. Artzt . . . promoting customer loyalty:* Tricia Kelly, "Looking into the Crystal Ball," *Quality Progress,* November 1992, p. 37.

8. *The demand for greater . . . a charitable donation:* Kelly, *id.,* pp. 37–38. Reprinted by permission of *Quality Progress.*

8. *Michael Treacy . . . the competition's reach:* Michael Treacy and Fred Wiersema, "Customer Intimacy and Other Value Disciplines," *Harvard Business Review,* January/February 1993, p. 84.

9. *Today's customers . . . dependability, and so on:* Treacy and Wiersema, *id.* Copyright © 1993 by The President and Fellows of Harvard College; all rights reserved. Reprinted by permission of *Harvard Business Review.*

9. *Dell Computer's . . . undermotivated intermediary:* Treacy and Wiersema, *id.,* pp. 85–86.

9. *Nike is an example . . . by the competition:* Treacy and Wiersema, *id.,* p. 84.

9. *Product leaders . . . another company will:* Treacy and Wiersema, *id.,* p. 91. Copyright © 1993 by The President and Fellows of Harvard College; all rights reserved. Reprinted by permission of *Harvard Business Review.*

9. *Its "business strategy . . . information and service":* Treacy and Wiersema, *id.,* p. 88. Copyright © 1993 by The President and Fellows of Harvard College; all rights reserved. Reprinted by permission of *Harvard Business Review.*

9. *In other words . . . additions they're planning:* Treacy and Wiersema, *id.*

9. *Treacy and Wiersema conclude . . . their industry:* Treacy and Wiersema, *id.,* p. 86.

10. *In a nutshell . . . defect to competitors:* "How to Create, Measure the Value of Customers," *Services Marketing Today,* May/June 1992, p. 3.

10. *"When a company . . . goes down":* Frederick F. Reichheld, "Loyalty-Based Management," *Harvard Business Review,* March/April 1993, p. 64. Copyright © 1993 by The President and Fellows of Harvard College; all rights reserved. Reprinted by permission of *Harvard Business Review.*

10. *For various reasons . . . can be developed:* Reichheld, *id.,* p. 66. Copyright © 1993 by The President and Fellows of Harvard College; all rights reserved. Reprinted by permission of *Harvard Business Review.*

10. *An example of . . . $1 billion:* David A. Aaker, "The Value of Brand Equity," *Journal of Business Strategy,* October 1992, p. 27.

11. *A recent study . . . is critically important:* "New Study Shows Americans' Changing Needs for Satisfaction," *Services Marketing Today,* September/October 1992, p. 1.

11. *REM Associates . . . recipe for disaster:* "How one Fortune 200 company used research to identify five customer satisfaction drives," *Executive Report on Customer Satisfaction,* January 15, 1993, pp. 1–3.

12. *Xerox shows . . . "customer delight" factors:* Xerox Service Diagram (Xerox Corporation, 1992).

12. *Trend watchers . . . relationship to continue:* "Value Marketing: Quality, Service, and Fair Pricing are the Keys to Selling in the '90s," *Business Week,* November 11, 1991, p. 133.

14. *Philip Kotler . . . delicate balance:* Thomas E. Caruso, "Kotler: Future Marketers Will Focus on Customer Data Base to Compete Globally," *Marketing News,* June 8, 1992, p. 21.

14. *At the Jacksonville . . . continued to decrease:* Frederick G. Schobert, Jr. and Charles L. Brown, "A Strategy for Continuous Improvement," *Quality Progress,* October 1990, pp. 69–70.

15. *PIMS Associates . . . of competitors:* George Binney, "Quality Pays," in *Making Quality Work: Lessons from Europe's Leading Companies* (London: The Economist Intelligence Unit, 1992), p. 2.

15. *"There is a clear . . . return on sales":* Binney, *id.,* p. 3.

15. *The businesses in . . . market share:* Binney, *id.,* pp. 3–4.

16. *In the long run . . . of the competitors:* Binney, *id.,* p. 4.

16. *The consulting firm . . . for competitors:* Binney, *id.,* p. 5.

16. *A good example . . . and its customers:* "Building Sales at Aikenhead's," *Sales and Marketing Manager Canada,* May 1992, p. 17. Reprinted by permission of *Sales and Marketing Manager Canada.*

16. *The way I . . . lost that $50,000 order:* "Building Sales at Aikenhead's," *id.,* p. 18. Reprinted by permission of *Sales and Marketing Manager Canada.*

17. *Although somewhat limited . . . employee satisfaction:* George Binney, "The Value of Total Quality," in *Making Quality Work: Lessons from Europe's Leading Companies* (London: The Economist Intelligence Unit, 1992), pp. 8–9.

17. *Intel CEO . . . didn't work out at all:* "Andy Grove: How Intel Makes Spending Pay Off," *Fortune,* February 22, 1993, p. 58.

17. *[You can't] hesitate . . . for someone else:* "Andy Grove: How Intel Makes Spending Pay Off," *id.,* p. 57. Reprinted by permission of *Fortune* © 1993 Time Inc. All rights reserved.

17. *Grove doesn't see . . . the postindustrial age:* "Andy Grove: How Intel Makes Spending Pay Off," *id.,* p. 57.

17. *First, you have to start . . . years from now . . . :* "Andy Grove: How Intel Makes Spending Pay Off," *id.,* p. 61. Reprinted by permission of *Fortune* © 1993 Time Inc. All rights reserved.

18. *Len Schelesinger . . . ". . . customer in mind":* "Good Service *and* Low Prices? Today's Burdened Buyers Are Looking for Both," *The Service Edge,* March 1992, p. 1.

18. *Another good example . . . worth paying for:* "Good Service *and* Low Prices? . . . ," *id.,* p. 2.

18. *With vigorous . . . production processes:* H. Thomas Johnson and Robert S. Kaplan, *Relevance Lost: The Rise and Fall of Management Accounting* (Boston: Harvard Business School Press, 1987), p. 3. Reprinted by permission of Harvard Business School Press.

18. *For the purposes . . . no apparent value:* Johnson and Kaplan, *id.,* p. 231. Reprinted by permission of Harvard Business School Press.

19. *A large life . . . for these processes:* Michael R. Ostrenga, Terrence R. Ozan, Robert D. McIlhattan, and Marcus D. Harwood, *The Ernst & Young Guide to Total Cost Management* (New York: John Wiley & Sons, 1992), p. 11.

19. *In a high-technology . . . from meetings:* Ostrenga et al., *id.,* p. 12.

20. *A management team . . . non-value-adding waste:* Ostrenga et al., *id.,* p. 14.

20. *Your pricing decisions . . . you have identified:* Ostrenga et al., *id.,* p. 28.

21. *For example, the Little Rock . . . non-value-added categories:* "Operations Input Critical in Successful Metrics Overhaul," *Profit Management,* June/July 1991, p. 1.

21. *Mark Rose . . . carrying costs:* "Operations Input Critical in Successful Metrics Overhaul," *id.,* p. 2.

21. *Motorola's obsession . . . are dropped:* "Future Perfect," *The Economist,* January 4, 1992, p. 61.

22. *Essentially, TQM boils . . . improvement or redesign:* Sandy Fife, "The Total Quality Muddle," *The Globe and Mail Report on Business Magazine,* November 1992, p. 64.

22. *For example, Douglas . . . ". . . American ground":* Jay Matthews with Peter Katel, "The Cost of Quality," *Newsweek,* September 7, 1992, p. 48.

22. *Florida Power & Light . . . excessive paperwork:* Matthews/Katel, *id.*

23. *The Wallace Company . . . bankruptcy protection:* Matthews/Katel, *id.*

23. *Despite these problems . . . keep track of progress:* "Five barriers to quality improvement block customer satisfaction," *Executive Report on Customer Satisfaction,* December 30, 1992, pp. 1–2.

23. *The Quality . . . is the goal:* Joseph H. Boyett and Henry P. Conn, "What's Wrong with Total Quality Management?", *Tapping the Network Journal,* Spring 1992, p. 10.

24. *ChemLawn, a $355-million . . . 20 percent per year:* Susan Caminiti, "Finding New Ways to Sell More," *Fortune,* July 27, 1992, pp. 101–102.

25. *In another example . . . several suppliers:* Caminiti, *id.,* p. 102.

25. *Great Plains, a software . . . great customer support:* Patricia Sellers, "Keeping the Buyers You Already Have," *Fortune,* Autumn/Winter 1993, pp. 57–59.

25. *"Great Plains has . . . a lot alike":* Sellers, *id.,* pp. 57–59. Reprinted by permission of *Fortune* © 1993 Time Inc. All rights reserved.

25. *Great Plains has . . . Version 7 revenues:* Sellers, *id.*

26. Accounting Today . . . *". . . should be handled":* Sellers, *id.* Reprinted by permission of *Fortune* © 1993 Time Inc. All rights reserved.

26. *When the television . . . for its products:* Richard C. Whiteley, *The Customer-Driven Company: Moving from Talk to Action* (Reading, MA: Addison-Wesley Publishing Co., 1991), p. 24.

27. *CEO Herbert Kelleher . . . job interviews:* Richard S. Teitelbaum, "Where Service Flies Right," *Fortune,* August 24, 1992, p. 115.

27. *Jeffrey E. Disend . . . needed extension:* Jeffrey E. Disend, *How To Provide Excellent Service in Any Organization: A Blueprint for Making All the Theories Work* (Radnor, PA: Chilton Book Co., 1991), p. 19.

28. *In a 1986 study . . . less money:* Disend, *id.,* p. 278.

28. *L. L. Bean . . . ". . . in customer service: Excellence Achieved: Customer Service Blueprints for Action from 50 Leading Companies* (New York: Simon & Schuster), p. 36.

28. *"Research has shown us . . . from you again": Excellence Achieved: Customer Service Blueprints . . . , id.,* p. 37.

28. *Susan Gagnon . . . serve customers better: Excellence Achieved: Customer Service Blueprints . . . , id.,* p. 38.

29. *When General Motors . . . consumer-advice article: Excellence Achieved: Customer Service Blueprints . . . , id.*

29. *The proof of GM's . . . target market: Excellence Achieved: Customer Service Blueprints . . . , id.*

29. *Experience and empirical data . . . solved immediately:* "Top 10 Service Attributes of Importance to Customers," *The Service Edge,* March 1992, p. 6.

30. *Kellogg's, the cereal maker . . . the competition:* "Time-to-Market," *Coopers & Lybrand, Solutions for Business,* p. 12.

30. *Markets based on style . . . its effects:* Joseph T. Vesey, "Time-to-Market: Put Speed in Product Development," *Industrial Marketing Management, 21* (New York: Elsevier Science Publishing Co., Inc., 1992), p. 151.

30. *Authors George Stalk, Jr. and . . . time-to-market can:* George Stalk, Jr. and Thomas M. Hout, *Competing against Time: How Time-Based Competition Is Reshaping Global Markets* (New York: The Free Press, 1990), p. 31.

31. *Wal-Mart has honed . . . industry benchmark:* Stalk and Hout, *id.,* p. 2.

31. *Thomasville Furniture ships . . . as profitable:* Stalk and Hout, *id.,* p. 3.

31. *Atlas Door fills . . . industry average:* Stalk and Hout, *id.,* pp. 2–3.

31. *A McKinsey & Company study . . . ". . . no longer recognizable":* Joseph T. Vesey, "Time-to-Market: Put Speed in Product Development," *Industrial Marketing Management, 21* (New York: Elsevier, 1992), p. 153.

32. *Ballistic Systems Division . . . from 1 : 15 to 1 : 20:* Vesey, *id.,* p. 152.

32. *Aleda Roth . . . ". . . were on quality":* Thomas A. Stewart, "Brace for Japan's Hot New Strategy," *Fortune,* September 21, 1992, p. 63. Reprinted by permission of *Fortune* © 1992 Time Inc. All rights reserved.

32. *In a Deloitte & Touche survey . . . low unit cost:* Stewart, *id.*

33. *Stalk and Hout . . . time-based advantage:* George Stalk, Jr. and Thomas M. Hout, *Competing against Time: How Time-Based Competition Is Reshaping Global Markets* (New York: The Free Press, 1990), pp. 35–36.

34. *Customers don't buy . . . it as excellent:* Speech delivered to Closing the Service GAP Conference, June 1991, Toronto, 1991. Quoted by Jim Clemmer, *Firing on All Cylinders: The Service/Quality System for High-*

Powered Corporate Performance, 2nd ed. (Toronto: Macmillan Canada, 1992), p. 27. Reprinted by permission of Macmillan Canada.

34. *Your customers' perceptions . . . are measured:* Clemmer, *id.,* p. 26. Reprinted by permission of Macmillan Canada.

34. *He suggests some excellent . . . in the computer field:* Clemmer, *id.,* pp. 118–120.

35. *Canadian Airlines . . . and so on:* Clemmer, *id.,* p. 125.

35. *In Argentina, . . . is 30 percent higher:* Michael E. Raynor, "Fantastic Things Happen When You Talk to Customers," *Marketing News,* February 15, 1993, p. 8.

Touchstone 2: Redesigning Business Processes

37. *By its contribution . . . preceding steps:* Geary A. Rummler and Alan P. Brache, *Improving Performance: How to Manage the White Space on the Organization Chart* (San Francisco: Jossey-Bass Inc., 1990), p. 45. Reprinted by permission of Jossey-Bass Inc.

37. *When Connecticut Mutual . . . months early:* David K. Carr, Kevin S. Dougherty, Henry J. Johansson, Robert A. King, and David E. Moran, *Break-Point: Business Process Redesign* (Arlington, VA: Coopers & Lybrand Publishing Division, 1992), p. 24.

38. *. . . a grouping . . . of improvement:* Robert B. Kaplan and Laura Murdoch, "Core Process Redesign." *The McKinsey Quarterly* (2), 1991, p. 27.

38. *Japanese manufacturers . . . process improvement:* Thomas G. Gunn, *21st Century Manufacturing: Creating Winning Business Performance* (New York: HarperCollins Publishers, 1992), p. 53.

38. *A Ford Motor Company . . . in production:* Gunn, *id.,* p. 55.

39. *The single most . . . their work:* H. James Harrington, "The Return of High Performance to the U.S. Workplace," *The Journal of Business Strategy,* July/August 1991, p. 23. Permission granted by Faulkner & Gray, 11 Penn Plaza, New York, NY 10001.

39. *Most enterprises today . . . cost, and time:* Tom Mueller, Russell Barss, and Chris Phillips, "Restructuring Organizations to Compete in the 1990's Global Market—The Application of Business Process Re-Engineering to Achieve Significant Performance Improvement." Technical Paper presented to the Northwest Regional Symposium of the Project Management Institute, March 1993.

39. *Hallmark Cards . . . more than 50 percent:* Thomas A. Stewart, "The Search for the Organization of Tomorrow," *Fortune,* May 18, 1992, p. 93.

41. *In small or new organizations . . . a liability:* Geary A. Rummler and Alan P. Brache, *Improving Performance: How to Manage the White Space on the Organization Chart* (San Francisco: Jossey-Bass Inc., 1990), p. 5. Reprinted by permission of Jossey-Bass Inc.

41. *Kaoru Ishikawa . . . and workers:* William A. Band, *Creating Value for Customers: Designing and Implementing a Total Corporate Strategy* (New York: John Wiley & Sons, Inc., 1991), p. 182.

42. *Creating shared values . . . are necessary:* Thomas A. Poynter and Roderick E. White, "Making the Horizontal Organization Work," *Business Quarterly,* Winter 1990, p. 73.

42. *Philip Selznick says . . . ". . . and commitment":* Poynter and White, *id.*

42. *Redefining managers' roles . . . and overall results:* Poynter and White, *id.*

42. *In* Horizontal Management . . . *operational levels:* D. Keith Denton, *Horizontal Management: Beyond Total Customer Satisfaction* (New York: Lexington Books/Macmillan, 1991), p. 36.

42. *A powerful method . . . someone else:* Denton, *id.*

43. *At Johnsonville Foods . . . profit pool:* "Team Rewards Rely on Internal-Customer Evaluations," *Total Employee Involvement,* May 1993, p. 9.

43. *Creative Professional Services . . . improve performance:* Susan Greco, "The ABCs of Internal Guarantees," *Positive Impact,* June 1993, p. 3. (Reprinted from *Inc.* magazine, March 1993. Copyright © 1993 Goldhirsh Group, Inc., 38 Commercial Wharf, Boston, MA 02110.)

44. *Before, almost half . . . real minutiae:* Greco, *id.* Reprinted from *Inc.* magazine, March 1993. Copyright © 1993 Goldhirsh Group, Inc., 38 Commercial Wharf, Boston, MA 02110.

44. *If you're thinking . . . of performance:* David K. Carr, Kevin S. Dougherty, Henry J. Johansson, Robert A. King, and David E. Moran, *BreakPoint: Business Process Redesign* (Arlington, VA: Coopers & Lybrand Publishing Division, 1992), p. 44.

45. *Medrad, a $60-million . . . rush orders:* Carr et al., *id.*

45. *In the early 1980s . . . a comeback:* Carr et al., *id.,* p. 6.

45. *Another example of . . . decrease in quality:* "'Breakthrough Strategy' Helps D&B Improve Service to Customers," *Executive Report on Customer Satisfaction,* May 15, 1993, p. 2.

46. *The "order faucet" . . . eliminated them:* "'Breakthrough Strategy' Helps D&B . . . ," *id.* Reprinted by permission of *Executive Report on Customer Satisfaction.*

46. *The following checklist . . . competitive advantage:* David K. Carr, Kevin S. Dougherty, Henry J. Johansson, Robert A. King, and David E. Moran, *BreakPoint: Business Process Redesign* (Arlington, VA: Coopers & Lybrand Publishing Division, 1992), p. 9.

47. *Andersen Consulting advocates . . . factor of ten:* Sid L. Huff, "Reengineering the Business," *Business Quarterly,* Winter 1992, p. 39. Reprinted by permission of *Business Quarterly.*

48. *Reengineering . . . through cost reduction:* Daniel Morris and Joel Brandon, *Re-Engineering Your Business* (New York: McGraw-Hill, 1993), p. 6. Reprinted by permission of McGraw-Hill, Inc.

48. *In answer, CSC Index's . . . "business as usual":* Rahul Jacob, "Thriving in a Lame Economy," *Fortune,* October 5, 1992, p. 44.

48. *Herman Miller CEO . . . ". . . constant turmoil":* Jacob, *id.* Reprinted by permission of *Fortune* © 1992 Time Inc. All rights reserved.

48. *But author Michael Hammer . . . ". . . and speed":* John A. Byrne, "Reengineering: Beyond the Buzzword," *Business Week,* May 24, 1993, p. 12.

49. *One management pundit . . . "overnight" improvement:* "The Newest Pet Rock Needs a Firm Foundation," *The Globe & Mail,* October 27, 1992, p. B30.

49. *In "Lessons from the Veterans. . ." ultimately fail:* Céline Bak, "Lessons from the Veterans of TQM," *Canadian Business Review,* Winter 1992, p. 17.

49. *Bak's investigation . . . understood by all:* Bak, *id.*

50. *A study of 1,005 firms . . . the aftermath:* "Downsizing: Many Firms Fall Short of Goals, Studies Show," *Total Quality Newsletter,* July 1992, p. 1.

50. *"Reengineering is to quality . . ." ". . . for most companies":* "Reengineering: A Process for Overhauling Your Business," *Total Quality Newsletter,* August 1992, p. 1. Reprinted by permission of Total Quality Newsletter, Lakewood Publications, 50 South Ninth St., Minneapolis, MN 55402. All rights reserved. Not for resale.

50. *There are five . . . of the enterprise:* Robert B. Kaplan and Laura Murdoch, "Core Process Redesign," *The McKinsey Quarterly* (2), 1991, p. 27.

51. *As an example, consider . . . (MTBF):* Henry J. Johansson, Patrick McHugh, A. John Pendlebury, and William A. Wheeler III, *Business Process Reengineering: BreakPoint Strategies for Market Dominance* (Chichester, England: John Wiley & Sons, Ltd., 1993), p. 52.

52. *The new division . . . responses in weeks:* Johansson et al., *id.,* p. 53.

52. *Andy Guarriello . . . quality by 1994:* Johansson et al., *id.*

52. *As the BPR . . . continuous improvements:* Johansson et al., *id.,* p. 54.

52. *Phase Two involves . . . measuring success:* Robert B. Kaplan and Laura Murdoch, "Core Process Redesign," *The McKinsey Quarterly* (2), 1991, p. 27.

53. *When Ford Motor Company . . . current ability:* Sid L. Huff, "Reengineering the Business," *Business Quarterly,* Winter 1992, p. 39.

53. *Phase Three . . . should be analyzed:* Robert B. Kaplan and Laura Murdoch, "Core Process Redesign," *The McKinsey Quarterly* (2), 1991, p. 27.

53. *The case of the IBM Credit Corporation . . . greatly reduced:* "The Promise of Reengineering," *Fortune,* May 3, 1993, p. 95. [Excerpt from: Michael Hammer and James Champy, *Reengineering the Corporation: A Manifesto for Business Revolution* (New York: HarperCollins Publishers, 1993).]

53. *Phase Four . . . time frames:* Robert B. Kaplan and Laura Murdoch, "Core Process Redesign," *The McKinsey Quarterly* (2), 1991, p. 27.

54. *A decline in net . . . on their behalf:* "Kodak and reengineering: A report from the trenches," *Executive Report on Customer Satisfaction, December 15, 1992, p. 1.*

54. *Running a minilab . . . satisfied customers:* "Kodak and reengineering: A report from the trenches," *Executive Report on Customer Satisfaction,* December 15, 1992, p. 1. Reprinted by permission of *Executive Report on Customer Satisfaction.*

55. *The Imaging Group . . . $138 million in savings:* "Kodak and reengineering: A report from the trenches," *Executive Report on Customer Satisfaction, id.*

55. *Phase Five . . . all key elements:* Robert B. Kaplan and Laura Murdoch, "Core Process Redesign," *The McKinsey Quarterly* (2), 1991, p. 27.

56. *Five factors must be . . . within the organization:* Johansson et al., *id.,* p. 192.

56. *All these leaders . . . best performance:* Johansson et al., *id.,* p. 193.

57. *The move from . . . their behalf:* Johansson et al., *id.,* pp. 199–200.

Touchstone 3: The New Enterprise Architecture

59. *The ubiquitous Tom Peters . . . ". . . we know it":* The Tom Peters Group, *The One Big Difference* (Palo Alto, CA: The Tom Peters Group, 1992), p. 1.

59. *EDS's goal is . . . systems capabilities:* Tom Peters, *Liberation Management: Necessary Disorganization in the Nanosecond Nineties* (New York: Alfred A. Knopf, 1992), p. 21.

60. *For each client . . . ". . . job done is":* Peters, *id.,* p. 21. Copyright © 1992 by Excel, a California Limited Partnership. Reprinted by permission of Alfred A. Knopf Inc.

60. *However, there are . . . ". . . designation or not":* Peters, *id.,* p. 25. Copyright © 1992 by Excel, a California Limited Partnership. Reprinted by permission of Alfred A. Knopf Inc.

60. *EDS is "loose . . . your 'responsibility'":* Peters, *id.,* p. 26. Copyright © 1992 by Excel, a California Limited Partnership. Reprinted by permission of Alfred A. Knopf Inc.

61. *. . . will bust through . . . improve upon it . . . :* Brian Dumaine, "The Bureaucracy Busters," *Fortune,* June 17, 1991, p. 36. Reprinted by permission of *Fortune* © 1991 Time Inc. All rights reserved.

61. *Raymond Miles . . . ". . . joint-venture partners":* Dumaine, *id.,* p. 38. Reprinted by permission of *Fortune* © 1991 Time Inc. All rights reserved.

61. *Apple Computer . . . around the world:* Dumaine, *id.,* p. 46.

61. *Harvard economist . . . ". . . with big ones":* Thomas A. Stewart, "The Search for the Organization of Tomorrow," *Fortune,* May 18, 1992, p. 93. Reprinted by permission of *Fortune* © 1991 Time Inc. All rights reserved.

61. *These new dimensions can . . . healthier pride prevails:* Larry Hirschhorn and Thomas Gilmore, "The New Boundaries of the 'Boundaryless' Company," *Harvard Business Review,* May/June 1992, p. 107.

63. *Authority in the . . . and effectiveness:* Hirschhorn and Gilmore, *id.,* p. 112. Copyright © 1992 by The President and Fellows of Harvard College; all rights reserved. Reprinted by permission of *Harvard Business Review.*

63. *This vice president . . . group effectively:* Hirschhorn and Gilmore, *id.,* pp. 113–115.

64. *Management observer Charles Handy . . . is finished:* Charles Handy, *The Age of Unreason* (London: Business Books Ltd., 1991), p. 71.

65. *D. Quinn Mills . . . ". . . performance declines":* D. Quinn Mills, *Rebirth of the Corporation* (New York: John Wiley & Sons, Inc., 1991), p. 29. Reprinted by permission of John Wiley & Sons, Inc.

65. *In Mills's vision . . . specific end-result:* Mills *id.,* p. 31.

66. *Autonomous work teams . . . operating styles:* David A. Nadler, Marc S. Gerstein, Robert B. Shaw [and Associates], *Organizational Architecture: Designs for Changing Organizations* (San Francisco: Jossey-Bass Inc., 1992), p. 5.

66. *Because the modern . . . as a team:* Peter F. Drucker, "The New Society of Organizations," *Harvard Business Review,* September/October 1992, p. 101. Copyright © 1992 by The President and Fellows of Harvard College; all rights reserved. Reprinted by permission of *Harvard Business Review.*

67. *As discussed in . . . changing tastes:* Thomas A. Stewart, "The Search for the Organization of Tomorrow," *Fortune,* May 18, 1992, p. 96.

68. *For example, there are . . . at corporate headquarters:* Stewart, *id.,* p. 94.

68. *Thomas A. Stewart . . . are the rule:* Stewart, *id.,* p. 93.

69. *A classic example . . . enriched as an individual:* Tom Peters, *Liberation Management: Necessary Disorganization for the Nanosecond Nineties* (New York: Alfred A. Knopf, 1992), p. 238.

69. *Johnsonville workers . . . make a better sausage:* Peters, *id.,* p. 239. Copyright © 1992 by Excel, a California Limited Partnership. Reprinted by permission of Alfred A. Knopf Inc.

69. *Self-management continues . . . strategic projects:* Peters, *id.,* p. 238.

70. *Johnsonville revenue . . . ". . . their full talents":* Peters, *id.,* p. 239. Copyright © 1992 by Excel, a California Limited Partnership. Reprinted by permission of Alfred A. Knopf Inc.

70. *This kind of structure . . . with greater ease:* Thomas A. Stewart, "The Search for the Organization of Tomorrow," *Fortune,* May 18, 1992, pp. 93–98.

70. *Says Xerox's Richard Palermo . . . hate each other:* Steward, *id.,* pp. 97–98. Reprinted by permission of *Fortune* © 1992 Time Inc. All rights reserved.

70. *Here are ten ideas . . . individual performance alone:* Stewart, *id.,* p. 96. (Source: McKinsey & Co.)

71. *An organizational architecture . . . and opportunities:* David A. Nadler, Marc S. Gerstein, and Robert B. Shaw [and Associates], *Organizational Architecture: Designs for Changing Organizations* (San Francisco: Jossey-Bass Inc., 1992), p. 118. Reprinted by permission of Jossey-Bass Inc.

71. *Whatever your own bias . . . and flat structure:* John O. Burdett, "A Template for Organization Design," *Business Quarterly,* Summer 1992, pp. 35–41.

71. *The Zoological Society . . . for visitors:* Thomas A. Stewart, "The Search for the Organization of Tomorrow," *Fortune,* May 18, 1992, p. 98.

72. *When the Cable News Network . . . the U.S. alone:* Tom Peters, *Liberation Management: Necessary Disorganization in the Nanosecond Nineties* (New York: Alfred A. Knopf, 1992), p. 31. Copyright © 1992 by Excel, a California Limited Partnership. Reprinted by permission of Alfred A. Knopf Inc.

73. *Turner's dream was . . . the "core":* Peters, *id.,* p. 32.

73. *CNN is a . . . larger puzzle:* Peters, *id.,* p. 40. Copyright © 1992 by Excel, a California Limited Partnership. Reprinted by permission of Alfred A. Knopf Inc.

73. *Turner's vision . . . in profit:* Peters, *id.,* p. 31.

74. *Customer-focused design . . . a changing environment:* David A. Nadler, Marc S. Gerstein, Robert B. Shaw [and Associates], *Organizational Architecture: Designs for Changing Organizations* (San Francisco: Jossey-Bass Inc., 1992), p. 120.

75. *The new design . . . of competitors:* Thomas A. Stewart, "The Search for the Organization of Tomorrow," *Fortune,* May 18, 1992, p. 95. Reprinted by permission of Fortune © 1992 Time Inc. All rights reserved.

75. *For example, the new Customer . . . ". . . to the customer":* Stewart, *id.,* p. 95.

75. *Empowered and autonomous . . . gain sharing:* David A. Nadler, Marc S. Gerstein, Robert B. Shaw [and Associates], *Organizational Architecture: Designs for Changing Organizations* (San Francisco: Jossey-Bass Inc., 1992), pp. 120–122.

75. *Ralph Heath, President . . . has paid off:* Tom Peters, *Liberation Management: Necessary Disorganization in the Nanosecond Nineties* (New York: Alfred A. Knopf, 1992), pp. 462–463. (Reprinted from Ken Brekke, *La Crosse Tribune,* September 2, 1991.)

76. *Empowering management . . . leaps of design:* David A. Nadler, Marc S. Gerstein, Robert B. Shaw [and Associates], *Organizational Architecture: Designs for Changing Organizations* (San Francisco: Jossey-Bass Inc., 1992), pp. 122–123.

Touchstone 4: The High-Involvement Workplace

77. *The concept of . . .* dissatisfaction: A. J. Vogl, "Bureaucracy Busting," *Across the Board*, March 1993, p. 23.

77. *I think the . . . no longer good enough:* Vogl, *id.*, p. 24. Reprinted by permission of The Conference Board, Inc.

78. *Approaches to employee . . . and/or the work process:* Edward E. Lawler III, *The Ultimate Advantage: Creating the High-Involvement Organization* (San Francisco: Jossey-Bass Inc., 1992), pp. 25–29.

78. *The key assumption in . . . their own behavior:* Lawler, *id.*, p. 29. Reprinted by permission of Jossey-Bass Inc.

78. *The high-involvement style . . . not just his or her hands:* Lawler, *id.*, p. 29.

78. *For example, Catharine . . . customer satisfaction:* Catharine G. Johnston and Carolyn R. Farquhar, *Empowered People Satisfy Customers: Strategies for Leaders, Lessons from the Canada Awards for Business Excellence Winners* (Ottawa: The Conference Board of Canada, 1992), p. 4.

79. *Eliminate fear, create . . . the solution:* Johnston and Farquhar, *id.*, p. 5.

79. *Each of the seven companies . . . employee attitudes:* Johnston and Farquhar, *id.*, p. 6.

80. *Another study, by . . . work toward as a team:* "Study Shows Strong Evidence that Participative Management Pays Off," *Total Quality Newsletter*, September 1992, p. 1. [Excerpt from Edward E. Lawler III, Susan Albers Mohrman, and Gerald E. Ledford, Jr., *Employee Involvement and Total Quality Management: Practices and Results in Fortune 1000 Companies* (San Francisco: Jossey-Bass Inc., 1992).]

80. *Individual incentives are . . . problem solving:* "Study Shows Strong Evidence . . . ," *id.*, p. 2. Reprinted by permission of *Total Quality Newsletter*, Lakewood Publications, 50 South Ninth St., Minneapolis, MN 55402. All rights reserved. Not for resale.

80. *Some companies . . . question management decisions:* "Open-Book Management: How to Turn Employees into Profit Makers," *Total Quality Newsletter*, March 1993, p. 1.

80. *We developed a . . . decision-making process:* "Open-Book Management: . . . ," *id.*, p. 2. Reprinted by permission of *Total Quality Newsletter*, Lakewood Publications, 50 South Ninth St., Minneapolis, MN 55402. All rights reserved. Not for resale.

81. *SMC then initiated . . . ". . . better things":* "Open-Book Management: . . . ," *id.* Reprinted by permission of *Total Quality Newsletter*, Lakewood Publications, 50 South Ninth St., Minneapolis, MN 55402. All rights reserved. Not for resale.

81. *Here's another example . . . gone out of control:* "Open-Book Management: . . . ," *id.*, p. 3.

81. *We presented the . . . powerful difference:* "Open-Book Management: . . . ," *id.* Reprinted by permission of *Total Quality Newsletter*, Lakewood Publications, 50 South Ninth St., Minneapolis, MN 55402. All rights reserved. Not for resale.

81. *After communicating . . . cost-sharing plan:* "Open-Book Management: . . . ," *id.*

81. *As participatory . . . within the hierarchy:* William H. Davidow and Michael S. Malone, *The Virtual Corporation: Structuring and Revitalizing*

the Corporation for the 21st Century (New York: Edward Burlingame Books/HarperBusiness, 1992), p. 187.

82. *The hazardous element . . . found in all employees:* Edward E. Lawler III, *The Ultimate Advantage: Creating the High-Involvement Organization* (San Francisco: Jossey-Bass Inc., 1992), p. 29.

82. *As a general rule . . . work in teams:* Lawler, *id.*, p. 53.

82. *Furthermore, the high-involvement . . . aren't necessary:* A. J. Vogl, "Bureaucracy Busting," *Across the Board*, March 1993, pp. 23–24.

82. *People who desire . . . decision-making skills:* Edward E. Lawler III, *The Ultimate Advantage: Creating the High-Involvement Organization* (San Francisco: Jossey-Bass Inc., 1992), p. 95.

82. *The high-involvement . . . just a job:* Lawler, *id.*, p. 227. Reprinted by permission of Jossey-Bass Inc.

83. *In 1911, . . . engineers with stopwatches:* "Return of the Stopwatch," *The Economist*, January 23, 1993, p. 69.

83. *"Taylorism" is now . . . a disciple of Taylor:* "Return of the Stopwatch," *id.*

83. *One aspect of . . . each task more efficient:* "Return of the Stopwatch," *id.*

84. *The reason that . . . the assembly line:* "Return of the Stopwatch," *id.*

84. *Chrysler has . . . marketers and salespeople:* "The Team Dream," *The Economist*, September 5, 1992, p. 69.

84. *GM's Saturn plant . . . traditional GM plants:* "Fall Sponsor Forum at Saturn," *QPMA Update*, November/December 1992, p. 1.

84. *The success of Saturn . . . the United States:* "Fall Sponsor Forum at Saturn," *id.*

84. *Each year, . . . were implemented:* D. Keith Denton, *Horizontal Management: Beyond Total Customer Satisfaction* (New York: Lexington Books/Macmillan, 1991), p. 112.

85. *Incentive magazine reports . . . each suggestion:* D. S. Ramelli III and Clifton Cooksey, "How to Run a Suggestion Program," *Incentive*, October 1991, pp. 103–108.

86. *The High-Reliability . . . of recognition:* "Fujitsu Oyama: Where Daily Work Equals Continuous Learning," *Total Employee Involvement*, October 1992, p. 8.

86. *Harris Corporation's . . . improving an enterprise:* "Nine Ways to Reward and Recognize Employees," *Total Quality Newsletter*, March 1992, p. 4.

88. *Infiniti, the luxury car . . . $25,000 per quarter:* "More Firms Link Pay, Cash Bonuses to Service to Sustain Long-Term Change," *The Service Edge*, May 1992, p. 1.

88. *Chrysler Corporation . . . form of bonuses:* "More Firms Link Pay, . . . ," *id.*

88. *Another example of the effect . . . executive approval:* Ann Walmsley, "Trading Places," *Report on Business Magazine*, March 1992, p. 20.

89. *There are six principles . . . for all those results:* "A Fresh Look at Recognition," *Commitment Plus*, January 1992, p. 1.

89. *The Baxter organization . . . budget was $613,000:* "Individual Incentives at Baxter Credit Union," *Commitment Plus*, February 1992, p. 1.

90. *The 1980s was the decade . . . of our people:* Robert H. Rosen, with Lisa Berger, *The Healthy Company: Eight Strategies to Develop People, Productivity, and Profits* (Los Angeles: Jeremy P. Tarcher, Inc., 1991), p. 125.

90. *Specific characteristics . . . part of managing oneself:* Rosen/Berger, *id.,* p. 129.

91. *Good employee "raw material"* . . . *the same period:* Ronald Henkoff, "Companies That Train Best," *Fortune,* March 22, 1993, pp. 62–64.

91. *Combining effective recruiting* . . . *rate of 96 percent:* Hal F. Rosenbluth and Diane McFerrin Peters, *The Customer Comes Second and Other Secrets of Exceptional Service* (New York: William Morrow and Company, 1992), p. 9.

92. *The reason why* . . . *really means:* Rosenbluth and Peters, *id.,* p. 18.

92. *To determine its employees'* . . . *form of communication:* Rosenbluth and Peters, *id.,* p. 21.

93. *We're not saying* . . . *everybody wins:* Rosenbluth and Peters, *id.,* p. 25.

93. *All too often* . . . *as their legacy:* Rosenbluth and Peters, *id.,* p. 9.

93. *You hear the word* . . . *stuff to me:* Ron Zemke, "With Clarity of Purpose, Employees Thrive," *The Service Edge,* December 1992, p. 8.

94. *How well do you* . . . *keep customers happy:* Zemke, *id.*

94. *A unique example of these* . . . *higher recognition:* "Don't Set Up Roadblocks to Service, Let Workers Run the Show," *On Achieving Excellence,* March 1992, p. 2.

95. *Employers who think* . . . *and other expenses:* Robert H. Rosen, with Lisa Berger, *The Healthy Company: Eight Strategies to Develop People, Productivity, and Profits* (Los Angeles: Jeremy P. Tarcher, Inc., 1991), p. 14.

95. *In addition, high job* . . . *health care expenses:* Rosen/Berger, *id.,* p. 23.

95. *Researchers at Northwestern* . . . *and productivity: The Service Edge,* April 1993, p. 6.

96. *Authors Tom Peters* . . . *". . . remain competitive?":* "The Death of Corporate Loyalty," *The Economist,* April 3, 1993, p. 63.

97. *Organize an intensive* . . . *is expected of them:* Scott Langdon, "How to Handle an "Internal Crisis," *DBM Communique,* Spring 1993, p. 2.

98. *By the year 2050* . . . *customers and suppliers:* John P. Fernandez, *Managing a Diverse Work Force: Regaining the Competitive Edge* (Lexington, MA: Lexington Books, 1991), p. 51.

98. *Canada's Honeywell Ltd. . . . her job performance:* Bruce Little, "A Factory Learns to Survive," *The Globe & Mail,* May 18, 1993, p. B22.

99. *You can use some* . . . *and disabled care:* John P. Fernandez, *Managing a Diverse Work Force: Regaining the Competitive Edge* (Lexington, MA: Lexington Books, 1991), p. 280.

99. *Carolina Fine Snacks* . . . *down to 5 percent:* "Disabled Workers Motivate an Able-Bodied Work Force," *On Achieving Excellence,* September 1992, p. 10.

Touchstone 5: Partnerships for Prosperity

101. *An Ernst & Young study* . . . *and foreign markets: John Kettle's FutureLetter,* January 1, 1993, p. 1.

101. *For most global businesses* . . . *Darwinian game:* Joel Bleeke and David Ernst, "The Death of the Predator," in Joel Bleeke and David Ernst, eds. *Collaborating to Compete: Using Strategic Alliances and Acquisitions in the Global Marketplace* (New York: John Wiley & Sons, Inc., 1993), p. 1. Reprinted by permission of John Wiley & Sons, Inc.

102. *The creation of . . . similar entities:* Charles C. Poirier and William F. Houser, *Business Partnering for Continuous Improvement: How to Forge Enduring Alliances among Employees, Suppliers and Customers* (San Francisco: Berrett-Koehler Publishers, 1993), p. 56. Reprinted by permission of Berrett-Koehler Publishers.

102. *The film industry . . . project is completed: John Kettle's FutureLetter,* January 1, 1993, p. 1.

102. *Partnering often refers . . . learn from failures:* Ron Zemke, "Partnering, Act II: An Evolving Concept," *The Service Edge,* February 1992, p. 8.

103. *The multilayered . . . firm in the industry:* "Decisions, Decisions," *The Economist,* February 27, 1993, p. 13.

103. *Even firms with a revolutionary . . . popular program:* "Decisions, Decisions," *id.*

104. *Every time a Childress . . . car washers:* "Auto Dealer Keeps 70 Percent of Service Customers Coming Back, Leaves Competitors Behind," *On Achieving Excellence,* May 1992, p. 5.

104. *Customers are amazed . . . service customers:* "Auto Dealer Keeps 70 Percent of Service Customers Coming Back . . . ," *id.*

104. *The Ritz-Carlton . . . keep a customer satisfied:* "How the Ritz-Carlton Hotel Company Delivers 'Memorable' Service to Customers," *Executive Report on Customer Satisfaction,* March 15, 1993, p. 1.

106. *AfterMarketing is the process . . . with all customers":* Terry G. Vavra, *AfterMarketing: How to Keep Customers for Life through Relationship Marketing* (Homewood, IL: Business One Irwin, 1992), p. 22. Reprinted by permission of Business One Irwin.

106. *Customers have a distinct life . . . from a firm:* Vavra, *id.,* p. 38. Reprinted by permission of Business One Irwin.

106. *Witness the turnaround . . . and market share:* John A. Swaim, "Customer Empowerment," *Quality Digest,* June 1992, p. 38.

106. *Since that time . . . customer satisfaction levels:* Swaim, *id.*

107. *Glen DeSouza . . . to attract new customers:* Glen DeSouza, "Designing a Customer Retention Plan," *Journal of Business Strategy,* March/April 1992, pp. 24–28.

108. *"The true cost . . . over a lifetime":* DeSouza, *id.,* p. 24. Permission granted by Faulkner & Gray, 11 Penn Plaza, New York, NY 11081.

108. *Measure customer retention . . . less than before:* DeSouza, *id.,* pp. 24–28.

108. *Interview former customers . . . ". . . market research":* DeSouza, *id.,* p. 25. Permission granted by Faulkner & Gray, 11 Penn Plaza, New York, NY 10001.

108. *In 1992, Air Canada . . . service failure:* Murray Wood and Gordon Pitts, "Zero Defections," *The Globe and Mail,* October 6, 1992, p. B28. Reprinted by permission of *The Globe and Mail.*

108. *This is what . . . our revenues:* Wood and Pitts, *id.* Reprinted by permission of *The Globe and Mail.*

108. *Price defectors are those . . . from Airbus:* Glen DeSouza, "Designing a Customer Retention Plan," *Journal of Business Strategy,* March/April 1992, pp. 24–28.

109. *Analyze complaint and . . . ". . . voice their complaints":* DeSouza, *id.* Permission granted by Faulkner & Gray, 11 Penn Plaza, New York, NY 10001.

109. *For example, in 1977 . . . number of customers:* DeSouza, *id.*

110. *Polaroid received . . . or dangerous, pattern:* DeSouza, *id.*

110. *Identify switching barriers . . . ". . . at a lower price":* DeSouza, *id.* Permission granted by Faulkner & Gray, 11 Penn Plaza, New York, NY 10001.

110. *Lotus Development Corporation . . . the technology link:* DeSouza, *id.*

111. *Strategic bundling is . . . in the bundle:* DeSouza, *id.* Permission granted by Faulkner & Gray, 11 Penn Plaza, New York, NY 10001.

111. *Cadet Uniform . . . given a solo route:* "How to Keep Customers for Life: Some Clues for Putting Theory into Practice," *The Service Edge,* September 1992, pp. 1–3.

111. *"Our compensation plan . . . a lot of money":* "How to Keep Customers for Life . . . ," *id.,* p. 1.

111. *Once accounts are . . . ". . . so dramatic":* "How to Keep Customers for Life . . . ," id., p. 2.

111. *An additional 28 percent . . . 22 to 23 percent annually:* "How to Keep Customers for Life . . . ," *id.,* p. 2.

111. *You have to love . . . with genuine interest":* "How to Keep Customers for Life . . . ," *id.,* p. 2.

112. *Supplier partnerships are . . . required from each other:* "Focus, The Supplier Partnership," *Service Report,* Vol. 1, Issue 10, May 1992, p. 1. Reprinted by permission of Anne Petite and Associates Ltd.

112. *One of the more challenging . . . to your competitor:* "Sears Supplier Quality Partnership Is a Partnership for Success," *Service Report,* Vol. 1, Issue 10, May 1992, p. 1. Reprinted by permission of Anne Petite and Associates Ltd.

112. *The role of each . . . to each other:* "Focus: The Supplier Partnership," *Service Report,* Vol. 1, Issue 10, May 1992, p. 2.

112. *Sears has developed . . . the supplier's management:* "Sears Supplier Quality Partnership Is a Partnership for Success," *Service Report,* Vol. 1, Issue 10, May 1992, p. 1.

113. *"By bringing assistance . . . competitive environment":* "Sears Supplier Quality Partnership . . . ," *id.* Reprinted by permission of Anne Petite and Associates Ltd.

113. *Cummins/Onan Corporation's . . . supplier for each job:* Vera K. Pang, "Scientifically Selecting Suppliers," *Quality Progress,* February 1992, p. 43.

114. *Supplier evaluation . . . as much as possible:* Charles C. Poirier and William F. Houser, *Business Partnering for Continuous Improvement: How to Forge Enduring Alliances among Employees, Suppliers, and Customers* (San Francisco: Berrett-Koehler Publishers, 1993), p. 183.

115. *Stage 1: Uncertainty . . . through shared savings:* Poirier and Houser, *id.,* p. 185.

115. *When a successful supplier . . . its client's sales staff does:* Personal interview.

116. *We have a mandate . . . didn't do yours:* Personal interview.

116. *Padulo Advertising . . . successful in this decade:* Personal interview.

116. *Padulo won hands down . . . fast as we do:* Personal interview.

116. *Review and update your . . . business with each other:* "Focus: The Supplier Partnership," *Service Report,* Vol. 1, Issue 10, May 1992, pp. 2–5.

117. *In the early 1980s . . . in the marketplace:* Louis P. Bucklin and Sanjit Sengupta, "Organizing Successful Co-Marketing Alliances," *Journal of Marketing,* April 1993, pp. 32–45.

117. *. . . IBM expands its . . . corporate computing:* Louis P. Bucklin and Sanjit Sengupta, "Organizing Successful Co-Marketing Alliances," *Journal of*

Marketing, April 1993, p. 32. Reprinted by permission of the American Marketing Association.

117. *Despite their potential . . . intellectual property:* Bucklin and Sengupta, *id.,* p. 33. Reprinted by permission of the American Marketing Association.

118. *Motorola is widely . . . with other services:* Charles Aubry II, "Business Partnerships: The New Opportunity," *Juran News,* Spring 1993, p. 1.

118. *The most successful . . . production operations:* David Severson, "Collaboration, Cooperation and Celebration," *Quality Progress,* September 1992, p. 63. Reprinted by permission of *Quality Progress.*

118. *World-class manufacturers . . . ". . . way to do something":* Severson, *id.,* p. 63.

118. *The Eli Lilly Tippecanoe . . . problem-free unit:* Severson, *id.,* p. 63.

119. *Engineers, line specialists . . . of improvement:* Severson, *id.,* p. 63. Reprinted by permission of *Quality Progress.*

119. *Indeed, the role of supplier . . . any Lexus dealership:* Thomas A. Stewart, "There Are No Products—Only Services," *Fortune,* January 14, 1991, p. 32.

119. *Commodore Business Machines . . . and customer:* Stewart, *id.*

119. *The evolution of interconnected . . . in the system:* "Becton Dickinson's Partnership Approach to Customer Satisfaction," *Executive Report on Customer Satisfaction,* May 15, 1993, pp. 3–5.

120. *Becton Dickinson is . . . total system cost:* "Becton Dickinson's Partnership Approach . . . ," *id.,* p. 3. Reprinted by permission of *Executive Report on Customer Satisfaction.*

120. *The company then . . . ". . . automatic replenishment":* "Becton Dickinson's Partnership Approach . . . ," *id.,* p. 3. Reprinted by permission of *Executive Report on Customer Satisfaction.*

120. *These features support . . . investment in inventory:* "Becton Dickinson's Partnership Approach . . . ," *id.,* p. 4.

121. *Corning's joint venture . . . any acquisition premium:* Joel Bleeke and David Ernst, "The Way to Win in Cross-Border Alliances," in Joel Bleeke and David Ernst, eds., *Collaborating to Compete: Using Strategic Alliances and Acquisitions in the Global Marketplace* (New York: John Wiley & Sons, Inc., 1993), p. 21.

121. *Crédit Suisse–First Boston . . . the early 1980s:* Bleeke and Ernst, *id.,* p. 19.

121. *It's crucial in strategic . . . mediocre performance:* Bleeke and Ernst, *id.,* p. 18.

121. *A lop-sided joint venture . . . the Japanese partner up:* Bleeke and Ernst, *id.,* p. 22.

122. *Companies are just beginning . . . to go it alone:* Kenichi Ohmae, "The Global Logic of Strategic Alliances," in Joel Bleeke and David Ernst, eds., *Collaborating to Compete: Using Strategic Alliances and Acquisitions in the Global Marketplace* (New York: John Wiley & Sons, Inc., 1993), p. 35. Reprinted by permission of John Wiley & Sons, Inc.

122. *Treat the collaboration . . . and independence:* Ohmae, *id.,* p. 46.

Touchstone 6: Transforming through Technology

124. *Information technology . . . to a new age:* Pierre Ducros, "Managing in a Knowledge-Based Canada," *Business Quarterly,* Spring 1993, p. 88. Reprinted by permission of *Business Quarterly.*

125. *A shift to knowledge . . . knowledge-based marketplace:* Ducros, *id.*

126. *Streamlining the business . . . can be reduced:* Norman Weizer, George O. Gardner III, Stuart Lipoff, Martyn F. Roetter, and Frederick G. Withington, *The Arthur D. Little Forecast on Information Technology and Productivity: Making the Integrated Enterprise Work* (New York: John Wiley & Sons, Inc., 1991), p. 41.

126. *Corporations such as . . . narrow specialties:* Weizer et al., *id.*, p. 12.

126. *As information spreads . . . able to reach:* Weizer et al., *id.* Reprinted by permission of John Wiley & Sons, Inc.

126. *Responding rapidly to . . . market trends:* Weizer et al., *id.*, p. 41.

126. *In Tokyo . . . to retailers:* Don Tapscott and Art Caston, *Paradigm Shift: The New Promise of Information Technology* (New York: McGraw-Hill, 1993), p. 69.

126. *Responding more rapidly . . . to a minimum:* Norman Weizer, George O. Gardner III, Stuart Lipoff, Martyn F. Roetter, and Frederick G. Withington, *The Arthur D. Little Forecast on Information Technology and Productivity: Making the Integrated Enterprise Work* (New York: John Wiley & Sons, Inc., 1991), p. 41.

127. *One major American . . . profitability of 15 percent: Trends in Information Technology, Fourth Edition: The Challenge of Business Integration,* Andersen Consulting, 1991, p. 35.

127. *Using resources more . . . from the other:* Norman Weizer, George O. Gardner III, Stuart Lipoff, Martyn F. Roetter, and Frederick G. Withington, *The Arthur D. Little Forecast on Information Technology and Productivity: Making the Integrated Enterprise Work* (New York: John Wiley & Sons, Inc., 1991), p. 41.

128. *While many complex . . . to be questioned:* Don Tapscott and Art Caston, *Paradigm Shift: The New Promise of Information Technology* (New York: McGraw-Hill, 1993), p. 26. Reprinted by permission of McGraw-Hill, Inc.

128. *For example, Cigna RE Corporation . . . as much as 40 percent:* Sid L. Huff, "Reengineering the Business," *Business Quarterly,* Winter 1992, p. 40.

129. *Increasing speed . . . expensive than labor:* Daniel Morris and Joel Brandon, *Re-Engineering Your Business* (New York: McGraw-Hill, 1993), p. 188.

129. *One of the biggest . . . cabinets' worth of paper:* Robert A. Cronkleton, "End of Paper Trail: Offices Do Everything via Computer," *Positive Impact,* March 1993, pp. 7–8. [Original source: *Kansas City Star,* January 25, 1993.]

130. *Many experts doubt . . . accomplish all three:* Cronkleton, *id.* [Original source: *Kansas City Star,* January 25, 1993.]

130. *Proponents of imaging . . . meaningful tasks:* Cronkleton, *id.*

130. *To better appreciate . . . on to the computer:* "Empowerment through Technology at USAA," *Commitment Plus,* July 1992, pp. 1–4.

131. *When a call comes in . . . done and when:* "Empowerment Through Technology at USAA," *id.* Reprinted by permission of the Quality & Productivity Management Association, Schaumburg, IL.

131. *While speaking . . . ". . . with our members":* "Empowerment Through Technology at USAA," *id.*

131. *In 1992, worldwide shipment . . . can't work:* Robert A. Cronkleton, "End of Paper Trail: Offices Do Everything via Computer," *Positive Impact,* March 1993, pp. 7–8. [Original source: *Kansas City Star,* January 25, 1993.]

132. *Assess current information . . . improve work processes:* Daniel Morris and Joel Brandon, *Re-Engineering Your Business* (New York: McGraw-Hill, 1993), p. 195.

132. *Personalized service . . . are most needed:* Blake Ives and Richard O. Mason, "Can Information Technology Revitalize Your Customer Service?" *Academy of Management Executive,* p. 52.

132. *K mart Corporation's . . . something to do:* "Asking Tough Questions Helps Match Right Technology to Service Initiatives," *The Service Edge,* April 1992, p. 1.

132. *Augmented service . . . of the product:* Blake Ives and Richard O. Mason, "Can Information Technology Revitalize Your Customer Service?" *Academy of Management Executive,* p. 55.

133. *United Parcel Service . . . next big advances:* "Asking Tough Questions Helps Match Right Technology to Service Initiatives," *The Service Edge,* April 1992, p. 2.

133. *Transformed service . . . business differentiation:* Blake Ives and Richard O. Mason, "Can Information Technology Revitalize Your Customer Service?" *Academy of Management Executive,* p. 63.

133. *Today, sophisticated . . . each recipient:* Ives and Mason, *id.,* p. 63.

133. *National, the car rental . . . handheld printer:* Don Tapscott and Art Caston, *Paradigm Shift: The New Promise of Information Technology* (New York: McGraw-Hill, 1993), p. 68.

134. *A Canadian daily . . . front door:* Tapscott and Caston, *id.,* p. 106.

134. *Toll-free 800-number . . . calls by 1997:* "The Customer Service Department of the Nineties: Integrating People, Technology and Quality," *Customer Service Newsletter,* February 1993, pp. 1–5.

135. *The CAC . . . service technician:* "The Customer Service Department of the Nineties: Integrating People, Technology and Quality," *Customer Service Newsletter,* February 1993, pp. 1–5.

135. *According to Cynthia Grimm . . . reach originally:* "Centralizing Service: Done Well, Fewer Employees Give Customers Better Care," *The Service Edge,* February 1993, p. 1.

135. *After implementing . . . actually increased:* "Centralizing Service: Done well . . . ," *id.*

136. *According to the 1992 . . . software are needed:* "Recipe for an Effective 800-Number Call Center," *The Service Edge,* February 1993, p. 1.

136. *In the highly competitive . . . and profits:* Blake Ives and Richard O. Mason, "Can Information Technology Revitalize Your Customer Service?" *Academy of Management Executive,* p. 52.

136. *Progress in information . . . life cycle:* Ives and Mason, *id.*

137. *For example, American Airlines . . . make sense:* William Fellows, The Coopers & Lybrand Consulting Group, "Opportunities for Enhancing Sales and Marketing Productivity Through the Use of Information Technology," presentation given at the Canadian Institute Smart Selling Conference, June 2, 1993, p. 17.

137. *Even Atlantic City casinos . . . gambling activities:* Fellows, *id.,* p. 13.

137. *Walden Books . . . software for cooking:* Fellows, *id.,* p. 14.

137. *Journey's End hotels . . . dialogue with buyers:* John Southerst, "Customer Crunching," *Canadian Business Review,* September 1993, pp. 28–35.

138. *Your customer database . . . when the promotion ran:* Southerst, *id.,* p. 30.

139. *Think of EDI as . . . you get in early:* "EDI or Die," *Issues for Canada's Future,* June 1992, p. 1.

139. *EDI is having . . . Eaton's client's account:* "EDI or Die," *id.*

140. *K mart Corporation . . . links with customers:* Don Tapscott, "Creating the Company without Borders," *Globe and Mail,* November 17, 1992, p. B24.

140. *When companies do not forge . . . to develop:* Tapscott, *id.*

140. *The economic impact . . . out the problem:* Mark Stevenson, "Virtual Mergers," *Canadian Business Review,* September 1993, pp. 20–26.

141. *Wal-Mart Stores Inc . . . Bentonville, Arkansas:* Stevenson, *id.*

141. *Procter & Gamble . . . actually delivered:* Stevenson, *id.*

141. *Author Ken Copeland . . . ". . . organization equation":* Ken Copeland, "Infotech: Shaping Management to Come," *Business Quarterly,* Spring 1993, pp. 125–128. Reprinted by permission of *Business Quarterly.*

142. *Information technology . . . manager's organization:* Copeland, *id.,* p. 125. Reprinted by permission of *Business Quarterly.*

142. *The internal focus . . . and visionaries:* Copeland, *id.* Reprinted by permission of *Business Quarterly.*

142. *New technologies are . . . called "subordinates":* Copeland, *id.*

142. *In the information age . . . more responsive:* Copeland, *id.,* p. 126. Reprinted by permission of *Business Quarterly.*

142. *Data entry . . . to selected audiences:* Don Tapscott and Art Caston, *Paradigm Shift: The New Promise of Information Technology* (New York: McGraw-Hill, 1993), pp. 248–250. Reprinted by permission of McGraw-Hill, Inc.

145. *LINK Resources . . . telecommuters in 1992:* Jocelyne Côté-O'Hara, "Sending Them Home to Work: Telecommuting," *Business Quarterly,* Spring 1993, pp. 104–109.

145. *Telecommuting can save on . . . save money:* "Telecommuting—Bringing Calls Home to CSRs," *Customer Service Newsletter,* February 1993, p. 1.

145. *Working from home . . . off-peak times:* Telecommuting—Bringing Calls Home . . . ," *id.*

145. *Letting workers telecommute . . . wants and needs:* Telecommuting—Bringing Calls Home . . . ," *id.*

145. *A 1985 study conducted . . . and working mothers:* Jocelyne Côté-O'Hara, "Sending Them Home to Work: Telecommuting," *Business Quarterly,* Spring 1993, pp. 104–109.

146. *Four years ago . . . computer company's books:* Côté-O'Hara, id., p. 104. Reprinted by permission of *Business Quarterly.*

146. *To help reduce . . . mail and faxes:* Côté-O'Hara, *id.,* p. 104.

146. *The benefits of telecommuting . . . marketplace:* Côté-O'Hara, *id.* Reprinted by permission of *Business Quarterly.*

146. *In a survey of over . . . productivity gains:* Côté-O'Hara, *id.,* p. 107.

147. *Do: Look for real . . . child care problem:* Côté-O'Hara, *id.,* p. 106.

148. *The global development . . . adopting them:* Roger A. More, "Managing New Technology Adoption," *Business Quarterly,* Spring 1992, pp. 69–74. Reprinted by permission of *Business Quarterly.*

148. *Often, a vast number . . . appeal or utility:* More, *id.*

148. *Important business factors . . . set of customer files:* Norman Weizer, George O. Gardner III, Stuart Lipoff, Martyn F. Roetter, and Frederick G. Withington, *The Arthur D. Little Forecast on Information Technology and Productivity: Making the Integrated Enterprise Work* (New York: John Wiley & Sons, Inc., 1991), p. 78.

149. *Improperly conceived and . . . or been relocated:* Thayer C. Taylor, "Back from the Future," *Marketing Executive Report,* August 1992, p. 10. [Reprinted from *Sales & Marketing Management,* June 1992.]

149. *We were naive . . . reps didn't help:* Taylor, *id.,* p. 11.

149. *Market share . . . total margin produced:* Roger A. More, "Managing New Technology Adoption," *Business Quarterly,* Spring 1992, pp. 69–74.

150. *The Gartner Group . . . infotech staff:* Ken Copeland, "Infotech: Shaping Management to Come," *Business Quarterly,* Spring 1993, pp. 125–128.

150. *Complete connectivity . . . and industrial spies:* Norman Weizer, George O. Gardner III, Stuart Lipoff, Martyn F. Roetter, and Frederick G. Withington, *The Arthur D. Little Forecast on Information Technology and Productivity: Making the Integrated Enterprise Work* (New York: John Wiley & Sons, Inc., 1991), p. 66.

Touchstone 7: Strategy Alignment

153. *A good example of . . . efforts were scattered:* "Moving Service from the Abstract to the Concrete: A Major Initiative at Aetna Life Insurance Company of Canada," *Service Report,* June/July 1992, p. 1.

153. *We needed to clearly . . . unrelated activities:* "Moving Service from the Abstract to the Concrete . . . ," *id.*

153. *Stojsic and Stephen . . . achieve that goal:* "Moving Service from the Abstract to the Concrete . . . ," *id.*

154. *Aetna will use . . . commitments (tangibles):* "Moving Service from the Abstract to the Concrete . . . ," *id.,* p. 2.

154. *Broken down into . . . employee commitment:* "Moving Service from the Abstract to the Concrete . . . ," *id.*

154. *"I believe that . . . very worthwhile":* "Moving Service from the Abstract to the Concrete . . . ," *id.*

154. *A value strategy . . . "customized economy":* Harry S. Dent, Jr., *The Great Boom Ahead* (New York: Hyperion, 1993), pp. 115–136.

155. *. . . consists of . . . assembly-line production:* Dent, *id.,* p. 135. Reprinted by permission of Hyperion.

155. *This approach has . . . "mass customization":* Dent, *id.*

155. *We've been creating . . . at lower cost:* Dent, *id.,* p. 136. Reprinted by permission of Hyperion.

155. *Dent proposes that . . . continue to fall:* Dent, *id.*

156. *Discount value . . . is rapidly growing:* Dent, *id.*

156. *Standard value . . . enough to compete:* Dent, *id.*

156. *Restructure to become . . . geographic markets:* Dent, *id.*

158. *Entering premium value . . . value players:* Dent, *id.*

158. *Buying into premium . . . from your competition:* Dent, *id.*

159. *. . . the goal is . . . eyes of the customers:* *Harvard Business Review,* March 1993, p. 62.

160. *The success of Honda . . . chief executive officer (CEO):* George Stalk, Philip Evans, and Lawrence E. Shulman, "Competing on Capabilities: The New Rules of Corporate Strategy," *Harvard Business Review,* March–April 1992, pp. 57–69.

160. *The starting point . . . strategic capabilities:* Stalk et al., *id.,* p. 57. Copyright © 1992 by The President and Fellows of Harvard College; all rights reserved. Reprinted by permission of *Harvard Business Review.*

160. *Shift the strategic . . . choice of merchandise:* Stalk et al., *id.*

161. *The real secret . . . customer needs:* Stalk et al., *id.*, p. 58. Copyright © 1992 by The President and Fellows of Harvard College; all rights reserved. Reprinted by permission of *Harvard Business Review.*

162. *Wal-Mart's goal was . . . system to implement:* Stalk et al., *id.*

162. *To make cross-docking . . . ROI criteria:* Stalk et al., *id.* Copyright © 1992 by The President and Fellows of Harvard College; all rights reserved. Reprinted by permission of *Harvard Business Review.*

162. *To make the system . . . retail strategies:* Stalk et al., *id.*

163. *. . . Wal-Mart emphasizes . . . dynamic rivals:* Stalk et al., *id.*, p. 60. Copyright © 1992 by The President and Fellows of Harvard College; all rights reserved. Reprinted by permission of *Harvard Business Review.*

163. *As more and more . . . essence of strategy:* Stalk et al., *id.*, p. 69. Copyright © 1992 by The President and Fellows of Harvard College; all rights reserved. Reprinted by permission of *Harvard Business Review.*

164. *Experts have a hard . . . ". . . corporate strategy":* "Strategy Has a Hard Time Getting Off the Chalk Board," *The Globe and Mail,* April 27, 1993, p. B22. [Reprinted from *The Economist.*]

164. *The concept of business . . . "strategic intent":* "Strategy Has a Hard Time . . . ," *id.*

165. *How a company views . . . their skills:* "Strategy Has a Hard Time . . . ," *id.*

165. *Traditional models . . . and objectives:* T. Wood Parker, "Total Quality Management Strategic Planning." Coopers & Lybrand, 1992.

165. *By contrast, newer ways . . . organization as a whole:* Parker, *id.*

166. *Conrail is a good . . . vision come true:* John M. Samuels, "Visioning" Conrail's foundation for Continuous Quality Improvement," *Tapping the Network Journal,* Fall/Winter 1991, pp. 17–18.

167. *The entire process . . . at all levels:* Samuels, *id.* Reprinted by permission of the Quality & Productivity Management Association, Schaumburg, IL.

167. *Once there was broad . . . irrelevant issues:* Samuels, *id.*

167. *John N. Younker . . . some reasonable boundaries:* John N. Younker, "Organization Direction-Setting: Key Concepts and Definitions," *Tapping the Network Journal,* Fall/Winter 1991, pp. 19–28.

167. *[Employees] will invest . . . contribute to them:* Younker, *id.*, p. 21. Reprinted by permission of the Quality & Productivity Management Association, Schaumburg, IL.

167. *"A statement that . . . of endeavor:"* Younker, *id.* Reprinted by permission of the Quality & Productivity Management Association, Schaumburg, IL.

168. *"It is a rather . . . marketplace conditions":* Younker, *id.* Reprinted by permission of the Quality & Productivity Management Association, Schaumburg, IL.

168. *Generally speaking . . . improve performance:* Younker, *id.*

168. *"A statement describing . . . for existence":* Younker, *id.* Reprinted by permission of the Quality & Productivity Management Association, Schaumburg, IL.

168. *The mission describes . . . are built:* Younker, *id.*

169. *"Statements identifying . . . its mission":* Younker, *id.*, p. 22. Reprinted by permission of the Quality & Productivity Management Association, Schaumburg, IL.

169. *Priorities serve to identify . . . the vision:* Younker, *id.*

169. *"Statements of short-term . . . that priority":* Younker, *id.* Reprinted by permission of the Quality & Productivity Management Association, Schaumburg, IL.

169. *Objectives state clearly . . . safety objectives, for example.* Younker, *id.*

169. *"A series of statements . . . and choices":* Younker, *id.* Reprinted by permission of the Quality & Productivity Management Association, Schaumburg, IL.

169. *Guiding principles are . . . management behavior:* Younker, *id.*

170. *"Statements that describe . . . its environment":* Younker, *id.,* p. 23. Reprinted by permission of the Quality & Productivity Management Association, Schaumburg, IL.

170. *These statements . . . organization's employees:* Younker, *id.*

170. *"The hard numbers . . . a successful entity":* Younker, *id.* Reprinted by permission of the Quality & Productivity Management Association, Schaumburg, IL.

170. *Business expectations usually . . . measured against:* Younker, *id.*

170. *A well thought-out . . . individual efforts:* Younker, *id.* Reprinted by permission of the Quality & Productivity Management Association, Schaumburg, IL.

170. *The front-end investment . . . cross-purposes decrease:* Younker, *id.*

170. *You can ask any . . . as top management:* "Setting Goals: Proper Mix of Planning, Doing Equals Success," *Total Quality Newsletter,* January 1993, p. 1. Reprinted by permission of Total Quality Newsletter, Lakewood Publications, 50 South Ninth St., Minneapolis, MN 55402. All rights reserved. Not for resale.

171. *These companies craft . . . that anymore:* "Setting Goals: Proper Mix of Planning, Doing . . . ," *id.* Reprinted by permission of Total Quality Newsletter, Lakewood Publications, 50 South Ninth St., Minneapolis, MN 55402. All rights reserved. Not for resale.

171. *The literal translation . . . competitive advantage: Policy Management: Executive Briefing Manual* (Dearborn, MI: American Supplier Institute, 1989), p. 7.

171. *. . . a step-by-step planning . . . business processes:* Greg Watson, "Understanding Hoshin Kanri," in Yoji Akao, ed., *Hoshin Kanri: Policy Deployment for Successful TQM* (Cambridge, MA: Productivity Press, 1988), p. xxi.

171. *Hoshin operates on two . . . the management process:* Watson, id.

172. *Companies that have used . . . the organization:* "Hoshin Planning: A Planning System for Implementing Total Quality Management (TQM)," GOAL/QPC Research Committee, p. 1.

172. *The Hoshin approach rests . . . simple cycle:* Bob King, *Hoshin Planning: The Developmental Approach* (Bob King–GOAL/QPC, 1989), p. 3.

173. *In 1989, GOAL/QPC . . . for the next year:* "Hoshin Planning: A Planning System for Implementing Total Quality Management (TQM)," GOAL/QPC Research Committee, p. 12.

176. *Associated with Hoshin . . . numerical information:* "Hoshin Planning: A Planning System . . . ," *id.,* p. 5.

178. *McDonnell Douglas Space . . . more customer-driven:* "Deploying TQM and Empowerment at McDonnell Douglas Space Systems Co.," *Commitment Plus,* October 1992, pp. 1–4.

179. *"We moved to four . . . customer satisfaction"*: "Deploying TQM and Empowerment . . . ," *id.*, p. 2. Reprinted by permission of the Quality & Productivity Management Association, Schaumburg, IL.

179. *Later, however the company . . . Horizontal Team:* "Deploying TQM and Empowerment . . . ," *id.*

179. *We told them . . . Horizontal Team:* "Deploying TQM and Empowerment . . . ," *id.* Reprinted by permission of the Quality & Productivity Management Association, Schaumburg, IL.

179. *Each Horizontal Team . . . their processes:* "Deploying TQM and Empowerment . . . ," *id.*, p. 2. Reprinted by permission of the Quality & Productivity Management Association, Schaumburg, IL.

179. *The Horizontal Teams . . . [government] audit:* "Deploying TQM and Empowerment . . . ," *id.* Reprinted by permission of the Quality & Productivity Management Association, Schaumburg, IL.

179. *The horizontal teams . . . the next 10 years:* "Deploying TQM and Empowerment . . . ," *id.*

180. *Next, each division . . . recognition program:* "Deploying TQM and Empowerment . . . ," *id.*, p. 3. Reprinted by permission of the Quality & Productivity Management Association, Schaumburg, IL.

180. *MDSSC's successful policy . . . by 40 percent:* "Deploying TQM and Empowerment . . . ," *id.*

181. *Leadership at the top . . . style and intent:* "Deploying TQM and Empowerment . . . ," *id.*, p. 4. Reprinted by permission of the Quality & Productivity Management Association, Schaumburg, IL.

181. *Overall, I'd say we're . . . been worth it:* "Deploying TQM and Empowerment . . . ," *id.* Reprinted by permission of the Quality & Productivity Management Association, Schaumburg, IL.

Touchstone 8: Fostering the Learning Organization

182. *The manager's job . . . and continuous development:* The Tom Peters Group, "The Essence of Learning," *Implementation: Start Small, Think Big,* July 1988, p. 16.

183. *A disturbing report . . . are all Japanese:* "Hotbed of Innovation?," *Total Quality Newsletter,* April 1992, p. 8.

183. *Where has all the . . . than big business:* Andrew J. Parsons, "Building Innovativeness in Large U. S. Corporations," *The Journal of Business & Industrial Marketing,* Fall 1992, pp. 33–48.

183. *The result is that . . . small American companies:* Parsons, *id.*, p. 35. Reprinted by permission of MCB University Press Ltd.

184. *The failure is an . . . against global competitors:* Parsons, *id.*, p. 36. Reprinted by permission of MCB University Press Ltd.

184. *Innovation and creativity . . . rather than the manufacturer:* Parsons, *id.*

185. *Conventional wisdom says . . . corporate imagination:* Gary Hamel and C. K. Prahalad, "Corporate Imagination and Expeditionary Marketing," *Harvard Business Review,* July–August 1991, p. 82. Copyright © 1991 by The President and Fellows of Harvard College; all rights reserved. Reprinted by permission of *Harvard Business Review.*

185. *Escape the tyranny of . . . up to a television:* Hamel and Prahalad, *id.*

186. *"New competitive space . . . and industry boundaries":* Hamel and Prahalad, *id.*, p. 83. Copyright © 1991 by The President and Fellows of Harvard

College; all rights reserved. Reprinted by permission of *Harvard Business Review.*

186. *Innovations can add . . . and camcorders:* Hamel and Prahalad, *id.*

186. *"Managers and product designers . . . competitive space":* Hamel and Prahalad, *id.,* p. 84. Copyright © 1991 by The President and Fellows of Harvard College; all rights reserved. Reprinted by permission of *Harvard Business Review.*

186. *Sony and JVC used . . . touch of a finger:* Hamel and Prahalad, *id.*

186. *The competition was left . . . ". . . construction process":* Hamel and Prahalad, *id.* Copyright © 1991 by The President and Fellows of Harvard College; all rights reserved. Reprinted by permission of *Harvard Business Review.*

186. *Get out in front . . . already under way:* Hamel and Prahalad, *id.*

187. *"If your company has . . . an organizational failure":* Andrew J. Parsons, "Building Innovativeness in Large U.S. Corporations," *The Journal of Business & Industrial Marketing,* Fall 1992, p. 42. Reprinted by permission of MCB University Press Ltd.

187. *Strategic failure may be . . . support innovation:* Parsons, *id.*

187. *"It is critical . . . to the approach":* Parsons, *id.,* p. 43. Reprinted by permission of MCB University Press Ltd.

187. *The so-called "big bang leader" . . . set of priorities:* Parsons, *id.*

187. *"Often traditional functional . . . project teams":* Parsons, *id.,* p. 44. Reprinted by permission of MCB University Press Ltd.

187. *Teams consisting of five . . . the PC-10:* Parsons, *id.*

187. *"Successful innovation doesn't . . . their ideas":* Parsons, *id.* Reprinted by permission of MCB University Press Ltd.

187. *The initial stage . . . of successful innovation:* Parsons, *id.*

188. *The problem often facing . . . innovation will be accepted:* "Joel Barker: Overcoming Resistance to Innovation," *Total Employee Involvement,* June, 1992, p. 5.

189. *A learning organization . . . processes and opportunities:* Jocelyne Traub, "Case Study I: Building Systems to Support Continuous Learning and Change at Xerox Canada Inc.," presented at Building the Learning Organization Conference, July 15, 1993, Toronto, Ontario. Cosponsors: PRAXIS and The Coopers & Lybrand Consulting Group.

189. *Witness some of the . . . ". . . to learn is to teach":* "To Become the Best, Make Learning Your Business," *On Achieving Excellence,* November 1992, p. 2.

189. *Each of the company's 12 . . . to new technology:* "To Become the Best . . . ," *id.*

190. *"Getting rich is very easy . . . all the time":* "To Become the Best . . . ," *id.*

190. *The essence of innovation . . . say, an entrepreneur:* Ikujiro Nonaka, "The Knowledge-Creating Company," *Harvard Business Review,* November–December 1991, p. 97. Copyright © 1991 by The President and Fellows of Harvard College; all rights reserved. Reprinted by permission of *Harvard Business Review.*

190. *The centerpiece of the Japanese . . . and its mission:* Nonaka, *id.* Copyright © 1991 by The President and Fellows of Harvard College; all rights reserved. Reprinted by permission of *Harvard Business Review.*

190. *Nonaka believes the four . . . from explicit to tacit:* Ikujiro Nonaka, *id.,* p. 98.

191. *New ideas are essential . . . own work activities:* David A. Garvin, "Building a Learning Organization," *Harvard Business Review,* July–August 1993, pp. 78–91.

191. *Peter Senge, author . . . ". . . taking in information":* Walter Kiechel III, "The Organization That Learns," *Fortune,* March 12, 1990, p. 133. Reprinted by permission of *Fortune* © Time Inc. All rights reserved.

191. *David Garvin, of the Harvard . . . 7 to 8 percent annually:* David A. Garvin, "Building a Learning Organization," *Harvard Business Review,* July–August 1993, pp. 78–91.

192. *. . . statistical methods, like design . . . ideas flowing:* Garvin, *id.,* p. 83. Copyright © 1993 by The President and Fellows of Harvard College; all rights reserved. Reprinted by permission of *Harvard Business Review.*

192. *Demonstration projects . . . once they were operating:* Garvin, *id.*

193. *Whether they are demonstration . . . unforeseen events:* Garvin, *id.,* p. 84. Copyright © 1993 by The President and Fellows of Harvard College; all rights reserved. Reprinted by permission of *Harvard Business Review.*

194. *Learning from mistakes . . . to discuss their need:* Garvin, *id.*

194. *"Benchmarking is one way . . . patterns of use":* Garvin, *id.,* p. 86. Copyright © 1993 by The President and Fellows of Harvard College; all rights reserved. Reprinted by permission of *Harvard Business Review.*

194. *"Ideas carry maximum . . . in a few hands":* Garvin, *id.,* p. 87. Copyright © 1993 by The President and Fellows of Harvard College; all rights reserved. Reprinted by permission of *Harvard Business Review.*

194. *Written, oral, and visual . . . areas of the business:* Garvin, *id.*

195. *Benchmarking is a process . . . improvement activities:* "Becoming the Best," *Benchmarking: A Tool for Continuous Improvement,* Coopers & Lybrand.

196. *In 1979, the modern . . . magazine had ever received:* Marc Hequet, "The Limits of Benchmarking," *Marketing Executive Report,* March 1993, pp. 17–19.

196. *Studies conducted by . . . comparators' primary advantages:* Jeffrey A. Schmidt, "The Link between Benchmarking and Shareholder Value," *Journal of Business Strategy,* 1992, p. 7.

198. *Florida Power & Light . . . secure cooperation:* Betsy Wiesendanger, "Benchmarking by Numbers," *Inside Guide,* February/March 1993, p. 9.

199. *What happens if your . . . customer complaints:* Beth Enslow, "The Benchmarking Bonanza," *Across the Board,* April 1992, pp. 16–22. Used by permission of The Conference Board, Inc.

200. *Proper benchmarking can lead to . . . most failures:* Michael J. Spendolini and Neil H. Thompson, "Benchmarking Etiquette," *Tapping the Network Journal,* Fall 1992, p. 11. Reprinted by permission of the Quality & Productivity Management Association, Schaumburg, IL.

200. *Many organizations are . . . to benchmark at all:* Spendolini and Thompson, *id.,* 12. Reprinted by permission of the Quality & Productivity Management Association, Schaumburg, IL.

200. *Here are some rules . . . permission has been granted:* Spendolini and Thompson, *id.*

202. *They brought with them . . . through two years:* Marc Hequet, "The Limits of Benchmarking," *Marketing Executive Report,* March 1993, pp. 17–19.

202. *The company then did . . . the lesson to heart:* Hequet, *id.*

202. *When somebody comes to . . . and our values:* Hequet, *id.,* p. 20.

202. *Three principal resources . . . application of results:* Beth Enslow, "The Benchmarking Bonanza," *Across the Board,* April 1992, pp. 16–22. Used by permission of The Conference Board, Inc.

202. *"Sharing the cost . . . is a real plus":* Enslow, *id.,* p. 19. Reprinted by permission of The Conference Board, Inc.

202. *Ameritech and Brown became . . . planning databases:* Enslow, *id.* Used by permission of The Conference Board, Inc.

203. *It's clear that . . . benchmarking standards:* Enslow, *id.,* p. 20. Reprinted by permission of The Conference Board, Inc.

203. *American Productivity and Quality Center . . . and Japan:* Enslow, *id.* Used by permission of The Conference Board, Inc.

203. A Training *magazine annual . . . 24 percent were executives:* Ray Wise, "The Boom in Creativity Training," *Across the Board,* June 1991, p. 38.

204. *Frito-Lay, a division of . . . training other employees:* Thomas Kiely, "The Idea Makers," *Technology Review,* January 1993, p. 33.

204. *Creativity training has been . . . weighs the results:* Ray Wise, "The Boom in Creativity Training," *Across the Board,* June 1991, p. 38. Reprinted by permission of the author.

204. *At Kodak, workers . . . the company's systems:* Thomas Kiely, "The Idea Makers," *Technology Review,* January 1993, p. 33.

205. *Fantasy, games, and dream . . . within the company:* Kiely, *id.*

205. *Fluency techniques help . . . half-baked suggestions:* Kiely, *id.,* p. 34.

205. *Creativity demands openness . . . however raw:* Kiely, *id.*

206. *. . . brainstorming has become . . . and prioritized:* Kiely, *id.*

206. *During a group brainwriting . . . for the boss:* Kiely, *id.,* p. 35.

206. *With open communication . . . eliminating redundancies:* Kiely, *id.*

206. *. . . participants in a group . . . of the flow:* Kiely, *id.*

206. *At Xerox PARC, researchers . . . fill everyday needs:* Kiely, *id.*

207. *In a creativity session . . . outside the problem:* Ray Wise, "The Boom in Creativity Training," *Across the Board,* June 1991, p. 38. Reprinted by permission of the author.

207. *Excursion session push . . . ". . . won't yet disclose)":* Thomas Kiely, "The Idea Makers," *Technology Review,* January 1993, p. 35.

207. *Another example is a group . . . the next decade:* Kiely, *id.*

208. *Pattern breakers force . . . to improve business:* Kiely, *id.,* p. 37.

208. *Shake-up exercises . . . loosen up and relax:* Kiely, *id.*

209. *Kids discover, and when . . . alternatives are possible:* Ray Wise, "The Boom in Creativity Training," *Across the Board,* June 1991, p. 38. Reprinted by permission of the author.

209. *Foster an environment . . . are suggested projects:* David A. Garvin, "Building a Learning Organization," *Harvard Business Review,* July–August 1993, pp. 78–91.

Touchstone 9: Mastering Change Management

211. *Few markets remain stable . . . soon follows:* Mark O'Hare, *Innovate!: How to Gain and Sustain Competitive Advantage* (Oxford: Basil Blackwell, 1988), p. 109.

211. *The burst of technical . . . are more sophisticated:* Tom Terez, "Change Management: Strategies and Tactics for Today's Change Leaders," *Business and Technology Consultant,* June 1990, p. 36.

211. *The essence of change . . . and processes:* Coopers & Lybrand, *Change Management: Taking Charge of Change,* 1993, p. II-1.

212. *Organizational change can be . . . future state:* Coopers & Lybrand, *id.,* p. II-2.

212. *York University's Gareth Morgan . . . to different products:* Charles Hampden-Turner, *Creating Corporate Culture: From Discord to Harmony* (Reading, MA: Addison-Wesley Publishing Co., 1990), p. 200.

212. *Attempting to change . . . the suggested changes:* Hampden-Turner, *id.,* p. 184.

213. *"Early in my career . . . 'What smell?'":* Quoted in "Smell? What Smell?, It's the Stench of Poor Service," *The Service Edge,* Lakewood Publications, August 1993, Vol. 6, no. 8, p. 6.

213. *Find the ones that . . . customer satisfaction:* Charles Hampden-Turner, *Creating Corporate Culture: From Discord to Harmony* (Reading, MA: Addison-Wesley Publishing Co., 1990), p. 185.

213. *DeLorean attacked this . . . ". . . rather than success":* Hampden-Turner, *id.* Text © 1990 by Charles Hampden-Turner. Reprinted by permission of Addison-Wesley Publishing Co., Inc.

214. *Bring conflicts into . . . within the business:* Hampden-Turner, *id.,* p. 188.

214. *The interviewees may be . . . trap for consultants:* Hampden-Turner, *id.* Text © 1990 by Charles Hampden-Turner. Reprinted by permission of Addison-Wesley Publishing Co., Inc.

214. *British Airways' Nick Georgiades . . . care of them:* Hampden-Turner, *id.,* p. 191.

214. *Much work in the service . . . to the culture:* Hampden-Turner, *id.,* p. 85. Text © 1990 by Charles Hampden-Turner. Reprinted by permission of Addison-Wesley Publishing Co., Inc.

214. *Play out corporate dramas . . . change this perception:* Hampden-Turner, *id.,* p. 193.

215. *Unearth your enterprise . . . see in their work:* Hampden-Turner, *id.,* p. 196.

216. *It is possible to change . . . from 1980 to 1982:* Hampden-Turner, *id.,* p. 155.

216. *The change in fortunes was . . . a French audience:* Hampden-Turner, *id.* Text © 1990 by Charles Hampden-Turner. Reprinted by permission of Addison-Wesley Publishing Co., Inc.

216. *Carstedt was faced with . . . values the same thing:* Hampden-Turner, *id.,* p. 198.

216. *Look at the symbols . . . to accomplish something:* Hampden-Turner, *id.,* p. 199.

216. *Create new ways of . . . can be formulated:* Hampden-Turner, *id.,* p. 202.

216. *British Airways (BA) took . . . "Putting People First" (PPF):* Hampden-Turner, *id.,* p. 81.

217. *Staff were encouraged . . . for such difficulties:* Hampden-Turner, *id.,* p. 85. Text © 1990 by Charles Hampden-Turner. Reprinted by permission of Addison-Wesley Publishing Co., Inc.

217. *Colin Marshall attended . . . designed and implemented:* Hampden-Turner, *id.*

217. *Another lesson in "change management" . . . passing it by:* William Echikson, "How Hart It Is to Change Culture," *Fortune,* October 19, 1992, p. 114.

218. *The problem is that . . . his Japanese foes:* Echikson, *id.* Reprinted by permission of *Fortune* © 1992 Time Inc. All rights reserved.

219. *Change is not perceived . . . over our environment:* Daryl R. Conner, *Managing at the Speed of Change: How Resilient Managers Succeed and Prosper Where*

Others Fail (New York: Villard Books, 1993), p. 70. Reprinted by permission of Villard Books.

219. *People's strong need . . . have macro implications:* Conner, *id.*, pp. 75–79.

220. *"Micro change is when . . . must change":* Conner, *id.*, p. 79. Reprinted by permission of Villard Books.

220. *He believes that, in order . . . stresses of change:* Conner, *id.*, p. 178.

220. *In fact, when resilient people . . . their objectives:* Conner, *id.*, p. 229. Reprinted by permission of Villard Books.

220. *Type-D or danger . . . ". . . their expectations":* Conner, *id.*, p. 231. Reprinted by permission of Villard Books.

220. *Type-D people . . . absolutely necessary:* Conner, *id.*

220. *Type-O or opportunity . . . ". . . to be avoided":* Conner, *id.*, p. 235. Reprinted by permission of Villard Books.

220. *They usually have a strong . . . strain of change:* Conner, *id.*

221. *"They view change . . . terrifying to avoid":* Conner, *id.*, p. 237. Reprinted by permission of Villard Books.

221. *Every successful change program . . . this effort:* Murray M. Dalziel and Stephen C. Schoonover, *Changing Ways: A Practical Tool for Implementing Change Within Organizations* (New York: American Management Association, 1988), p. 21.

221. *Is there a motivation . . . can be misconstrued:* Dalziel and Schoonover, *id.*, p. 31.

222. *In dealing with radical . . . where it will lead:* Paul Strebel, *Breakpoints: How Managers Exploit Radical Business Change* (Boston: Harvard University Press, 1992), p. 71.

222. *The case of Niagara Mohawk Power . . . a meter reader:* Stephanie Losee, "Revolution from Within," *Fortune,* June 1, 1992, pp. 112–115.

222. *"The whole system . . . had to change":* Losee, *id.*, p. 112. Reprinted by permission of *Fortune* © 1992 Time Inc. All rights reserved.

222. *The process convinced . . . supply and delivery:* Losee, *id.*, p. 113. Reprinted by permission of *Fortune* © 1992 Time Inc. All rights reserved.

222. *No matter how well . . . submerged resistance:* Losee, *id.* Reprinted by permission of *Fortune* © 1992 Time Inc. All rights reserved.

222. *Donlon confronted this issue . . . Niagara negotiated:* Losee, *id.*

223. *In two years of talks . . . over five years:* Losee, *id.*, p. 114. Reprinted by permission of *Fortune* © 1992 Time Inc. All rights reserved.

223. *The results? Donlon's . . . dropped by 27 percent:* Losee, *id.*

223. *Niagara's management . . . deep, lasting change:* Losee, *id.*, p. 115. Reprinted by permission of *Fortune* © 1992 Time Inc. All rights reserved.

223. *A young person fresh . . . when placing calls:* Joel Arthur Barker, *Future Edge: Discovering the New Paradigms of Success* (New York: William Morrow and Co., 1992), p. 57.

224. *New paradigms put . . . by changing paradigms:* Barker, *id.*, p. 69.

224. *New paradigms can both . . . the change is logical:* Barker, *id.*, p. 84.

224. *Unitel Communications Inc. . . . existing service contracts:* Lawrence Surtees, "Hung Up on Service," *The Globe and Mail,* January 5, 1993, p. B20.

225. *Mr. Harvey set to . . . on market needs:* Surtees, *id.*

225. *In late 1988, the company . . . measurements and software:* Surtees, *id.*

226. *There's nothing mysterious about . . . harmonize with it:* Denis E. Waitley and Robert B. Tucker, *Winning the Innovation Game* (New York: Berkley Books, 1989), p. 12.

226. *Here's a list of the . . . friends, and advisers:* Waitley and Tucker, *id.*

228. *"The biggest single factor . . . primary roles":* Coopers & Lybrand, *Change Management: Taking Charge of Change,* 1993, p. II-5.

233. *The Aggressive Corporation . . . high-performing team:* Coopers & Lybrand, *id.,* p. Vb-46.

233. *There are spots in . . . change will fail:* Daryl R. Conner, *Managing at the Speed of Change: How Resilient Managers Succeed and Prosper Where Others Fail* (New York: Villard Books, 1993), p. 70. Reprinted by permission of Villard Books.

223. *If an initiating sponsor . . . change will fail:* Conner, *id.* Reprinted by permission of Villard Books.

234. *Reduce uncertainty . . . all affected parties:* Tom Terez, "Change Management: Strategies and Tactics for Today's Change Leaders," *Business and Technology Consultant,* June 1990, p. 37.

Touchstone 10: The New Spirit of Leadership

236. *In fact, one study of . . . ". . . leadership at the top":* John P. Kotter and James L. Heskett, *Corporate Culture and Performance* (New York: The Free Press, 1992), p. 84. Copyright © 1992 by Kotter Associates, Inc. and James L. Heskett. Reprinted by permission of The Free Press.

236. *This theme is echoed . . . ". . . few can change it":* Michael Grant, "The Principles of Leadership," *Canadian Business Review,* Autumn 1993, p. 89.

237. *Peter Drucker believes . . . the leader's as well:* Peter F. Drucker, *Managing for the Future: The 1990s and Beyond* (New York: Truman Talley Books/Dutton, 1992), p. 120.

237. *It's hard to tell if . . . compassion and accountability:* Hyler Bracey and Warren Smith, "Leaders Who Manage from the Heart Can Transform the Workplace," *Total Quality Newsletter,* February 1993, p. 7. Reprinted by permission of *Total Quality Newsletter,* Lakewood Publications, 50 South Ninth St., Minneapolis, MN 55402. All rights reserved. Not for resale.

237. *The old paradigm enterprise . . . two tenets:* Bracey and Smith, *id.*

237. *Meaningful work . . . ". . . to the world":* Bracey and Smith, *id.* Reprinted by permission of *Total Quality Newsletter,* Lakewood Publications, 50 South Ninth St., Minneapolis, MN 55402. All rights reserved. Not for resale.

237. *Health relationships . . . one reason cited:* Bracey and Smith, *id.*

237. *"The best people won't . . . colleagues and friends":* Bracey and Smith, *id.* Reprinted by permission of *Total Quality Newsletter,* Lakewood Publications, 50 South Ninth St., Minneapolis, MN 55402. All rights reserved. Not for resale.

237. *Bracey and Smith report . . . in order to grow:* Bracey and Smith, *id.*

238. *"The best managers . . . skill and compassion":* Bracey and Smith, *id.* Reprinted by permission of *Total Quality Newsletter,* Lakewood Publications, 50 South Ninth St., Minneapolis, MN 55402. All rights reserved. Not for resale.

238. *Honoring these five . . . motivation, and innovation:* Bracey and Smith, *id.*

238. *As we looked deeper into . . . the heart:* James M. Kouzes and Barry Z. Posner, *The Leadership Challenge: How to Get Extraordinary Things Done in*

Organizations (San Francisco: Jossey-Bass, Inc., 1993), p. 7. Reprinted by permission of Jossey-Bass Inc.

238. *When they "challenged the process" . . . or a reorganization:* Kouzes and Posner, *id.,* p. 8.

239. *Leaders are pioneers . . . of doing things:* Kouzes and Posner, *id.* Reprinted by permission of Jossey-Bass Inc.

239. *They may not be the . . . successes and mistakes:* Kouzes and Posner, *id.*

239. *When Stanley Gault . . . wet roads (hydroplaning):* John Greenwald, "Is Mr. Nice Guy Back?" *Time,* January 27, 1993, p. 43.

239. *"The teams at Goodyear . . . because of it ":* Greenwald, *id.*

239. *Every organization . . . ever created before:* James M. Kouzes and Barry Z. Posner, *The Leadership Challenge: How to Get Extraordinary Things Done in Organizations* (San Francisco: Jossey-Bass, Inc., 1993), p. 9. Reprinted by permission of Jossey-Bass Inc.

239. *Leaders must understand . . . the entire enterprise:* Kouzes and Posner, *id.*

240. *Exemplary leaders enlist . . . empower others:* Kouzes and Posner, *id.,* p. 10. Reprinted by permission of Jossey-Bass Inc.

240. *The effect of enabling . . . extraordinary results:* Kouzes and Posner, *id.* Reprinted by permission of Jossey-Bass Inc.

240. *In order to lead . . . respect for them:* Kouzes and Posner, *id.,* p. 11. Reprinted by permission of Jossey-Bass Inc.

240. *Being a role model means . . . and make suggestions:* John W. Johnstone, "A Point of View: Life in a Fishbowl, A Senior Manager's Perspective on TQM," *National Productivity Review,* Spring 1992, pp. 143–146.

240. *Leaders who "encouraged . . . " ". . . they can win":* James M. Kouzes and Barry Z. Posner, *The Leadership Challenge: How to Get Extraordinary Things Done in Organizations* (San Francisco: Jossey-Bass, Inc., 1993), p. 12. Reprinted by permission of Jossey-Bass Inc.

241. *Those who become the best . . . participants in change:* Kouzes and Posner, *id.,* p. 277. Reprinted by permission of Jossey-Bass Inc.

241. *When leaders followed the five . . . performing teams:* Kouzes and Posner, *id.,* p. 281.

241. *Anticipatory skills . . . of information sources:* Richard E. Byrd, "Corporate Leadership Skills: A New Synthesis," *Organization Dynamics,* 1987, p. 36.

241. *Foresight is fundamental . . . constantly changing:* Byrd, *id.*

241. *Leaders with these skills . . . with these issues:* Byrd, *id.*

241. *Anticipatory skills, then . . . trust and influence):* Byrd, *id.,* p. 37.

242. *These abilities allow . . . about new ideas:* Byrd, *id.,* p. 37.

242. *It's the job of leaders . . . toward current reality:* Peter M. Senge, "The Leader's New Work: Building Learning Organizations," in John Renesch, ed., *New Traditions in Business: Spirit and Leadership in the 21st Century* (San Francisco: Berrett-Koehler Publishers, 1992), p. 85.

242. *"The principle of . . . a desired future":* Senge, *id.* Reprinted by permission of Berrett-Koehler Publishers.

242. *Helping your staff to . . . questions such as:* Chris Lee, "Followership: The Essence of Leadership," *Training,* January 1991, p. 34.

243. *If the plant were . . . its internal customers?:* Lee, *id.* Reprinted with permission from the January 1991 issue of *Training* Magazine. Copyright 1991,

Lakewood Publications, 50 South Ninth St., Minneapolis, MN 55402. All rights reserved. Not for resale.

243. *After considering . . . than two days:* Lee., *id.*

243. *One of the characteristics . . . described as visionary:* David R. Gaster, "A Framework for Visionary Leadership," in John Renesch, ed., *New Traditions in Business: Spirit and Leadership in the 21st Century* (San Francisco: Berrett-Koehler Publishers, 1992), p. 162. Reprinted by permission of Berrett-Koehler Publishers.

243. *Federal Express is an . . . ". . . its employees perform":* Chris Lee, "Followership: The Essence of Leadership," *Training,* January 1991, p. 32. Reprinted with permission from the January 1991 issue of *Training* Magazine. Copyright 1991, Lakewood Publications, 50 South Ninth St., Minneapolis, MN 55402. All rights reserved. Not for resale.

243. *Fed Ex knows that . . . more consistent quality:* Lee, *id.*

244. *. . . A manager should . . . throughout the organization:* Richard E. Byrd, "Corporate Leadership Skills: A New Synthesis," *Organization Dynamics,* 1987, p. 40.

244. *The experience of Chrysler . . . keeping vision "short":* "Crystal Balls Out, Nuts and Bolts In," *The Globe and Mail,* October 5, 1993, p. B1.

244. *Internally, we don't use . . . one can quantify:* "Crystal Balls Out . . . ," *id.*

244. *Far from being . . . the entire time:* "Crystal Balls Out . . . ," *id.*

244. *Eaton, a very different . . . ". . . run your business":* "Crystal Balls Out . . . ," *id.*

245. *Value-congruence skills . . . organization's values:* Richard E. Byrd, "Corporate Leadership Skills: A New Synthesis," *Organization Dynamics,* 1987, p. 40.

245. *One of the greatest pitfalls . . . in values arise:* Byrd, *id.*

245. *All great leaders stand . . . leadership of these men:* Charles F. Kiefer, "Leadership in Metanoic Organizations," in John Renesch, ed., *New Traditions in Business: Spirit and Leadership in the 21st Century* (San Francisco: Berrett-Koehler Publishers, 1992), p. 176. Reprinted by permission of Berrett-Koehler Publishers.

245. *"For a leader . . . harm than good":* Richard E. Byrd, "Corporate Leadership Skills: A New Synthesis," *Organization Dynamics,* 1987, p. 40.

245. *Leaders should be eager . . . for those limitations:* Byrd, *id.*

246. *Self-understanding skills . . . arouse motivation:* Byrd, *id.,* p. 42.

246. *A passion for seeking . . . influence others; diplomacy:* John W. Thompson, "Corporate Leadership in the 21st Century," in John Renesch, ed., *New Traditions in Business: Spirit and Leadership in the 21st Century* (San Francisco: Berrett-Koehler Publishers, 1992), p. 219.

246. *William G. Pagonis . . . and Desert Farewell:* William G. Pagonis, "The Work of the Leader," *Harvard Business Review,* November–December 1992, p. 118.

246. *I've concluded that leadership . . . from the start:* Pagonis, *id.* Copyright © 1992 by The President and Fellows of Harvard College; all rights reserved. Reprinted by permission of *Harvard Business Review.*

247. *He has been groomed . . . to become more productive:* Pagonis, *id.*

247. *. . . a leader is not simply . . . block of leadership:* Pagonis, *id.* Copyright © 1992 by The President and Fellows of Harvard College; all rights reserved. Reprinted by permission of *Harvard Business Review.*

247. *His philosophy on leadership . . . to achieve mastery:* Pagonis, *id.*

247. *I can think of no leader . . . generalist's realm:* Pagonis, *id.,* p. 120. Copyright © 1992 by The President and Fellows of Harvard College; all rights reserved. Reprinted by permission of *Harvard Business Review.*

247. *Empathy also plays . . . ". . . other person's shoes":* Pagonis, *id.*

247. *During the Gulf War . . . walking across that land:* Pagonis, *id.*

247. *We put ourselves in the . . . respect and cooperation:* Pagonis, *id.* Copyright © 1992 by The President and Fellows of Harvard College; all rights reserved. Reprinted by permission of *Harvard Business Review.*

248. *During the Gulf War . . . his side at all times:* Pagonis, *id.,* p. 123.

248. *By definition, leaders . . . conducive context:* Pagonis, *id.* Copyright © 1992 by The President and Fellows of Harvard College; all rights reserved. Reprinted by permission of *Harvard Business Review.*

248. *For Pagonis, the day begins . . . cards per day):* Pagonis, *id.,* p. 124.

248. *Formal methods of . . . communication channels:* Pagonis, *id.,* p. 125. Copyright © 1992 by The President and Fellows of Harvard College; all rights reserved. Reprinted by permission of *Harvard Business Review.*

248. *What was the point of . . . seem to come easily:* Pagonis, *id.,* p. 126. Copyright © 1992 by The President and Fellows of Harvard College; all rights reserved. Reprinted by permission of *Harvard Business Review.*

249. *Progressive companies are . . . in leadership training:* Chris Lee, "Followership: The Essence of Leadership," *Training,* January 1991, p. 34.

249. *All employees need to . . . aren't going forward:* Chris Lee, "Followership: The Essence of Leadership," *Training,* January 1991, p. 34. Reprinted with permission from the January 1991 issue of *Training* Magazine. Copyright 1991, Lakewood Publications, 50 South Ninth St., Minneapolis, MN 55402. All rights reserved. Not for resale.

249. *Call them sponsors . . . practices upside down:* Brain Dumaine, "The New Non-Manager Managers," *Fortune,* February 22, 1993, pp. 80–84. Reprinted by permission of *Fortune* © 1993 Time Inc. All rights reserved.

249. *The trend for the past 35 . . . "middle" or "upper":* Peter F. Drucker, *Managing for the Future: The 1990s and Beyond* (New York: Truman Talley Books/Dutton, 1992), p. 157.

249. *The American Management . . . front-line employees:* Brian Dumaine, "The New Non-Manager Managers," *Fortune,* February 22, 1993, pp. 80–84.

250. *"If you can't say why . . . you're out":* Dumaine, *id.,* p. 80. Reprinted by permission of *Fortune* © 1993 Time Inc. All rights reserved.

250. *Tomorrow's top corporate jobs . . . that managers receive:* Dumaine, *id.*

251. *Steve Jobs, founder . . . ". . . and strategic plans":* Dumaine, *id.,* p. 82. Reprinted by permission of *Fortune* © 1993 Time Inc. All rights reserved.

251. *At Next, everyone is . . . the payroll list:* Dumaine, *id.*

251. *There is a profound difference . . . from subordinates:* Dumaine, *id.*

252. *. . . the trick to working . . . jobs, skills, and needs:* Dumaine, *id.,* p. 83. Reprinted by permission of *Fortune* © 1993 Time Inc. All rights reserved.

252. *A cross-functional team . . . their respective departments:* Dumaine, *id.*

252. *I had to build trust . . . I had to cajole:* Dumaine, *id.* Reprinted by permission of *Fortune* © 1993 Time Inc. All rights reserved.

252. *Because fast innovation is . . . ventures going at once:* Dumaine, *id.*

252. *Consultants say any new . . . and fickle markets:* Dumaine, *id.* Reprinted by permission of *Fortune* © 1993 Time Inc. All rights reserved.

252. *Lombardo and his people . . . four to six years:* Dumaine, *id.*

252. *Lombardo says the key . . . ". . . the market demands":* Dumaine, *id.* Reprinted by permission of *Fortune* © 1993 Time Inc. All rights reserved.

252. *Okidata's John Ring . . . product of the year:* Dumaine, *id.*

253. *When times were flush . . . anything he can:* Dumaine, *id.,* p. 80. Reprinted by permission of *Fortune* © 1993 Time Inc. All rights reserved.

253. *The original idea came . . . previous experience:* Dumaine, *id.*

253. *Being a new manager . . . his or her career:* Dumaine, *id.,* p. 84. Reprinted by permission of *Fortune* © 1993 Time Inc. All rights reserved.

254. *Most people in our culture . . . a learning experience:* Anthony Robbins, *Unlimited Power: The New Science of Personal Achievement* (New York: Simon & Schuster, 1986), p. 76.

Index